Blushing and the Social Emotions

Blushing and the Social Emotions

The Self Unmasked

W. Ray Crozier

palgrave
macmillan

First published in 2006 by
PALGRAVE MACMILLAN
Houndmills, Basingstoke, Hampshire RG21 6XS and
175 Fifth Avenue, New York, N.Y. 10010
Companies and representatives throughout the world.

PALGRAVE MACMILLAN is the global academic imprint of the Palgrave Macmillan division of St. Martin's Press, LLC and of Palgrave Macmillan Ltd. Macmillan® is a registered trademark in the United States, United Kingdom and other countries. Palgrave is a registered trademark in the European Union and other countries.

ISBN-13: 978–1–4039–4675–1 hardback
ISBN-10: 1–4039–4675–2 hardback

This book is printed on paper suitable for recycling and made from fully managed and sustained forest sources.

A catalogue record for this book is available from the British Library.

Library of Congress Cataloging-in-Publication Data

Crozier, W. Ray, 1945–
    Blushing and the social emotions : the self unmasked / W. Ray Crozier.
        p. cm.
    Includes bibliographical references and index.
    ISBN 1–4039–4675–2 (cloth)
        1. Blushing. 2. Emotions – Physiological aspects. 3. Emotions – Social aspects. 4. Self-consciousness. I. Title.

QP401.C76 2006
152.4—dc22   2005055272

10 9 8 7 6 5 4 3 2 1
15 14 13 12 11 10 09 08 07 06

Transferred to digital printing in 2007.

To Sandra, John and Beth

Contents

List of Tables and Figure

Tables

Figure

Acknowledgements

I am grateful to Sandra Crozier for her support while writing this book. I thank Alison Davies, Alison Garbert-Jones and Delia Russell who worked with me on projects discussed in this book. I am grateful to Beth Crozier, Judith Marshall, Dr Val Rees and the anonymous participants for their contributions to the questionnaire study described in Chapter 5; details of the study appeared in the *Journal for the Theory of Social Behaviour*, 2004, 18, 121–8, published by Blackwell Publishers Ltd. Table 7.1 is based on the theory of the blush by Cristiano Castelfranchi and Isabella Poggi that appeared in their chapter, 'Blushing as a discourse: Was Darwin wrong?' published in W. R. Crozier (ed.) (1990) *Shyness and Embarrassment: Perspectives from Social Psychology* (pp. 230–51), New York: Cambridge University Press.

Introduction

Blushing is a ubiquitous but little understood phenomenon that presents many puzzles. It is a visible change in our most conspicuous feature – the face – yet often coincides with lowering the head and avoiding eye contact, actions that seem to have more to do with hiding than with drawing attention to ourselves. We blush when we wish 'the ground would open up and swallow us' but we also do so when we are praised, congratulated, thanked or presented with a prize. Blushing is involuntary and uncontrollable. An actor might simulate tears, laughter or surprise but not a blush. We are not always sure whether we are blushing, as we do not usually see our own face and rely on feeling hot or a tingling sensation.

Until recently the blush attracted scarcely any systematic scientific attention. It is a difficult phenomenon to study: it is a fleeting, situation-specific reaction, and its measurement is not straightforward. One scientist who took blushing seriously was Charles Darwin who devoted a chapter to it in *The Expression of the Emotions in Man and Animals*. For many years this provided the sole detailed account of blushing and his observations and analysis are still pertinent today. Darwin claimed that we blush when we think we are the object of others' attention particularly, but not exclusively, when we think that they are deprecating us. Unsurprisingly, he proposed that the causes of the blush have evolved. Originally, people blushed when they thought about what others thought of their appearance (and this is why it is the face, the most conspicuous part of the body, that reddens) but through habit and association they have come to blush when their conduct is the object of attention. Darwin argued that blushing accompanies shame, guilt, shyness and modesty, all of which share heightened sensitivity to the opinion of others. These have come to be known as the 'social' or 'self-conscious' emotions. This volume aims to review what is known about the blush and to relate it to these emotions. It draws upon recollections of the circumstances of blushing and analysis of fictional descriptions, and it reviews the literature on laboratory studies of social interaction and the measurement of facial blood flow and skin temperature. The book comprises four parts.

The first part has two chapters on emotion. The first of these locates the blush within the study of the facial expression of emotion. It examines Darwin's thesis within the context of his defence of evolution against the position that the blush represents evidence of divine design. It considers how research into emotional expression has marginalised the blush and the emotional states associated with it. The second chapter considers different approaches to the conceptualisation and study of self-consciousness. It evaluates empirical research into self-focused attention and its relationships with social anxiety. Finally, it introduces the social or self-conscious emotions, which are considered in more detail in the third part of the book.

The second part comprises three chapters on the nature of the blush. Chapter 3 provides an account of what is known about the psychophysiology of the blush and reviews research that has been stimulated by recent technological advances in its measurement. Chapter 4 compares alternative theories of the causes of blushing. It considers explanations in terms of unwanted social attention and exposure of the self and evaluates its role as a signal of apology or submission. Chapter 5 provides an analysis of the circumstances in which people blush. It draws upon a questionnaire study of recollections of blush-making episodes and references to blushing in literary sources. The findings are related to the explanations discussed in Chapter 4.

Chapters in the third part examine the relation of the blush to the social emotions: embarrassment, shame, guilt and shyness. The blush has been regarded as the 'hallmark' of embarrassment yet there is no consensus among researchers as to whether it invariably accompanies embarrassment and whether it accompanies the other social emotions as well. Chapter 6 discusses the nature of embarrassment, its visible display and the circumstances that elicit it. Chapter 7 examines shame and the relation between embarrassment and shame and asks whether people blush with shame. It considers shame in the broader sense used by theorists such as Sylvan Tomkins and Helen Block Lewis and analyses the blushing episodes from the study in Chapter 5 in terms of this broader conception. Chapter 8 considers the relation between shame and guilt and asks whether we blush with guilt. It discusses the relations between shame and anger and considers how the blush differs from the flush of anger. This raises questions about why we should blush at all. Shyness is the subject of Chapter 9. It discusses the relation of shyness to shame and anxiety, and asks whether a distinction between fearful and self-conscious shyness helps understand the role of the blush.

The fourth part reports on individual differences in tendency to blush. Many regard their blushing in a negative light; they interpret it as a sign of weakness or evidence of social incompetence and this can lead those who believe they are susceptible to blushing to adopt a range of coping strategies including the avoidance of social situations. These anxieties are heightened by the awareness that blushing is beyond conscious control. Chapter 10 looks at personality characteristics, particularly the trait of self-consciousness, that are associated with a tendency to blush. It considers whether people who are anxious about their blushing actually blush more than less anxious people do. Concerns about blushing lead many to seek professional help and there has developed a range of psychological approaches to intervention, including cognitive behaviour therapy and pharmacological treatments. Chapter 11 discusses the relation between fear of blushing and the clinical category of social phobia before outlining and evaluating interventions to help people overcome their fear of blushing, including recent controversies about surgical treatment.

A brief chapter brings the book to a close. It asks whether the research reviewed in previous chapters has clarified the puzzle of the blush, highlights themes that have emerged and offers interpretations of some central features of this phenomenon. The study of the blush is still in its infancy; it is hoped that this book will stimulate interest among readers and encourage research into this intriguing phenomenon.

I
Emotion in Social Life

1
Emotion and its Expression

Charles Darwin wrote extensively on emotion in his notebooks and in his book *The Expression of Emotion in Man and Animals*, published in 1872. The book included a chapter on blushing that for many years provided the only extended account of the phenomenon in scientific literature, and it is common even today for articles on blushing to cite this chapter. Discussion of emotion and the facial expression of emotion seems a natural starting point for consideration of the blush but it raises the immediate problem of how to deal with a topic that has attracted so much theorising and research, indeed so much controversy. For many years the dominant approach construed the expression of emotion as the visible manifestation of a distinct internal state; more recently there is growing recognition of the social nature of emotion accompanied by an interpretation of expressions as signs that serve communicative functions for the self and others. The first section of the chapter discusses Darwin's analysis of the blush; the second section considers how the study of emotion and its facial expression has marginalised the blush and asks how much this owes to Darwin's influence.

Darwin on the blush

Expression of the Emotions

The facial expression of emotion was of longstanding interest to Darwin and he assembled relevant evidence over many years. The study of the facial expression of character and of emotion had begun to attract scientific attention by the middle of the nineteenth century. The British psychiatrist Diamond applied the emerging technology of photography to psychiatric diagnosis (photographs were still uncommon when

Darwin was preparing *The Expression of the Emotions in Man and Animals* [hereafter abbreviated as *Expression*] but Darwin drew upon them as a source of evidence and included several in the book, and of course later research has relied heavily upon the medium). Another source of photographic evidence known to Darwin were experiments conducted by G. B. Duchenne de Boulogne in 1862, which recorded changes in expression brought about by electrical stimulation of individual facial muscles.

Darwin kept diaries of his children's development and these include observations of their facial expressions. For example, he reflects on his son's shyness (1877, p. 292):

> No one can have attended to very young children without being struck at the unabashed manner in which they fixedly stare without blinking their eyes at a new face; an old person can look in this manner only at an animal or inanimate object. This, I believe, is the result of young children not thinking in the least about themselves, and therefore not being in the least shy, though they are sometimes afraid of strangers. I saw the first symptom of shyness in my child when nearly two years and three months old: this was shown towards myself, after an absence of ten days from home, chiefly by his eyes being kept slightly averted from mine; but he soon came and sat on my knee and kissed me, and all trace of shyness disappeared.

Darwin made notes of observations of his pet dogs and visited London Zoo in order to observe the animals and to speak to zookeepers. He sent questionnaires to correspondents around the world seeking information on cross-cultural similarities in expressions. In the following excerpt from his notebook he reflects on blushing, wondering whether this occurs in all human groups and in different species.

> Does a negress blush – I am almost sure Fuegia Basket did ((& Jeremy when Chico plagued him)). Animals I should think would not have any emotion like a blush.[1]

Later in the notebook, Darwin offers an explanation of blushing in terms of self-attention, which he elaborated in the chapter in *Expression*. A reproduction of it reads,

> Blushing is intimately concerned with thinking of ones appearance – does the thought drive blood to surface exposed, face of man, face,

neck, /upper/bosom in women: like erection I shyness is certainly very much connected with thinking of oneself. – /blushing/ is connected with sexual, because each sex thinks of what another thinks of him, than of any one of his own sex –. Hence, animals, not being such thinking people, do not blush. – sensitive people apt to blush.

Darwin's writing on blushing is worthy of examination in some detail. He raised issues that we are only now beginning to address through the collection of systematic empirical evidence. His explanation still deserves our attention. In order to understand this explanation it is useful to relate *Expression* to Darwin's researches into evolution and his defence of his controversial thesis. It is useful too to understand the positions that Darwin challenged and something of the evidence that was available to him.

The *Origin of Species* was published in 1859 and set out the thesis that the evolution of a species was driven by the mechanism of natural selection operating upon variation among its members. It paid little attention to humans although its implications were clear, for example, the notion that 'man' and 'beasts' are descended from a common ancestor was taken up by Bishop Wilberforce in his attack on Darwin during the Oxford debate with T. H. Huxley in 1860 and in the ensuing article published in the *Quarterly Review*. Darwin had been interested in the implications of his theory for humans since at least the 1830s, including the topic of the facial expression of emotions in human and other species: he had begun recording his newborn son's expressions from 1839. Thus it has been argued (Gruber, 1974; Browne, 1985) that Darwin's fundamental ideas about the mechanisms of the expression of emotion were already in place before he conducted the surveys that figure so largely in *Expression*. It has also been argued that these ideas have to be understood in the context of his attempt to make a case against critics of the *Origin of Species*, particularly his defence against the argument that effective adaptation is itself evidence of the perfection of divine design.

The theory set out in the *Origin of Species* offered a profound challenge to the literal truth of the creation story in the Bible and to accepted beliefs that the various species were separately created by God, that their forms were unchanged since their creation, and that the adaptation of an animal to its niche proves the perfection of its design. That the human species is also subject to processes of evolution was even more shocking, given the belief that man occupies a unique place in the world, as set out in Genesis 1:26 – 'Then God said, "Let us make man in our image, in our likeness, and let them rule over the fish of the sea and the birds of the air, over the livestock, over all the earth, and over all the creatures that move along the ground." ' Darwin anticipated the reaction that publication of the *Descent of Man* would attract. He explained in a letter to Alfred Russel Wallace, who had been working independently on natural selection, that it was better to omit the subject of human evolution from the *Origin of Species* as it was 'so surrounded with prejudice; though I fully admit that it is the highest and most interesting problem for the naturalist'.[2]

Expression was written in only four months and was published in 1872, the year after *The Descent of Man* appeared. Darwin had intended to include the subject of emotion in *The Descent of Man* but decided that the material he had collected was too lengthy and warranted a separate publication in its own right. *Expression* concentrated on the expression of emotion, on postures, gestures and facial expressions. Darwin aimed to bolster his application of evolutionary principles to humans by showing that the expression of emotion was similar throughout the world and in different 'races', which would imply their common descent from a single ancestor. Similarity in expressions of emotion across the animal world would support the thesis that human and non-human species had common origins. Darwin also sought to develop a counter-argument against creationist responses to evolution (particularly the argument from design, which holds that all creatures have been designed by God, thus explaining the effective adaptation of biological structure). It was essential for Darwin to establish continuity between human and non-human species and he collected evidence on this as well as on similarities in expression across cultures.

Principles of expression

Darwin had also to show how expressive behaviour could be transmitted from one generation to the next. He was unaware of Mendelian principles of heredity (Mendel had published his research into the mechanisms of inheritance in 1866 but his work was not disseminated until the beginning of the twentieth century). Darwin drew upon Lamarck's thesis that acquired traits and habits are transmitted to offspring. He proposed three explanatory principles for the expression of emotion: the 'Principle of Serviceable Associated Habits'; the 'Principle of Antithesis'; the 'Principle of Direct Action of the Nervous System'. These principles emphasise the transmission of instincts and acquired habits. The first maintained that gestures and postures that are acquired are repeated from one generation to another until these habits become fixed and inherited. They continue to be performed even when they no longer serve any useful function (Darwin, 1872, p. 28):

> Certain complex actions are of direct or indirect service under certain states of mind, in order to relieve or gratify certain sensations, desires etc.; and whenever the same state of mind is induced, however feebly, there is a tendency through the force of habit and association for the same movements to be performed, though they may not then be of the least use.

The second principle maintained that some expressions are the opposite of patterns of gestures and expressions that were once useful. Submissive gestures are opposite to aggressive and dominant gestures; making oneself small and shrinking close to the ground is the opposite of aggrandisement and standing tall; in cats the submissive flat back is the opposite of an arched back. According to the third principle, there is an 'overflow' of energy under conditions of extreme excitement, which leads to involuntary expressions like trembling, writhing, grimaces, and the clenching and gnashing of teeth as well as activity of the autonomic nervous system resulting in perspiration or urination.

Darwin's claim that movements will be performed whether or not they are of any use has been variously interpreted. Frijda (1986) takes from Darwin that expressions are of use in some, albeit not all, conditions, and thus should not be regarded as mere remnants of actions that once had adaptive significance: they can have current functional significance in facilitating interaction with the environment. On the other hand, Fridlund (1994) has concluded that the principles attach little significance to the adaptive significance of emotional expression. Fridlund suggests that Darwin adopted this position because he realised that claims for adaptive significance could be taken as support for the 'argument by design' thesis that the facial muscles had been designed *for* the expression of emotion. Fridlund illustrates the position that Darwin challenged by providing two quotations from Sir Charles Bell's *Essays on the Anatomy of Expression in Painting*.

> It is obvious thus to observe how the muscles, by producing distinct impressions, afford a new occasion of distinguishing the tribes of animals; and, as signs of superior intelligence, become proofs of the higher endowments of man, and a demonstration of the peculiar frame and excellence of his nature. (Bell, 1806, p. 141)

> In man there seems to be a special apparatus, for the purpose of enabling him to communicate with his fellow creatures, by that

natural language which is read off the change of his countenance. There exist in his face ... a peculiar set of muscles to which no other office can be assigned than to serve for expression. (ibid., p. 121)

In taking up a contrary position Darwin set out to show that expressive behaviours do not distinguish man from animals and that they do not serve primarily for communication with his fellow creatures. Although he could demonstrate that humans and dogs shrink with fear and bare their teeth when angry, and he could construct an evolutionary explanation for these similarities among species, he did not develop the argument that this similarity exists *because* these behaviours have adaptive value. The expressions do have functional origins, for example, the wide eyes of surprise represent the attempt to see more of the unexpected stimulus but their continuing appearance in humans and other animals is due to habit and association, not to any current functional value. Thus, the sneer is the descendant of an ancestor's baring the teeth in aggression, an expression that is still seen in dogs.

Nevertheless, as we have noted, Frijda believes that this argument is over-stated, and characterises Darwin's principle of 'serviceable habits' in terms of behaviours that affect the contact between the organism and some other organism or the environment – they modify sensitivity to information from the environment, enhance readiness for action, communicate to others, and so on. He also points out that there is a thin line between expression and actions that bring about change, between shrinking with fear and hiding, the angry look and the threatening stare. The claim that expressive displays have adaptive value has characterised subsequent accounts of behaviour within an evolutionary perspective.

The meaning of the blush

Darwin's chapter on the blush differs from the other chapters in his book. Whereas they focus on a single emotion and its characteristic expression, this chapter takes a single expression as its theme and considers that it is induced by three mental states: shyness, shame and modesty. Darwin concluded that it is 'the thinking of what others think of us which excites a blush'. He emphasised a process of self-attention, reiterating a theme that was rehearsed in the *N Notebook* of 1838 (Gruber, 1974, p. 344):

Whenever we know, or suppose, that others are depreciating our personal appearance, our attention is strongly drawn toward ourselves, more specifically to our faces ... whenever we know, or imagine, that any one is blaming, though in silence, our actions, thoughts, or character; and, again, when we are highly praised.

The blush offered a particular challenge to Darwin's position. First, it appears to be a uniquely human reaction. Whereas his surveys yielded evidence that it is present in different races it seemed to have no equivalent in other species: 'Monkeys redden from passion, but it would require an overwhelming amount of evidence to make us believe that any animal could blush' (Darwin, 1872, p. 310). This conclusion was consistent with the view on blushing advanced by Thomas Burgess, whose publication, *The Physiology or Mechanism of Blushing*, published in 1839, is cited throughout Darwin's chapter. According to Burgess, the blush is a sign of the moral dimension of human nature and provides evidence that man has an innate conscience. Thus the blush is peculiar to man because he alone has a conscience. Furthermore, because it signifies shame and is involuntary, and hence not under the control of man's will, it demonstrates the innateness of his sense of guilt. Burgess argued that this arrangement is evidence of the perfection of design, writing (1839, pp. 24–5; emphasis in original):

[The] Creator of man endowed him with this peculiar faculty of *exhibiting* his internal emotions, or more properly speaking, of the internal emotions exhibiting themselves, for no individual blushes voluntarily ... in many cases it will control the individual from violating the laws of morality, and this affords us a beautiful instance of the design, wisdom, and goodness of Providence.

The blush is revealing of good character. As Browne (1985, p. 317) puts it, 'All the higher qualities of man, all the Victorian virtues of modesty, innocence, and sensibility, were dramatically revealed by the flustered self-consciousness of an outright blush'. Similar themes are apparent in studies of the blush by literary critics. O'Farrell (1997) draws attention to nineteenth-century novelists' interest in the blush and the various ways in which they saw it as expressive of character (because it is involuntary, it tells the truth about who we are, and even betrays us when the truth is something we wish to conceal) as well as being the appropriate response to certain social circumstances (for example, a breach of modesty).

An admission that the blush is at the service of a moral sense would undermine Darwin's evolutionary account and would strengthen the position of advocates of man's unique place in nature. Darwin's task was to show how the blush could be specifically human without abandoning his general principles about the expression of emotion. He did so by emphasising the role of self-attention and denying that the blush originally served a moral function, writing, 'Attention directed to personal appearance, and not to moral conduct, has been the fundamental element in the acquirement of the habit of blushing' (Darwin, 1872, p. 326). Self-attention requires an awareness of self and hence blushing would not be observed among those who lacked this awareness, young children or the insane. Darwin corresponded with a Crichton Browne, the physician in charge of an asylum in Yorkshire, who had made observations among the 'idiots and the deranged'. Browne wrote to Darwin to confirm that these patients did not blush: 'Dr Crichton Browne observed for me those under his care, but never saw a genuine blush, though he has seen their faces flush, apparently from joy, when food was placed in front of them, and from anger'.

This explanation lacked a mechanism for translating self-attention into the blush. Darwin proposed that mental attention paid to any part of the body would cause increased blood flow in that region and he appealed to the principles of association and habit in order to show how self-attention would produce increased blood flow in the capillaries lying close to the surface of the skin of the face. According to this explanation, if we attend to our face, this will increase circulation. Thus, by processes of association and habit, whenever we believe that others are attending to our face, this belief will increase blood flow:

> Now as men during endless generations have had their attention often and earnestly directed to their personal appearance, and especially to their faces, any incipient tendency in the facial capillaries to be thus affected will have become in the course of time greatly strengthened through the principles ... namely, nerve-force passing readily along accustomed channels, and inherited habit. (Darwin, 1872, p. 345)

Chapter 3 examines more recent thinking on the physiology of the blush and its measurement. However, this is perhaps an appropriate place to report a recent study by Drummond and Mirco (2004) who tested Darwin's hypothesis that attention to a site on the face increases blood flow at that site, as sitting beside a hot fire would redden the side of the face closer to the fire. The study addresses an observation made by Campbell (1890, p. 147) of a man who 'is very liable to blush at dinner;

if talking to a person at his side will *blush on this side only!*' Cheek temperature was measured while participants carried out either an embarrassing activity (singing aloud) or a less embarrassing activity (reading aloud) while being stared at by the experimenter. Measures of temperature were made separately for each cheek while the experimenter stared at one or other cheek. It was found that the temperature increase was significantly greater in the cheek being stared at, and this was the case for both activities. These findings provide support for Darwin's claim that staring produces vasodilation of the facial capillaries and hence blushing. Time (and further research) will tell whether this is a significant clue in understanding the blush, or is a false trail.

Darwin's legacy

Subsequent to Darwin's chapter and Campbell's monograph the blush remained a neglected topic in the psychology of emotion. Ironically, the success of Darwin's account of emotion and its expression is largely responsible for this. The chapters of *Expression* are devoted to separate emotions and this encouraged research aimed at the identification of emotions that are basic or universal. Darwin's success in identifying facial expressions of emotions prompted research here too, and facial expression contributed to the definition of basic emotions. The emergence of evolutionary psychology led to greater attention to the communicative functions of expression but here too the emphasis has been on basic emotions.

Basic emotions

In his classic 1884 article 'What is an emotion?' William James distinguished between 'standard' emotions, which have a distinct bodily expression, such as anger, fear or shame, and other emotions, which, he argued, do not. James made this distinction in the course of an argument about the process involved in emotional experience. He adopted a position that was counter to the conventional view that the perception of eliciting circumstances (for example, the sight of a bear) gives rise to an emotion (fear) that in turn gives rise to bodily changes (trembling, increase in heart rate) and actions (running away). James proposed instead that the perception gives rise to the bodily changes and it is the awareness of the bodily state that gives rise to the feeling of emotion: I feel fear because I tremble or because my heart is pounding (I feel embarrassed because I am blushing). This implies an inherent connection between the stimulus and the bodily change, since these changes occur directly without mediation.

James acknowledged that the theory faced problems with emotions that are not associated with bodily changes. One solution would have been to argue that all emotions involve bodily reactions, but not all enter conscious awareness. However, James dealt with this problem by qualifying the application of the theory, restricting it to those 'coarser' emotions that do have a distinctive bodily expression. The theory implies that each emotion is associated with a specific pattern of bodily reaction. Otherwise we would not know which emotion we were experiencing – the sight of the bear might give rise to pride in a zoologist who had been searching for a representative of this genus. Both implications – the direct connection between stimulus and bodily response and the existence of distinct patterns of reactions – were challenged, and have generated an enormous amount of research.

Some argue that there are no distinct patterns of bodily reaction other than a heightened level of generalised arousal and what distinguishes emotions are the person's appraisals of the eliciting circumstances, memories of similar events, attributions about the causes of events and so on. These cognitions cannot be isolated from the individual's cultural context, since this profoundly influences his or her understanding of the meanings of events. Researchers working on brain structures and processes adopt an alternative position and seek to identify the central and autonomic nervous system processes involved in specific emotions. These studies have concentrated on the basic emotions, thus there has been extensive research into mapping the neural pathways involved in fear, and the role of specific brain structures has been identified, in particular the nuclei of the amygdala, which plays a central role in emotional processing (LeDoux and Phelps, 2000). The research has yielded a finding that is potentially of considerable relevance to James's thesis. There seem to be two pathways from the emotional stimulus to the amygdala. The 'low road' or 'quick and dirty' route from sensory input to the lateral nucleus of the amygdala bypasses the cortex and permits rapid registration of potential threat and alerts the amygdala to information that arrives more slowly by the 'high road'. The high road sends information via the cortex and involves more detailed processing of the input.

Damasio (2004) reviewed research into the brain using the technique of positron-emission tomography (PET scans). For example, one study asked participants to think about episodes from their life where they had experienced anger, fear, happiness or sadness and to signal to the researcher if and when they were experiencing the emotion. Measures of autonomic responses – heart rate and skin conductance – were recorded during the procedure to check if the imagination of the episode was accompanied by physiological changes consistent with emotional arousal. The PET scans showed that the different emotions were associated with activation in different regions of the brain. Such findings offer a challenge to claims that research has failed to identify distinct physiological correlates of individual emotions.

Recent findings implicate the amygdala in processing information about the facial expression of the social emotions. Adolphs *et al.* (2002) reported that patients with damage to the amygdala were particularly impaired when deciding what emotion was expressed by admiring, arrogant, flirtatious and guilty faces and experienced greater difficulty with these faces than with expressions of anger, disgust, distress, fear, happiness, sadness and surprise.[3] This attention to the social emotions is overdue and welcome. Nevertheless, despite recent technological advances the methods available to study physiological changes in emotion are crude relative to the complexity of the system. Thus, while the amygdala can be represented as a box in simple flow diagrams of neural circuitry it is known to have 700 inputs and outputs (Schulkin *et al.*, 2003).

A problem for the concept of basic emotions is the discrepancy between the small number of basic emotions that is proposed and the richness of emotional experience as represented in the large number of emotion words in ordinary language. Although any scheme can encompass more emotions by adding degrees of variation in the intensity of feeling (so that, say, rage and irritation are variations of anger), this is hardly sufficient to account for the wide range of emotions that can be differentiated or for the subtlety of feeling that characterises, say, the aesthetic experience aroused by a piece of music or the sight of a landscape or a sunset. A favoured solution is to explain this diversity in terms of combinations or mixtures of basic emotions. An obvious analogy is with colour mixture, where a small set of primary colours, whether of light or pigment, can be combined to produce a huge array of discriminable colours, many, but not all, of which can be labelled. Someone with normal colour vision can distinguish among 10,000 hues, but there seems to be at most 4000 colour words in English to label these.

Research into emotion words and facial expressions has used the semantic differential measurement technique, where people rate target stimuli (emotion words or photographs of faces) on bipolar rating scales (for example, pleasant versus unpleasant) or group them in terms of their perceived similarities. These studies tend to find that two, at most three, dimensions underlie judgments, corresponding to valence (degree of pleasantness – the dimension that explains most variation in judgments), arousal and intensity. Here too, there is an analogy with research into colour perception where colours have been mapped in terms of two and three dimensions. There is debate whether to study emotion by classifying emotional states in terms of dimensions of valence and arousal or by assuming the existence of distinct emotions.[4]

Although such analysis of emotions and colours has its scientific and technological uses, it is an abstraction. In everyday life we are mostly unaware of the precise colours that surround us even though they may influence our mood, how warm or cool we feel and so on. We do not see the world in terms of discrete areas of colour; the phenomenon of colour constancy shows that we tend to perceive an object as having the same colour on different occasions despite marked changes in the wavelength of light that it reflects. Similarly, psychological conceptions of emotion are abstractions. Embarrassment is an abstraction from experience: there are embarrassing situations and moments, embarrassed people and so on. Nevertheless, it is useful for some purposes to isolate specific emotions and this is the approach taken in this volume.

The longstanding division between those emotions that are identified as fundamental, basic or primary, and those regarded as secondary, learnt or of higher order is ingrained in 'common sense'. Demoulin *et al.* (2004) report pertinent findings from a study of understanding of primary and secondary emotion words. More than 1000 students, speakers of four languages (French, Spanish, Dutch and English), resident in three countries, rated a total of 448 emotion words on a set of scales. Statistical analysis of the ratings located the words along a continuum. At one end of the continuum were 'primary emotions', which were judged to be common to human and non-human species, experienced in a similar way by all people, caused by external events, visible, of short duration, appearing early in development and less likely to involve moral judgment and cognitive processes. They include fear, pain, surprise, anger, pleasure and happiness. At the other end were 'secondary' emotions, uniquely human, more likely to vary across cultures, be acquired later in development, lasting long, generated by internal characteristics, requiring cognitive processing, and informative about the individual's moral nature. Characteristic secondary emotions are optimism, tenderness, love, hope, embarrassment, guilt, remorse, shame and humiliation. These lay judgments are consistent with conclusions reached in psychological research and, as noted below, with findings from studies of the facial expression of emotion.

Yet the four languages scarcely represent the world's linguistic and cultural variation, and Wierzbicka (1992) has criticised basic emotions research for its ethnocentrism and its assumption that emotions coded in Western languages are universal. She points out that other cultures take different emotions to be basic, and gives the example of the Ilongot language of the Philippines which has no word for the supposed universal emotion anger yet has a word *liget* for a basic emotion that does not correspond to any English word; she concludes (ibid., p. 287) that 'there are *no* universal emotion concepts, lexicalised in all the languages of the world'. I return to the issue of language in later chapters.

Emotion in the face

The expression of emotion in the face is central to several definitions of emotion. Thus, Tomkins (1963) defines affect in terms of facial expression. Izard (1972, p. 2) defined fundamental emotions in terms of '(a) a specific innately determined neural substrate, (b) a characteristic neuromuscular expressive pattern, and (c) a distinct subjective or phenomenological quality'. Here an emotion is regarded as fundamental because it is associated with a distinctive and universal facial expression (the definition excludes facial colour changes). According to facial feedback theory the emotional stimulus elicits facial muscular activity and autonomic processes, and it is the sensory feedback from these that gives rise to the subjective state.

The study of facial expression has played a significant role in the classification of basic or fundamental emotions. Ekman and Friesen (1978) constructed a coding scheme for emotion based on painstaking research into the facial musculature and this has been used to arrive at a set of basic emotions that are universally recognised, namely anger, disgust, fear, happiness, sadness and surprise. The list has considerable overlap with everyday conceptions of primary emotions. Early research was obliged to rely upon the identification of posed emotions in still photographs but subsequently has drawn upon advances in film, videotape and computer technology to provide finer grained analysis of movement of the facial musculature and in particular of the rapid sequential processes involved in facial expression. Unfortunately this technology has not been used to examine facial changes other than those brought about by the musculature, and until recently there has been no systematic investigation of changes associated with facial colouring, whether blushing or blanching. This is due in part to technological limitations in measurement (see Chapter 3) but it also reflects the lack of attention paid by psychologists to the emotional experiences that are commonly associated with the blush.

A seminal investigation of the universality of facial expressions that draws upon the identification of emotion from pictures was carried out in Papua New Guinea, among the South Fore people who had been isolated from foreign cultural influences; for example, they had no experience of photographs or film. In this study (Ekman, 1972) people were presented with stories where various emotions might be experienced and were asked to select from a set of photographs of Western facial expressions the photograph that best depicted what the characters in the stories would be feeling. For example, the story might involve a sudden, unexpected event and a photograph depicting surprise would be presented alongside two photographs depicting other emotions. Despite their unfamiliarity with the medium and with Western faces the participants agreed with Western people as to the emotions experienced by the characters in the story. This consensus was confirmed when Ekman photographed the participants from New Guinea as they posed the emotions and carried out a parallel investigation with a sample of Americans, asking them what emotions were being posed.

Nevertheless, despite the undoubted value of this research for understanding the facial expression of emotion, the relation between emotion and its expression is not straightforward. Emotions are subject to 'display rules' that regulate their expression. Thus Ekman (1972) found that Japanese and American students showed similar facial expressions while watching a film of surgical procedure when they were on their own; however, in the presence of the researcher their expressions differed, and Japanese students tended to hide their expression behind a smile. These differences are not idiosyncratic but reflect cultural values about the appropriate display of emotion. There are gender differences in the acceptable display of emotion evident, for example, in the reactions to failure or disappointment of professional men and women athletes. Display rules involve the amplification of expressions as well as their inhibition or attenuation. The public display of grief following the death of Diana, Princess of Wales in 1997 surprised many commentators, not merely because it resembled hysteria but because it seemed incompatible with 'traditional' British reserve. Commentators questioned the legitimacy of the experience; they wondered whether people really were experiencing grief and were bothered by the remarks of individuals who claimed that they experienced more sadness about the Princess's death than they had following the death of a member of their own family.

It is tempting to conclude that there is an unambiguous distinction between feeling an emotion and displaying it. To consider an example from sport, spectators at a sports event who are elated at their team's triumph may suppress the expression of this if surrounded by opposing supporters, producing a mismatch between what they feel and what they show. This seems to represent an obvious example of a display rule, however, as Fridlund (1994) points out, the spectator's neutral expression does not necessarily constitute evidence for a disparity between experience and display. The spectator may be experiencing additional emotions because of the proximity of these other people, for example, apprehension or embarrassment, thus the lack of correspondence between emotion and expression cannot necessarily be attributed solely to the operation of display rules.

The social nature of emotion

Fridlund draws attention to the social nature of expression, highlighting the individual's awareness of the reaction of others. An emotion is social in a number of respects: emotional expression plays an important communicative role in social interactions; it is shaped by sociocultural factors; more radically, it has no existence outside social and linguistic practices, as Lupton (1998, p. 15) puts it: 'emotional states are viewed as purely contextual and cannot be reified as separate entities: they are not inherent or pre-existing, waiting to be studied by the observer'. Mead (1934) was influenced by Darwin's book but he construed expression not as an indicator of an inner emotion but as a 'social gesture' that plays a key role in social interaction and in the acquisition of self-consciousness (see Chapter 2). The meanings of gestures are shared by social actors and this allows the individual to put himself in the place of another to understand how his behaviour looks to the other: 'the individual's consciousness depends on his thus taking the attitude of the other toward his own gestures' (ibid., p. 47).

Some emotions – shame, embarrassment and shyness – are evidently social in that they are experienced in the actual or imagined company of others. Furthermore, any visible sign of emotion has social consequences; it is judged to be appropriate or excessive and so on, and it informs others about the characteristics of the person showing it. As discussed in Chapter 4, the belief that emotional expression cannot be controlled or readily feigned makes it an effective cue for identifying people's motives and for predicting their behaviour, for example in bargaining, where negotiators strive to keep an expressionless 'poker' face.

Emotions are social in another sense. Societies arrange ceremonies to mark significant events in the lives of individuals and these relate to worldviews and values that are held by those societies and the social structures and institutions that are set up to sustain those views and values. Bar mitzvahs, weddings and funerals are ceremonies and what is done and 'felt' there relates the individual to organised social systems.

Emotions are social in that they are described in language, which is used to communicate about bodily feelings, subjective states and the meanings of events. The way a language codes emotional experiences relates to the common sense or 'folk' theories that a culture constructs about the nature of emotion, for example about where the emotions are located, in the body or in the brain. It is well known that different languages code emotions differently, and some languages group together emotions that others treat as distinct. Research into emotion relies on language: interviewing people about their experiences, having them complete questionnaires and rating scales and asking them to provide labels for photographs of facial expressions. This is problematic when it is undertaken with people of different cultures, languages and dialects but it has the less obvious but more fundamental problem that, as Wierzbicka (1992) argues, psychological theories are themselves framed in language and in the concepts of their culture.

A more extreme position on the role of language is that it does more than provide labels for emotions; rather, emotions are constructed through language or 'discursive practices'. Thus, when we fall in love, we don't invent this experience but appropriate our culture's understanding of romantic love as we know it through books, songs, television and so on. In short, emotions are socially constituted. As Lupton (1998, p. 16) characterises this perspective, 'emotion is thus viewed as an intersubjective rather than an individual phenomenon, constituted in the relations between people'. Emotions are experienced as internal states but they are produced in and through social interactions. According to Averill (1982, p. 7), 'any emotional syndrome represents the enactment of a transitory social role'. The behaviours associated with grief and romantic love are examples of emotional roles or 'scripts'; the patterns of behaviour and feeling involved in both are culturally and historically specific. Consider the unease that many in Western societies express about the notion of an arranged marriage and their intuition that this cannot be a genuine relationship because it is not based on 'falling in love'. Yet the contemporary notion of romantic love is relatively recent in Western culture; arranged marriages have been common in the history of Western society, and Western folk wisdom acknowledges that passion does not necessarily provide a sound basis for an enduring relationship. Responses in Britain to the death of Princess Diana illustrate the significant influence that sociocultural factors have on the experience and display of emotion, but does this necessarily lead to the conclusion that emotion is entirely defined by these influences? The pattern of behaviours that is seen is not arbitrary but is evident in other cultures and in British society in the past (during the Victorian period, for example).

Plausible as these examples may be, many would object to the characterisation of emotion as a role. One objection is that we normally contrast playing a role with being sincere and distinguish between feigning an emotion and feeling it. We know what it is like to adopt the persona of someone who feels an emotion and we sense that this is a different experience from actually feeling it. There are subtle differences between spontaneous and feigned expressions (Ekman, 1997). Another objection is that while characterising it as a role draws attention to the social nature of emotion, it fails to specify what distinguishes emotional roles from other roles or, for that matter, what differentiates a shame role from a guilt or embarrassment role.

Intense emotion, such as fear or grief, can be overwhelming; it is experienced as something that happens *to* us and is inescapable, and is not a role we can choose whether or not to play. It is difficult to believe that our grief following a close bereavement feels differently from that suffered by individuals in other societies, even though we accept that its display is influenced by culturally and historically specific factors.

Psychological research holds to a realist conception of emotion and this has influenced approaches to understanding the blush. One position on the blush, perhaps the consensual one, is that embarrassment is an emotional state that has its own distinctive expressive pattern, and one element of this pattern is localised change in skin colour and temperature. Certainly the blush constitutes a social event in the sense that the blusher is aware of his or her colouring and is frequently unhappy about it, since it is feared that others who notice the blush will make judgments about the psychological state of the blusher and perhaps about his or her character. Observers reach these judgments in accordance with their culturally influenced interpretation of the prevailing circumstances and their just-acquired insight into the blusher's psychological state. The blusher, in turn, responds to the others' reactions to his or her blush and takes steps to influence the impression that it has created.

As this volume illustrates, perspectives on the blush reflect these different positions on emotion. Some emphasise the psychophysiology of the blush while others focus on its interpersonal nature. There are social constructionist positions on the blush although at present these are represented in literary criticism (for example, O'Farrell, 1997) rather than in psychological investigations. The dominant psychological position owes much to Darwin.

Conclusion

Darwin has influenced two approaches to the study of emotional expression. The predominant one has sought to identity expressions for basic, universal emotions. Another has interpreted expressions as acts of communication. Neither approach has paid much attention to the blush, although there have been recent empirical studies of blushing in response to embarrassing circumstances and the influence of the blush on interpretations of people's conduct. Part II examines this research.

Darwin proposed that blushing evolved with self-consciousness since it is found in all races but is absent in those individuals who lack self-awareness and in other species. Thus, he was able to account for the unique position of man and the absence of continuity between man and other species without yielding his position on human evolution. An appeal to self-attention also enabled Darwin to weaken the connection that Burgess had made between shame, guilt and blushing. Darwin argued that it is our sense of how we appear to others rather than our conscience that originally caused us to blush. Darwin's position quickly became accepted. By 1890 Campbell had provided an analysis of blushing that quoted Darwin extensively and concluded (p. 138) that 'self-consciousness is the essential mental condition underlying blushing'. The argument has proved durable. *Expression* has been continuously in print ever since its publication; in contrast, Burgess's account has had little influence and his book has never been reprinted.

Research has concentrated on a small number of basic emotions that exclude the states most commonly associated with the blush – embarrassment, guilt, modesty, shame and shyness. This bias is reinforced by research into facial expression, itself influenced by Darwin, which has identified a small set of universal emotions that overlaps substantially with the basic emotions. Embarrassment, guilt, shame and shyness occupy an uncertain place in this set. Early studies of expression relied upon monochrome still photographs, which of course would fail to capture a blush. Subsequent research examined changes in expression brought about by the musculature; this inevitably neglected colour changes.

Taken together, these trends in research into emotional expression have resulted in neglect of the blush. This neglect seems unwarranted: as reported in later chapters, there is evidence that the blush is a universal sign of human emotion; indeed it meets many of Ekman's (1972) criteria for the definition of a basic emotion.

The extensive psychophysiological research into emotion has almost completely ignored the blush, nevertheless its findings are of relevance. For instance, the distinction made in fear research between fast and slow routes from stimulus to emotion suggests how a blush might be triggered before there is time for extensive cognitive analysis of a potential social predicament: to anticipate an example presented in Chapter 8, we can sometimes be surprised to find ourselves blushing.

The expression of emotion is subject to display rules. As discussed earlier, these rules vary across cultures, between sexes and across social contexts. The expression of the basic emotion of sadness provides an illustration. Ceremonies and behaviours associated with grieving are different in different cultures. In British society there are social pressures on everyone to put a brave face on grief and loss yet it has been more acceptable for women to shed tears of grief or disappointment than it has been for men to do so. Rules are not just about inhibiting emotions; they can lead us to simulate an expression and 'put on' a sad face when commiserating with someone.

Display rules imply a degree of control over emotional expression and this raises questions about the blush, which is generally assumed to be uncontrollable. It must be said that this assumption has not been put to empirical test and there is no evidence that it cannot be controlled or is less controllable than other facial expressions. Other expressions can be difficult to mask and it can be hard to adhere to display rules: tears break through and contradict the attempt at a smile. Nevertheless, if it is the case that the onset of a blush cannot be prevented, this has implications for the construction of display rules involving the blush and for the interpretation of facial reddening by the blusher and those who observe it. These issues are addressed in Chapter 4.

A blush contributes to a social encounter in numerous ways and the concept of display rule represents only one tool for understanding how it does so. Unfortunately, other approaches to the social nature of the blush have been scarcely developed. In part, the dearth of such studies reflects a more general trend in research into emotion of concentrating upon the analysis of the reactions of individuals in psychological experiments to the neglect of the social context. An orientation to study facial signs of emotion during social encounters other than in the laboratory could scarcely ignore the blush.

2
Self-consciousness and Emotion

The self has generated a seemingly endless number of philosophical enquiries, theoretical expositions and empirical investigations and yet remains a complex and controversial topic. In the process it has become increasingly elusive, as the consensus position in scholarship, which may broadly be characterised as social constructionist, is to deny that there is any 'essential' self: the self comprises a multiplicity of identities and roles. Yet it is clear that we will not be able to understand the blush without taking the self into account. Darwin and Campbell associated the blush with the mental state of self-consciousness; this too remains little understood, and uncertainties about terminology contribute to this state of affairs in no small measure. The chapter begins by considering various meanings of self-consciousness as the term has been used by psychologists, and goes on to examine a conceptualisation of self-consciousness as self-focused attention that has attracted considerable psychological and clinical research. Finally, it introduces the self-conscious emotions, which are considered individually in later chapters.

Self-consciousness

There are two principal themes in the study of self-consciousness. One is that it is inextricably linked with personhood and personal identity. The second is that social processes are the precondition for self-consciousness, that the self is inherently social. This position in social psychology is associated with Mead (1934) who proposed:

> Self-consciousness involves the individual's becoming an object to himself by taking the attitudes of other individuals toward himself within an organized setting of social relationships, and that unless

the individual had thus become an object to himself he would not be self-conscious or have a self at all.

However, we also think of self-consciousness not just as personhood but as a distinctive mental state where the self is focal in awareness. Campbell (1890, p. 141) distinguished self-consciousness in the sense of selfhood – 'subject consciousness' or awareness of our existence as individuals – from self-attention, 'the critical contemplation by an individual of his body, and of his mental life – of his past life, his moral responsibility, his future destiny (= introspection)'. In this second sense, self-consciousness is directed either to 'the mental being' or to the body, whether physical appearance or bodily functions. Campbell followed Darwin in arguing that the blush is caused primarily by self-consciousness of physical appearance and not by moral conduct, although it is also caused by undue self-consciousness of mental being: 'he fancies others forming unfavourable opinion of his abilities, character or conduct – that they can read his consciousness and see him as he sees himself, or that they are ridiculing his acts' (ibid., p. 147).

Psychologists have tended to use the term in a more restricted sense, consistent with the Concise Oxford Dictionary definition of a 'person embarrassed or unnatural in manner from knowing he is observed by others', and have emphasised one or other elements of this definition. Harré (1983, p. 166) alludes to unnaturalness of manner when he defines self-consciousness as the state where 'the normal intentionality of actions in which they are thought of as ends or outcomes is suspended and the self-conscious actor focuses on the actions he or she is performing'. Csikszentmihalyi (1990) also refers to the disruption of ongoing behaviour and contrasts this with the 'flow' of experience that is characteristic of immersion in a task; when this flow is disrupted, attention is directed away from involvement in the task and becomes focused on the self. Goffman (1972, p. 118) writes of self-consciousness as occurring when the actor gives attention to 'himself as an interactant at a time when he ought to be free to involve himself in the content of the conversation'. Goffman argues that it not necessarily self-consciousness when the self is the topic of conversation: it is possible to be self-centred without being self-conscious. He also refers to the close relation between self-consciousness and the fluster and inaction of embarrassment.

None of these statements regards the actual attention of others as essential for self-consciousness. Nevertheless it is a common experience that being watched while carrying out some activity can lead to feeling awkward and increases the likelihood of making clumsy movements and mistakes; this is reflected in the dictionary definition, which gives being observed by others as the source of embarrassment and unnaturalness of manner. As noted in Chapter 1, Darwin regarded the attention of others as the original cause of the blush.

Tomkins (1963) and Harris (1990) follow Campbell in relating the blush to self-consciousness. As discussed later in this chapter, Tomkins found the blush problematic for his account of shame; nevertheless he too suggested that it is associated with heightened self-consciousness. Not only is the self the subject and object of shame, the judge and the accused, but shame is perceived as close to the experiencing self because 'the self lives in the face' (1963, p. 133). He continues,

> Shame turns the attention of the self and others away from other objects to this most visible residence of self, increases its visibility and thereby generates the torment of self-consciousness ... Blushing of the face in shame is a consequence of, as well as a further cause for, heightened self- and face-consciousness.

Harris argues that embarrassment is accompanied by public self-awareness (and blushing) and that these are 'two sides of the same coin' and relate to the common sense notion of the state of self-consciousness. He labels this state as 'acute negative public self-attention' (ANPS-A) and, as the wording implies, he regards this as an inherently unpleasant experience: it is negative because we are aware of a discrepancy between our current self-image and our ideal self-image, and public because the experience is dominated by our sense of how we appear in the eyes of others. Social anxiety is experienced when we anticipate that we are likely to experience ANPS-A. It is our self-consciousness that we fear, not, as other theories propose, what other people might think of us. As Harris portrays it, ANPS-A is inherently unpleasant (it has aversive properties and motivates us to avoid it) and is associated with self-presentation failures. This interpretation of self-consciousness goes beyond the common sense notion of, say, blushing, since a person may blush when praised and thanked. Embarrassment, which also involves self-consciousness and blushing, is not necessarily acute or negative since it seems to vary in intensity and duration, from mild or transient fluster, perhaps accompanied by humour, to the prolonged agony of wishing the floor would open and swallow us. Harris regards the blush as the hallmark, not of embarrassment, but of ANPS-A, and thus also of shame and shyness, since both of these are labels that may be applied to ANPS-A. This is a position I am sympathetic towards, and I pick up the notion that the blush is characteristic of self-consciousness rather than of embarrassment in several places in this volume.

While I am not persuaded that the state is as inherently intensely aversive as Harris and Tomkins suggest, I believe Harris is correct to identify it as a distinctive state, one dominated by our sense of how we appear in the eyes of others. Self-consciousness is a palpable experience with its own phenomenological character, where the self is conscious of acting in the gaze of others. Sartre (1966) gives the example of a voyeur who is absorbed in spying through a keyhole when he suddenly becomes aware of what he is doing, as seen through the eyes of another, which gives rise to self-consciousness and shame.

I remember several occasions of intense self-consciousness. Once, as a child, I went out for the first time in a new coat and imagined (how foolish and self-centred this was) that the coat (and its wearer) was the object of everyone's attention. On another occasion, when I was 17, I rode a motor scooter for the first time; the engine was much noisier than I had anticipated and I imagined that all the pedestrians were looking at me. These memories are vivid even though nothing untoward happened and I was the object of no one's attention but my own, and they attest to the intensity of the experience of self-consciousness. I did not necessarily expect that people would think badly of me for wearing the coat or riding the scooter but in each case I felt exposed. The experience contrasts with feeling proud of my coat or scooter; here I might also be conscious of the gaze of others but this would not be the unpleasant state of exposure. Who did I imagine was paying attention to me? The 'other' that is credited with doing the observing is not necessarily a particular individual or group although, of course, it can be. People frequently remark to someone whose behaviour or appearance seems to them to be inappropriate in some way, 'what will people say?' or 'what would people think?' – expressions that do not specify which people they have in mind but nonetheless convey the sense that there exists a point of view 'out there'. Yet the source of this 'other' is the imagination of the self-conscious person. I would not have felt self-conscious if I had not been wearing a new coat, yet who else would have known that it was new. I was attributing to others knowledge that I had about myself, assuming that because I knew this, they would too. This bias in thinking has been researched by clinical psychologists studying the cognitive processes involved in social phobia, and is discussed below and in Chapter 11.

Self-focused attention

I return to the distinctive nature of this state when the self-conscious emotions are introduced later in this chapter but I now turn to its interpretation as self-focused attention, a conceptualisation which, along with its associated methodology, has captured the attention of researchers in social and clinical psychology. I ask whether this interpretation does justice to the notion of the observing other.

The distinction between attention focused on the self and attention directed towards the environment has given rise to an immense body of research. Duval and Wicklund (1972) published their seminal theory of *objective self-awareness*, which proposed that attention could be focused inwards, on the self, or outwards, to some aspect of the environment. Their most enduring contribution has been the introduction of an experimental paradigm where the researcher influences the direction of participants' attention by manipulating the presence or absence of mirrors, audiotape recorders and television cameras or by having participants write essays using first-person pronouns. Research established that inducing objective self-awareness, or self-focused attention as it soon came to be labelled, elicited predictable changes in cognitions and behaviour. Buss (1980) further distinguished between attention paid to private aspects of the self, which can be induced by looking at oneself in a small mirror, and that paid to public aspects of the self, which is induced by arranging circumstances so that the participant hears an audiotape recording of his or her own voice or sees his or her image in a large mirror or on a television screen. Public self-awareness is also produced when we are observed and, Buss suggests, believe we are shunned.

Research has identified individual differences in the predisposition to focus attention inwards or outwards. Fenigstein *et al.* (1975) constructed a self-report questionnaire to measure this predisposition and this has been widely used in research, including studies of blushing. The questionnaire provides scores on three factors: *private self-consciousness*, where items refer to a tendency to focus attention upon private thoughts and feelings, *public self-consciousness*, a tendency to focus on the self as a social object, and *social anxiety*, where the items refer to shyness and embarrassment.[1] Chapter 10 reviews research into the relations between these measures and blushing. Suffice it to point out here that results using this measure parallel findings in studies that induce a transient increase in self-focused attention through systematic manipulation of camera or mirror.

Buss (1980) drew upon this research to produce one of the first comprehensive accounts of the similarities and differences among shyness, shame and embarrassment. He identified these as distinct forms of social anxiety (adding audience anxiety as a fourth member of the set), based on the assumption that all entail acute public self-awareness. This state is the cornerstone of the model, the property that all four forms of social anxiety share. What distinguish the forms are their unique patterns of causes, whether conspicuousness, novelty, disclosure or anxiety about being evaluated, the degree of self-blame involved, gestures like covering the face and gaze aversion, and autonomic system reactions. Buss was explicit that the blush is specific to embarrassment and is not associated with shyness or shame. This claim is controversial, since many people report that they do blush when they feel shy. Buss has gone on to make an influential distinction between fearful and self-conscious shyness (discussed later in this chapter and in Chapter 9), with the implication that the blush is specific to the latter form. This distinction is reminiscent of that made by Harris between anxiety and ANPS-A although he distinguished between these on a temporal dimension: anxiety is anticipatory and self-consciousness reactive. Rather than advocating distinct types of shyness, Harris proposed that shyness – unlike embarrassment, which is reactive – could be either anticipatory or reactive.

Attention and anxiety

The construct of self-focused attention has been taken up in cognitive models of social anxiety, and in approaches to the treatment of social phobia based on these models (see also Chapter 11). Duval and Wicklund proposed that objective self-awareness leads us to compare our current state with our standards, and a perceived discrepancy produces either positive or negative affect depending on its direction. In general, however, it leads to negative affect since it is more likely that we perceive ourselves to fall short of our ideals. Carver and Scheier (1987) modified this model to argue that detection of a discrepancy initiates attempts to reduce it and negative affect is linked to a pessimistic appraisal of the likely success of this process.

These models predict that tendencies towards self-focused attention would be associated with negative mood and depression. The evidence seems to support this. Mor and Winquist (2002) conducted a meta-analysis of 221 studies involving clinical and non-clinical samples that presented data on links between self-focused attention and anxiety, depression and depressed mood. They included both experimental research

(72 studies) and correlational research drawing upon the self-consciousness scales (149 studies). Across the set of studies as a whole, there were moderate effect sizes for public and private self-focused attention in both experimental and correlational designs although this overall trend masked a significant interaction effect where correlational studies are concerned.[2] Anxiety was correlated with public self-consciousness (the effect size statistic $d = 0.73$; 6 studies) but not with private self-consciousness ($d = 0.08$; 4 studies). Conversely depression was correlated with private self-consciousness, $d = 0.67$ (34 studies). While the pattern of findings seems coherent, several of the comparisons are based on a very small number of studies, and only in the case of the link between private self-consciousness and depression does the sample of studies seem adequate to indicate robust trends. Furthermore, while public self-focused attention is more closely associated with negative affect than is the private form, and this difference is statistically significant, the effect sizes are comparable in magnitude, for example, in studies with a correlational design the respective values of d are 0.63 and 0.55.

Clark and Wells (1995) drew upon the concept of self-focused attention in their cognitive process model of social phobia, which assigns a central place to 'processing of the self as a social object'. They propose that socially anxious individuals tend to direct attention to observation and monitoring of the self. This tendency creates problems for anxious individuals since they use this information to infer how they appear to other people, leading to distorted judgments about what others are thinking. For example, if I know from internal cues that I am blushing and I feel uncomfortable about this because I regard the blush as a sign of lack of poise, I infer not only that my blushing is noticeable to others but that they will form an adverse judgment of me because of it. Clark (2005) provides an overview of experimental and correlational research that has been undertaken within this paradigm. Individuals diagnosed as meeting clinical criteria for social phobia tend to make negative inferences about how they appear to others. They over-estimate the visibility of their anxiety-related behaviours. The more they are aware of bodily sensations the more negative they infer the judgments of others to be. They believe that they blush more than others do even when physiological measures indicate that they do not do so (this research is discussed in Chapters 3 and 10). For example, Mellings and Alden (2000) related measures of social anxiety and self-focused attention to the inferences that people make about how they appear to others. The undergraduates who participated in the study were selected on the basis that they obtained either high or low scores on a social anxiety questionnaire. Each student interacted for ten minutes with another individual (who was actually a confederate of the researcher) and subsequently rated him or herself on questionnaire measures of self-focused attention and the presence of anxious behaviours (pauses, eye contact, fidgeting) and body sensations (this measure included one item on blushing). Socially anxious students reported more self-attention and also more anxiety-related behaviours and bodily sensations than did their less anxious counterparts. When they were tested the following day on their memory of details of the encounter, they recalled more negative information about themselves and less information about the person with whom they had interacted. They also over-estimated the signs of anxiety they were giving off relative to estimates made by observers of the interaction.

This research implies that self-focused attention would influence awareness of blushing, but Bögels *et al.* (2002) failed to find this. Their study tested whether inducing self-focused attention by means of a mirror would increase blushing in socially anxious individuals who were interacting with another person (a confederate of the researcher) who was supposedly evaluating them. Blushing was measured by physiological recording on three occasions – prior to, during and after the interaction. Participants high in social anxiety obtained higher scores on the physiological measure than those low in anxiety, but the mirror manipulation had no significant effect on the measure. Similarly no effect of mirror was obtained for self-rated or confederate-rated blushing. Increasing self-awareness did not mediate the influence of social anxiety on rated blushing or the physiological measure. It is possible that the presence of the mirror heightened private self-awareness, perhaps leading to a more accurate assessment of the physiological arousal. The study showed that socially anxious individuals do blush more than less anxious individuals do, and they do not simply exaggerate their colouring, at least in the conditions of this experiment. However, other studies (discussed in Chapters 3 and 10) have found no difference in physiological measures associated with anxiety about blushing.

The findings about the role of self-awareness in mediating the relation between blushing and anxiety are equivocal and many questions are left unanswered. Further research is needed to show why all studies do not find that socially anxious individuals exaggerate their blushing. There has been much discussion of the role of self-awareness in blushing but there is little direct evidence on this (see also Chapter 10). Chapter 11 considers the application of research into self-focused attention related to the development of interventions for individuals seeking help for their fear of blushing.

The principal psychological construct in this research has been social anxiety. The items on the questionnaires that assess appearance and bodily sensations refer to signs and symptoms of anxiety, and blushing appears among these items along with sweating and trembling. The emotions that are elicited by the anticipation and the experience of interacting with other people belong to the fear family: anxiety, apprehension and nervousness. This emphasis is consistent with Buss's (1980) model, which classes shyness and embarrassment as forms of anxiety. However, an alternative approach regards these states as members of a family of self-conscious emotions, which, as the term suggests, also have self-focused attention and self-consciousness at their core.

The self-conscious emotions

Writers on emotion have consistently grouped together shame, guilt and pride in terms of the central role that self-appraisal plays in each. The set of emotions is variously labelled social emotions, moral emotions, attachment emotions, emotions of self-approval and self-disapproval, self-conscious emotions, self-reflexive emotions, self-sentiments and emotions of self-assessment. They have also been termed higher cognitive or cognition-dependent emotions because they are presumed to require more extensive processing by the cerebral cortex than do basic, lower or cognition-independent emotions, such as fear and sadness. Tangney and Fischer (1995) assembled an influential collection of chapters under the over-arching title of the self-conscious emotions, and this term seems likely to endure.

Several issues continue to be debated in this field, including which emotions comprise the 'family' of self-conscious emotions, which of these are distinct emotions, and what are the criteria for distinguishing among them. There have been two general approaches to this. One considers shame to be the fundamental emotion, with embarrassment and shyness as variants. Tomkins identified shame, shyness and guilt as a single affect, namely shame-humiliation. Helen Block Lewis (1971) and Scheff and Retzinger (2001) regard shame as the 'master emotion' and treat embarrassment and shyness as variants (see Chapter 7).

The second approach differentiates the self-conscious emotions in terms of the pattern of attributions that is made. Michael Lewis (1992; 2000) set out an influential 'cognitive attribution' model that makes claims about their development in the life of the child. Lewis argues that three criteria define the self-conscious emotions of shame, guilt/regret, pride and hubris: (i) awareness that there are standards and rules for conduct; (ii) evaluation of the success or failure of actions, thoughts and feelings relative to these standards and rules; (iii) attribution of success or failure to the self, specifically to either global or specific dimensions of the self. Shame and guilt are produced by an assessment of failure to meet standards; they are distinguished in that the failure in the case of shame is attributed to global aspects of the self whereas in guilt it is attributed to specific actions. In the former case, 'the self becomes embroiled in the self. It becomes embroiled because the evaluation of the self by the self is total. There is no way out' (M. Lewis, 2000, p. 628). In the case of guilt the self is not so embroiled, and the focus of the person's attention is on the specific act that has brought about the failure; it is possible to make good the failure or excuse or justify it in some way.

The model is extended to incorporate embarrassment, where Lewis distinguishes between two forms, one emerging earlier in life than the other. The earlier appearing form, exposure embarrassment, is produced simply by exposure to others and does not necessarily involve negative self-evaluation. The second form, evaluative embarrassment, is a less intense form of shame, and is produced by the same combination of evaluation and self-attribution of outcome as is shame. Shyness, like exposure embarrassment, is not construed in terms of self-evaluation and Lewis regards it as a form of social discomfort in the presence of unfamiliar people. It emerges prior to the development of the capacity for self-evaluation of the social self, and behaviours can be observed in other species that resemble the expressions, gestures and actions characteristic of human shyness.

Tracy and Robins (2004) have published a review of research on these emotions and constructed a 'process model' that aims to integrate existing findings and to propose testable hypotheses about the nature of these emotions and the relations among them. The model distinguishes them from basic emotions, which, it is claimed, serve survival goals, whereas the self-conscious emotions serve 'identity goals'. It is further proposed that embarrassment, shame, guilt and pride (the last is separated into hubris and 'achievement-oriented pride') can be distinguished in terms of the specific appraisal and attribution processes involved. The same issue of the journal in which the article appears carries commentaries from many of the researchers who have made significant contributions to the study of the self-conscious emotions. Regrettably, but telling for understanding contemporary conceptualisations of self-consciousness, blushing does not figure in the target article or in any of the commentaries. Indeed, Tracy and Robins claim that no self-conscious emotion has a distinct facial expression; they argue that this helps to define this class of emotions. They use the term expression to refer specifically to expressions produced by the facial musculature, distinguishing these from changes in posture and body movements such as lowering the head or averting the gaze.

The self in self-conscious emotion

The title of Tracy and Robins' article refers to 'putting the self into self-conscious emotions'. This section considers what the article has to say about the self, taking shame as an illustration although any of the other emotions would do as well. According to Tracy and Robins, the starting point for the process is that an event triggers self-attention and produces awareness of failure to live up to some actual or ideal self-representation. This results in a specific identity-goal incongruent emotion. For example, if a man believes that he is not tall enough and some event, say a comment he overhears on short people, causes him to become aware of and focus his attention on his shortcomings, he will experience shame. One might think that rather than experience shame, he would feel disappointment, regret, sadness or anger at being dealt a cruel hand by his genetic endowment. Disappointments can attract descriptions in terms of shame – 'What a shame that you couldn't make it', 'Isn't it a shame that the shop has closed down'. A convincing theory of shame should be able to specify whether these alternative reactions are different from shame and how they are different.

It is evident that the perspective that is being taken on the failure to live up to standards is that of the ashamed person himself. Tracy and Robins (ibid., p. 105) make this point explicitly about the self-conscious emotions in general:

> Thus, the primary distinctive characteristic of self-conscious emotions is that their elicitation requires the ability to form stable self-representations (me), to focus attention on those representations (i.e., to self-reflect; I), and to put it all together to generate a self-evaluation.

However, when Tracy and Robins write on shame (ibid., p. 108), they extend this definition beyond self-representations to include the internalisation of 'an external, societal, or parental perspective on those self-representations; and reflect on the discrepancy between his or her own behavior, external evaluations of that behavior, and various self-representations'. The notions of different perspectives on the self and of a discrepancy in perceptions are central to many accounts of shame (and the self-conscious emotions more generally). A crucial question, it seems to me, and one that has generated extensive discussion in the literature on shame, is that of which perspective is involved: according to several writers, this seems to be the decisive issue for understanding shame. There is widespread recognition that there is a dual role for the self, it is both the subject and the object in shame. Tangney *et al.* (1996a, p. 1257) wrote that, 'the self is both agent and object of observation and disapproval, as shortcomings of the defective self are exposed before an internalized observing "other" '. Leary (2004, p. 130) also refers to the internalised observing 'other':

> Specifically, all self-conscious emotions require reflection on how one is being perceived and evaluated by other people, either people with whom one is interpersonally engaged or people whose evaluations one only imagines. Thus, stable self-representations and self-appraisals are not the central features of self-conscious emotions, but rather reflected representations and reflected appraisals – how people believe they are being perceived and evaluated by others.

The concept of reflected appraisal recalls Cooley's point that what 'moves us to *pride* or *shame* is not the mere mechanical reflection of ourselves, but an imputed sentiment, the imagined effect of this reflection upon another's mind (Cooley, 1902/1983, p. 184). Cooley famously proposed the concept of the 'looking-glass self' but this conceptualisation pre-dates the twentieth century and was influenced by Adam Smith's *Theory of Moral Sentiments*, first published in 1759.

> We suppose ourselves the spectators of our own behaviour, and endeavour to imagine what effect it would, in this light, produce upon us. This is the only looking glass by which we can, in some measure, with the eyes of other people, scrutinize the propriety of our conduct. (Smith, 1759/2002, p. 131)

Smith also emphasises the duality of the self:

> When I endeavour to examine my own conduct ... I divide myself into two characters, as it were into two persons; and that I, the examiner and judge, represent a different character from that other I, the person whose conduct is examined into and judged of. The first is spectator, whose sentiments with regard to my own conduct

I endeavour to enter into, by placing myself in his situation, and by considering how it would appear to me, when seen from that particular point of view. (ibid., p. 131)

Seeing ourselves from another point of view requires an act of imagination. But which other's viewpoint should we take? Other people will have different perceptions of our conduct and they have no direct access to our motives, intentions and so on. Cooley pointed out that we might be ashamed if our deficiency were perceived by one person but not if the same deficiency were perceived by another. Others have their own motives and intentions that will inevitably influence their judgments of us. H. B. Lewis (1971, p. 202) writes of the 'implied hostile watcher' in shame; as her wording indicates, the hostility is attributed to the observer by the ashamed person. Smith proposed that we imagine an ideal disinterested judge, an 'impartial spectator'. We judge our own conduct through the eyes of the impartial spectator and feel ashamed if it falls short in the spectator's judgment. This concept is similar to that of a 'possible detached observer-description' proposed by Taylor (1985), writing on shame and the self-conscious emotions. Taylor describes (ibid., p. 57) the ashamed person feeling 'exposed: she thinks of herself as being seen through the eyes of another', and characterises this (ibid., p. 66) in terms of:

The agent's becoming aware of the discrepancy between her own assumption about her state or action and a possible detached observer-description of this state or action, and of her being further aware that she ought not to be in position where she could be so seen, where such a description at least appears to fit.

It is this internalisation that allows shame to operate as a powerful means of social control, and the force of this control is that the ashamed person identifies with the critical view held in this observer-description even if he or she thinks the evaluation is undeserved. Smith writes of shame in terms of the dread of attracting the hatred and contempt of others. Even if it were unlikely that others would discover what the person had done, he or she would still experience shame because the dread would be present.

In my view it is this activation of the mental representation of the self in the eyes of the 'other' that allows us to distinguish shame from other emotions that might be experienced in circumstances where an individual feels that he or she has fallen short of standards. For example,

I might catch sight of myself in a mirror and become aware of a discrepancy between my appearance and how I wished I looked. My attention is focused on myself and a self-representation of public aspects of myself is activated, yet while I might become depressed by awareness of this failure to live up to my ideal I don't think I would necessarily be ashamed. If I am disappointed with myself or depressed about my appearance the judgment comes from me and it might persist even when other people were to compliment me on my appearance or even try to disabuse me of any notion of my inadequacy, were I to share my concerns with them.

Does the construct of self-focused attention do justice to this sense of self-consciousness? The dominant conceptualisation in the literature on self-focused attention is that of the individual's reflection on different *aspects* of the self. Mor and Winquist (2002) write that, 'in discussing self-focus types, we do not imply different attentional systems with different biological or anatomical underpinnings but rather different aspects of the self that one can attend to'. As we have noted, the distinction between public and private aspects has been an important one in research, but this distinction has been blurred in recent studies of social anxiety. For example, items written for a self-focused attention scale by Mellings and Alden (2000) refer to aspects that are public (such as previous social failures), that are private (internal bodily states) and that could be either public or private depending on whether they were visible to others, such as trembling. Their research shows that all of these are used to infer the public self, how one appears to others.

Recent empirical research has moved from concentration on aspects of the self to consider perspectives that can be taken on these aspects. This development has drawn upon studies of autobiographical memory which distinguish between a 'field perspective' (looking out at the world) and an 'observer perspective', seeing oneself from an external viewpoint (Nigro and Neisser, 1983); these studies conclude that self-focused attention and self-consciousness tend to induce an observer perspective. Research finds that individuals diagnosed with social phobia tend to recall social situations from an observer perspective rather than from a field perspective (Hackmann *et al.*, 1998). Clark (2005, p. 202) writes of social phobics forming 'distorted observer-perspective images of how they think they appear to others when in feared social situations'. Hirsch *et al.* (2003, p. 910) argue that 'when attention shifts onto the self, negative images that involve seeing one's self as if from an external observer's perspective are synthesised'. This body of clinical research implies that the perspective that is attributed to the observer is itself biased by the individual's anxieties, so that he or she is primed to notice or exaggerate any possible negative reactions or adverse judgments on the part of any observers who are present, a process that creates a vicious circle from which it is difficult to extricate oneself. The terminology in these accounts resembles Taylor's description of the ashamed person who takes a detached observer perspective on the self. Is current clinical research edging towards a position where the central emotions in social phobia will be seen as shame and the fear of shame?

The position advocated here is that self-consciousness is not equivalent to self-focused attention and that the latter is a necessary but not a sufficient condition for the former. Rather, self-consciousness involves a shift in perspective. The observer perspective is itself a mental representation but it has a palpable quality – it does feel as if you are seen from an external viewpoint – and, I suggest, it has a distinctive bodily manifestation: the blush.

Cultural variation

Cognitive models tend to generate emotion categories that correspond to English words for emotions. An exception is M. Lewis's analysis, which yields two forms of embarrassment that do not have separate English words. Tracy and Robins distinguish two forms of pride, although there is a (relatively uncommon) English word available – hubris – to label the alternative form. The status of emotion categories is complicated by cultural and historical differences in how emotional states are labelled. In English it is only relatively recently that embarrassment has been used to refer to self-consciousness and fluster in social encounters. Many non-western languages do not distinguish among members of the family of self-conscious emotions, for example between shame and embarrassment or between shame and guilt, or else they have a number of different terms for what English would describe as a single emotion. Li *et al.* (2004) draw attention to cultural differences in words for shame explaining, for example, that there is no salient category of words for shame in Indonesia whereas, in contrast, Chinese culture emphasises shame and has a rich terminology: a dictionary search identified 83 shame-related terms.

In Arabic there are two words for shyness, *khajal* and *haya*. *Khajal* seems to correspond more closely to shyness as an undesirable quality, a limitation on effective social interaction as evident, for example, in responses to the Stanford Shyness Survey made by English-speaking Americans (Zimbardo, 1977), whereas *haya* is a more positive quality and refers to desirable and appropriate behaviour, to the rejection of what is bad and immoral, including shyness about saying something wrong or immoral. This sense is perhaps more closely related to shyness in its meanings of modesty, reserve or good manners, describing, for example, the appropriate way for a child to behave towards a parent or a woman to behave in the company of unfamiliar men. It is also related to shame, since a person who lacks *haya* would say anything regardless of its effect on others, someone we would describe in English as shameless or unblushing. European languages also have different concepts corresponding to the same word in English, for example, the distinction in Greek between shame as disgrace and shame as modesty is found in other modern European languages apart from English (Scheff and Retzinger, 2001).

Cultural differences aren't solely linguistic. Cohen and Gunz (2002) compared perspectives on the self held by North American and Asian participants in a study of autobiographical memory. Participants recalled instances of different situations (for example, being embarrassed) and were asked to distinguish between first-person memories and third-person memories. The descriptions of situations manipulated whether the participants, who were supposed to imagine themselves the actor in the episode, were or were not the centre of others' attention. Participants were presented with alternative sets of instructions. In one set of instructions, they were told: 'in your memory, you imagine the scene from your original point of view, not as an external observer would see it'; in the other set they were told: 'in your memory, you imagine the scene as an observer might see it. Such an observer would see you as well as other aspects of the situation'. Participants then rated each memory on a scale anchored by these alternative descriptions. Asian participants reported more third-person memories when the actor was the focus of attention relative to when the actor was not the centre of attention. However, the responses of North American participants were not influenced by this manipulation of descriptions. In a second part of the study, involving the identification of emotions in pictures of facial expressions, North Americans showed more egocentrism when judging the emotional expressions, that is they were more likely to project their own emotion onto the picture; on the other hand, Asian participants did not show this bias. Cohen and Gunz (ibid., p. 59) suggest that the findings demonstrate that:

> under the right circumstances, in looking at a social situation they [Easterners] construct a spontaneous social reality from a less egocentric, more overarching vantage point than Westerners do. Not only

does this vantage point make situations look different to the imagery of their mind's eye, but it causes them to understand the world differently.

Clearly the self-conscious emotions have different significance and meanings in different cultures. It would be surprising if this were not the case, given cultural variation in the concept of the self, for example between Eastern and Western societies, and given the view, that seems to be widely shared by researchers, that the self-conscious emotions appear later in life than 'basic' emotions and involve self-evaluation relative to standards. The standards, the dimensions of the self that are considered relevant to evaluation of the self and the implications of any incongruence between self and standards can be expected to vary across cultures and over time within a given culture.

How much weight should be attached to differences between languages? Pinker (1994) argues that differences are often over-stated. While emotions are organised differently in the lexicon of different languages, it is possible to translate from one to another and to understand the distinctions that are being made. To pick up on an example provided by Harré, while it is difficult for us to grasp what is meant by the emotion *accidie*, an emotion that was readily understood in our society in the past, and it is certainly difficult to define it succinctly, it is nevertheless possible for us to understand it in its historical context and to discuss it. Similarly, there is no single English equivalent word for *Schadenfreude* yet English speakers understand the concept and import the word.

Nonetheless, it has to be acknowledged that not only are emotions captured differently in language but the connotations of, say, shame, in one culture will not be the same as the connotations in another. As Li *et al.* (2004, p. 769) point out, 'shame to the Chinese is not a mere emotion, but also a moral and virtuous sensibility to be pursued'. The significance of emotion has to be judged in a wider cultural context. The analysis of the emotional experiences that are labelled pride, shame, guilt or embarrassment requires consideration of how these experiences are understood and labelled in cultures other than the English-language culture that has dominated psychological enquiry. It is difficult to escape entrenched preconceptions about the self and about the relation between mind and body if research is narrowly based in one culture and relies upon a small number of languages with common origins. There have been numerous attempts to identify the characteristics that distinguish shame from embarrassment or shame from guilt without acknowledgement that these terms are not signs of emotions but are culturally bound ways of speaking about experience.

Conclusion

Darwin considered that the blush is produced by self-attention. Psychological research has construed self-consciousness in four ways: as a distinctive mental state; as self-focused attention; as embarrassment; as a family of emotions. It is feasible that the blush is the expression of any or all of these. There is no evidence that self-focused attention in itself produces a blush, and it is argued in this chapter that this construct does not assign sufficient weight to the other-perspective that seems to be intrinsic to the state of self-consciousness and which may be essential for a blush to occur. It is possible that people only blush if they see themselves as if from the perspective of another. Darwin emphasised the blusher's consciousness of what the other would think of his or her action, as evident in his notebook[3] (reproduced here as given in his notebook):

> Let a person have committed any /concealed/ action he should not, & let him be thinking over it with any sorrow, – let the possibility of his being discovered by anyone, especially if it be a person, whose opinion he regards, <see> feel how the blood gushed into his face, – "as the thought of his knowing /it/, suddenly came across her, the blood rushed to her face." – One blushes if one thinks that any one suspects one of having done either good or bad action, it always bears some reference to thoughts of other person.

Psychological accounts consider that the self-conscious emotions share common features. They involve the self. The event that triggers emotion induces focus of attention on the self; this involves a comparison between the self and standards for behaviour; the cause of any congruence or discrepancy between self and standards is attributed to the self. The emotion is accompanied by a pattern of cognitive processes, physiological responses, visible bodily changes and action tendencies. These can represent and contribute to the individual's attempts to claim or reclaim social status, to make him or herself larger and more visible (to swell with pride) or smaller and less visible (to shrink with shame). They can influence the reactions of others, for example, the changes in posture that accompany shame and embarrassment are interpreted as attempts to show submission or appease others and thereby deflect aggression or social rejection. Correspondingly the blush can be interpreted as a bodily change that accompanies emotion or as a form of communication that influences the reactions of others.

Perhaps the blush is associated with some self-conscious emotions but not others, with embarrassment but not, say, with pride or guilt. The chapters in Part II of this volume focus on what is known about the blush, about its physiology, the circumstances that elicit it, and its significance for social relationships. Part III examines the principal self-conscious emotions separately, discusses the circumstances that give rise to each emotion and considers whether the blush is an idiosyncratic expression of that emotion.

II
The Nature of the Blush

3
What is a Blush?

The nature of the blush

Darwin was aware that the redness of the face, ears, neck and upper chest – the 'blush region' – is due to increased blood flow in that region brought about by vasodilation of the capillaries lying just under the skin. The mechanism responsible for this reddening was not understood at the time and while we now know a great deal more about the cardiovascular system and have learnt a little more about the physiology of the blush, the process remains mysterious. The blush is rarely discussed in textbooks of the cardiovascular system and if it is mentioned, it is typically to acknowledge how little it is understood. This chapter locates the blush within the context of what is known about the system and considers explanations that have been proposed. The final section examines measurement issues.

Several questions suggest themselves at the outset. First, is the change in colour and skin temperature that occurs in blushing distinct from other instances of reddening or flushing? Faces redden when we are hot, take exercise or imbibe alcohol; or when we are angry and indignant as well as when we are embarrassed. Flushing, associated with rapid temperature rise, palpitations and perspiration, can occur around the time of the menopause, be persistent and cause distress.[1] Do we label redness of the face a 'blush' only because of the circumstances in which it occurs or is there a distinctive physiological pattern? If, say, Anna Kournikova is photographed red-faced when a 'streaker' interrupts her tennis match, is it a blush that we see (as the article accompanying the picture claims) or simply the flush of exertion? When a visibly red-faced Prince Harry was involved in an altercation with a photographer outside a London nightclub, attracting, as a youthful member of the British royal family would do, extensive media coverage, he was variously described as red-faced and flushed, never as blushing.[2] Do we rely on the context to decide that a red face is a blush?

Is there more than one kind of blush? Leary *et al.* (1992) distinguish between the *classic* blush (as we have been considering so far) and the *creeping* blush. The latter spreads slowly over a period of several minutes, and is 'blotchy' in appearance and can spread to the neck and upper chest. It tends to be seen when someone is performing in front of others over an extended period of time. I have observed it in a university setting when a student is a candidate in an interview or a *viva voce* examination, or when a lecturer or student is making a presentation to a group. Its onset does not seem to coincide with either the anticipation of the performance or its beginning – the latency can be of several minutes – and it persists for a long time, although the colouring fades soon after the person leaves the situation. Although this type of blush typically appears when the individual is aware of being the object of sustained attention, as in these examples, it does not seem to require a specific precipitating incident, such as making a faux pas, which characteristically triggers the 'classic' type.

The classic blush can also persist, particularly if the person continues to ruminate on the circumstances, as this quotation from a participant in my research indicates. She started to blush while she was giving a speech to her classmates:

> I began fairly confidently, but gradually I became more aware of the silence except for my voice, and the fact that everyone was watching and listening to me. I felt nervous and started to shake while hurrying my speech. This caused me to blush. For ages afterwards (while the others were doing their speeches) I was still shaking and felt very hot. I could not concentrate on what they were saying as I was too concerned with thinking about my speech and how annoyed I was for getting so nervous. My red face did not disappear instantly – the moment the attention was no longer on me – because my thinking about it caused me to blush still.

Nevertheless, the similarities and differences between the two types, if indeed there are two, are not yet understood, nor do we have available accounts of any differences in mechanism. Campbell (1890) made careful observations of the spread of a blush and concluded that there are diverse ways in which redness is distributed. In some instances it starts with a dot of redness on the cheek which becomes triangular in form;

another triangle of redness anterior to the ear then appears and the two patches join. In other instances an initial patch appears and then expands, or else distinct patches appear and merge. A mild blush, he suggests, is restricted to the cheeks whereas a more intense blush extends to the ears, the neck, the forehead and the upper regions of the chest and back. Little attention has been paid to the patterns that the reddening can take, presumably reflecting an assumption that they are of little psychological significance.[3]

Is the blush the outcome of increased sympathetic nervous system activity or is it, as some theorists (for example, Buss, 1980) have claimed, associated with heightened parasympathetic activity? If it is the product of sympathetic activity, it targets limited areas of the body (it is possible, of course, that skin colouring and temperature changes occur elsewhere but are most noticeable, or are only detectable, in the 'blush region'). This specificity is in contrast to the sympathetic activity involved in fear, where there are widespread bodily changes: increases in heart rate, blood pressure, blood flow to skeletal muscles, sweating, constriction of blood vessels in the gut and so on. Blushing is not reliably correlated with other indices of sympathetic arousal. There is evidence that it is associated with a reduction in heart rate in embarrassing situations (Keltner and Buswell, 1997), implying inhibited sympathetic and increased parasympathetic nervous system activity. Stein and Bouwer (1997) also make the point that lower heart rate and blood pressure accompany blushing while Drummond (1999) reported a negative correlation between measures of forehead blood flow and diastolic blood pressure. On the other hand, there are arguments that embarrassment, like anxiety, gives rise to heightened sympathetic activity. A substantial proportion of respondents to surveys on blushing claim that increased heart rate, sweating and the sensation of 'butterflies in the stomach' accompany their blushing (for example, Simon and Shields, 1996). A similar picture is evident in responses to surveys on shyness. Respondents to the Stanford Shyness Survey indicated a number of typical symptoms of shyness that included blushing, perspiration, increased pulse, heart pounding and butterflies in the stomach (Zimbardo, 1977).

Laederach-Hofmann *et al.* (2002) investigated whether individuals with pronounced fear of blushing (erythrophobia) could be distinguished from a control group on indices of sympathetic and parasympathetic nervous system regulation. Those with fear of blushing showed a higher increase in heart rate than the control group in the baseline measurement condition and when completing a stressful intellectual task. This result is consistent with findings from studies of shyness and inhibition where shy individuals show increased heart rate in a stressful (unfamiliar) situation (see Chapter 9). However, research into shyness also tends to report a decrease in heart rate variability in stressful circumstances, whereas those with fear of blushing in this study showed a smaller reduction in heart rate variability in the stress condition compared to the control group, implying greater parasympathetic influence. Interpretation of differences among studies is difficult because the measures of heart rate variability are different and it is not clear whether the pattern identified by Laederach-Hofmann *et al.* is specific to erythrophobia or reflects social anxiety more generally. It would be instructive to compare the erythrophobia group with a group that was socially anxious, but not about blushing.

There is evidence that performing in front of other people, for example, in public speaking, gives rise to heightened sympathetic arousal (Beidel *et al.*, 1985). Gerlach *et al.* (2003) induced embarrassment in two groups of participants – a group obtaining high scores on social phobia scales and a control group – by having them watch, in the company of two other people, a videotape recording of themselves singing a children's song. Measures of increased heart rate and skin conductance (which are sympathetically controlled) and respiratory sinus arrhythmia (RSA; an index of parasympathetically mediated vagal nerve activity[4]) showed no heightened parasympathetic activation while watching the tape, but there was evidence of heightened sympathetic activity (and of a difference in this between the two groups, with the social phobic group showing higher heart rate).

A problem with interpreting these findings is that tasks such as speaking in front of others provoke anxiety as well as embarrassment, and hence they may trigger a complex pattern of physiological reactivity. In the experiment reported by Gerlach and associates, the participants with social phobia reported high levels of anxiety as well as embarrassment, and greater anxiety when first meeting their viewing companions (anticipating embarrassment) and when viewing the videotape (experiencing embarrassment). It is difficult to disentangle the effects of anxiety and embarrassment. Relevant evidence would seem to be provided by the control group in the study, whose members reported a statistically significant increase in embarrassment in both phases of the procedure relative to the baseline measure but did not report increased anxiety. In principle, this group should show more clearly the physiological correlates of embarrassment without the confounding factor of elevated anxiety. In support of the hypothesis that this group would not show greater parasympathetic arousal, there was no evidence of increases in RSA across the phases of the experiment. On the other hand, the levels of embarrassment reported were modest, a mean of 2.5 on a rating scale that ranged from 1 (not at all embarrassed) to 10 (extremely embarrassed). A more rigorous test of the hypothesis would require evidence of intense embarrassment accompanied by a low level of arousal.

Leary *et al.* (1994 cited by Miller, 1996, p. 16) tested whether embarrassment would produce a sequential pattern where an immediate increase in sympathetic reaction – initial surprise and arousal – would be followed by an increase in parasympathetic activity. In their study, the body fat of young women was measured and the procedure resulted in an initial increase in heart rate and blood pressure followed by a decrease in these measures along with an increase in facial skin temperature. However, Gerlach and associates were unable to replicate this pattern in their study among either the social phobic participants or the control group. They suggested that the measurement of body fat involved the tester making physical contact with the women's bodies and this might have contributed to physiological changes, complicating interpretation of the measures. These are difficult issues and the measurement and interpretation of physiological changes are far from straightforward in any study. There are complex, dynamic relations between sympathetic and parasympathetic processes.

Nevertheless, Leary *et al.*'s point that to be embarrassed it to be frozen in inaction is a plausible one. There is surely heuristic value for physiological research in Frijda's (1986, p. 168) proposal that:

> In all instances of blushing, then, there seems to be an action tendency that is stopped, blocked, or suppressed. Blushing thus could be a response of sudden inhibition of some tendency to act. Why this should become manifest in vasodilation, however, remains obscure.

How does the mental activity entailed in recognising or imagining that you are the object of others' attention result in vasodilation? How can thought alter the circulation of blood? The embarrassment that is frequently associated with a blush involves appreciation of the situation in which you find yourself and a sense of how you are seen, or could reasonably be seen, by others. How is this sense translated into increased blood flow in the facial region? To be sure, the blush is not the only instance of the power of the imagination to affect blood flow; another example is the enlargement of the clitoris or penis in sexual arousal. Erection of the sex organ is brought about by the relaxation of vascular muscle, which allows the arteries of the organ to fill with blood, increasing blood pressure and producing enlargement of the clitoris or penis. Sexual arousal can be induced by imagination or memory.[5] Darwin mentioned the connection between the erection and the blush in his notebooks (see Chapter 1) although, perhaps for reasons of modesty, he did not pursue the topic.

Psychoanalytic perspectives link the blush with sexual excitement, for example, Feldman (1941, [quoted by Karch, 1971, p. 44]) argues that women (but not, it seems men, where the picture is allegedly 'more complex') blush to 'prove their innocence and chastity, and ... to indicate sexual excitement and reveal their interest in sex'. The psychoanalytic position is more complex than regarding the blush as an indication of sexual arousal. Because it involves mechanisms of repression and displacement, its meaning is never the obvious one. The conspicuousness of the blush is linked with exhibitionism and voyeurism, the wish to display and to see the genitals. Because of the fear of castration the repressed wish to exhibit the genitals is displaced to the face, which is our most conspicuous feature – 'A displacement from below upward phallicizes the face, whereby unconscious exhibitionistic and punishment wishes are satisfied' (Bergler, 1944, p. 43).

The aroused sexual organ and the blush have more than a physiological connection, since shame and embarrassment play an important role in inhibiting sexual activity. While Western society has become more tolerant of depictions of nudity there is still a taboo on the display of the erect penis and it is only in the last few years that male and female masturbation have been acted in television and cinema drama. While there is more open discussion of masturbation and slang expressions and gestures are commonplace, the topic still has the capacity to cause a blush.

Physiology of the blush

What physiological mechanisms are involved in blushing? The circulation of blood is involved in regulation of body temperature. A basically hairless species like ours[6] relies on the circulation of blood close to the skin, particularly at the face, hands and feet, in order to adapt to environmental changes in temperature and to maintain the temperature of the brain and the other principal internal organs at 37.0 to 37.5°C. The skin is some 1.0 to 2.0 mm thick, although its thickness varies at different locations. It comprises a thinner outer layer, the epidermis, which contains no blood vessels, and a thicker inner layer, the dermis, beneath which is a layer of subcutaneous tissue.

Because of its vital role in temperature regulation the system of skin blood vessels has a distinctive, specialised structure. Blood flows along the arteries and resistance vessels (the smaller arteries and arterioles) in the subcutaneous layer into the capillaries in the epidermis; these form loops under the dermis before flowing via the venules into an extensive network of veins, the venous plexus. This network carries a large proportion of the volume of blood that flows close to the skin. The subcutaneous arteries have direct links to the venous plexus via vessels known as arteriovenous anastomoses, so that blood can be 'shunted' directly from arterioles to venules without passing through the capillary beds, thereby facilitating blood flow by reducing resistance. Thus the structure of subcutaneous vessels ensures that a substantial volume of blood can quickly be moved close to the skin so that heat can be lost.

The blush region has a distinctive anatomical structure that lends itself to the blush. Facial skin has large numbers of capillary loops in the dermis, the venous plexus holds a large amount of blood and the blood vessels are close to the surface of the cheek. The increased blood flow is apparent in the reddening of the skin that we notice on a hot day or that typically accompanies physical exercise. Redness of the skin is caused by engorgement of the capillaries in the dermis with blood, and the colour is due to haemoglobin, the pigment that carries oxygen in the blood.

How is vasodilation produced to increase blood flow to the facial skin and result in a blush? This is a difficult question to answer; there are several mechanisms, and none of them has been shown to produce a blush. Messages transmitted from temperature regulation centres in the hypothalamus via sympathetic adrenergic nerves[7] maintain a high degree of basal tone in the arteries and a much smaller degree of basal tone in the arteriovenous anastomoses (which have little basal tone in comparison with arteries). The neurotransmitter norepinephrine, which is released at the terminus of these nerves, binds to α receptors in the muscle cells of the blood vessels to produce constriction of the vessels.[8] Therefore, vasodilation can be produced by a decrease in sympathetic adrenergic activity, which relaxes constriction. Activity of the sympathetic nervous system also innervates the adrenal glands, located just above the kidneys, causing the medulla (central part) of the adrenal to secrete two hormones, epinephrine and norepinephrine, into the blood stream. Most of the norepinephrine is transformed to epinephrine, which is carried around the body in the blood and acts upon all those organs that have appropriate receptors. It produces vasoconstriction, including constriction of blood vessels at the skin, by activating α-receptors.

Thus the effect upon the muscles that constrict or dilate the blood vessels at any one site is influenced by the amount of norepinephrine or epinephrine at that site, and this comes either (i) from the binding of the neurotransmitter (predominantly norepinephrine) and receptor at the junction between nerve terminal and muscle or (ii) from the hormone circulating in the blood stream (predominantly epinephrine). A third route involves the release of paracrine hormones from cells adjacent to blood vessels (as opposed to endocrine hormones that are carried by the blood stream). This process plays little part in dilation of the arteriovenous anastomoses, since these are largely controlled by sympathetic nervous system activity, but the resistance vessels are dilated by release of bradykinin, which acts upon bradykinin receptors that stimulate nitric oxide formation. Activation of sweat glands by cholinergic nerves originating in temperature regulation centres in the hypothalamus stimulates the sweat glands to secrete enzymes including kallikrein, which is transformed into the kinins, kallidin and bradykinin. These cause dilation of arterioles: intravenous infusion of bradykinin produces visible flushing of the face (Bell *et al.*, 1976, p. 349).

These explanations relate facial reddening to activity of the temperature regulation centre, whether directly via relaxation of vasoconstriction or indirectly via activation of the sweat glands. None relates specifically to blushing – facial reddening triggered by emotional stimuli – and none proposes a mechanism for direct sympathetically controlled vasodilation of the blood vessels. An influential study by Mellander *et al.* (1982) implicated sympathetic innervation of β-adrenoceptors in blushing. It investigated the effects of drugs upon a section of facial vein from the cheek region that had been removed for medical reasons during neck surgery. The effects of the administration of phenoxybenzamine (hypothesised to block α-adrenoceptors) and propranolol (hypothesised to block β-adrenoceptors) were measured. It proved possible to initiate contraction in the facial vein specimens, but not in other skin vein specimens, by physical stretching of the specimen. This contractile response was unaffected by the pharmaceutical blockade of α-adrenoceptors and was therefore interpreted as representing basal vasoconstrictor tone. Electrical stimulation of the vein affected α-adrenoceptors in some specimens, producing constriction of the vein, or β-adrenoceptors in others, producing dilation. The dilation response occurred rapidly, within 5 to 10 seconds of stimulation; it was eliminated by the administration of propranolol (the beta-blocker drug), producing vasoconstriction. Furthermore, a drug (isoproterenol) that activated β-adrenoceptors elicited relaxation of the vein and a maximal dose of the drug eliminated the basal tone.

Mellander *et al.* (1982) concluded that both α- and β-adrenoceptors are present in the facial vein and they speculated (ibid., p. 398) that 'the neural adrenergic dilator control of the facial vein in man, when present, might be involved in the reaction of emotional blushing'. Their data also indicated individual differences in reaction, which they interpreted as differences in the relative quantities of the two types of receptors. Post-study interviews with participants revealed that those with a more probable dilator response to stimulation reported frequent blushing, unlike those who showed a constrictor response.

Drummond (1996; 1997) studied the effect of pharmacological blockade in a test of Mellander *et al.*'s hypotheses about the involvement of β-adrenoceptors in blushing and the link between the relative density of receptors and individual variation in propensity to blush. Skin blood flow was recorded with a laser Doppler flowmeter[9] attached to either side of the forehead. One side of the forehead was pre-treated with the administration of either an α-agonist (norepinephrine), an β-antagonist (phentolamine), a β-agonist (isoprenaline) or a β-antagonist (propranolol). The pharmacological pre-treatment had an immediate effect. Phentolamine induced a local increase in blood flow relative to baseline, which can readily be interpreted as inhibition of the effect of norepinephrine on α-adrenoceptors, releasing vasoconstrictor tone. The α-antagonist pre-treatment followed by administration of the α-agonist norepinephrine inhibited the normal constrictor response to norepinephrine, and also resulted in increased blood flow. Pre-treatment with the β-antagonist had no effect on blood flow. Administration of the β-agonist isoprenaline produced vasodilation, resulting in increased blood flow; increase was inhibited if this had been preceded by pre-treatment with isoprenaline. This pattern of findings suggests the role of both α- and β-adrenoceptors in vasodilation of blood vessels at the forehead.

Drummond (1997) extended the experiment to study the effect of embarrassment on blood flow. Two tasks were designed to induce embarrassment: failure to solve arithmetic problems and singing children's rhymes while making the appropriate animal noises. Participants rated their positive and negative affect, embarrassment and self-consciousness on four-point scales. Participants were identified as frequent or less frequent blushers on the basis of their scores on Leary and Meadows' (1991) measure of blushing propensity (see Chapter 4). More frequent blushers reported a significantly greater increase in negative affect and in self-consciousness than less frequent blushers during both tasks. Both groups reported an increase in embarrassment following failure on the mental arithmetic task; in the singing task the increase in embarrassment was greater among the more frequent blushers.

Measured blood flow increased during both tasks on the side of the forehead that had not been treated with the antagonist drug. That is, both tasks induced blushing on the untreated side. However, the administration of the drugs had differential effects on blushing at the treated side. The α-antagonist did not increase blood flow on the treated site relative to the untreated site, implying that the release of sympathetic vasoconstrictor tone is not responsible for blushing. Conversely, the results suggest that β-adrenoceptors are involved in blushing, albeit in ways that depended on the task and on the group. During the singing task the increase in blood flow was smaller at the pre-treated site than at the untreated site. This partial reduction in blushing was identified in both groups for this task. Where the mental arithmetic task was concerned, the β-antagonist prevented an increase in blood flow but only among the less frequent blushers.

This study offers support for the hypothesis about the involvement of β-adrenoceptors in blushing, although the finding that there was a substantial increase in blood flow despite the pharmacological blockade suggests that vasodilator mechanisms in addition to β-adrenoceptors are involved. Replication of the research is necessary to clarify the meaning of the interaction effect between self-reported blushing propensity and the nature of the embarrassing task. Singing children's songs certainly seems an embarrassing thing to do and has been demonstrated to induce increased self-ratings of embarrassment in other studies. However, it is feasible that failure at a task that is diagnostic of ability could elicit a more complex emotional reaction among university students: arranging for failure at a cognitive task has proved an effective anxiety-inducing manipulation in experimental studies of test anxiety. Moreover, it is likely that anxiety would be heightened in this study since failure on an item was accompanied by an unpleasant noise and the failure rate was set at 50 per cent of the items, thereby creating uncertainty on each problem.

Measuring the blush

One of the principal obstacles to scientific research into the blush has been the difficulty of measuring it. The first problem is to induce it reliably. Folklow and Neil (1971, p. 455) describe their frustrations at arranging sessions for the measurement of blushing only to find that, whatever methods they used to induce a blush, the participants would not do so during the experiment, yielding no usable measures, but would blush intensely when the experiment was completed and they were thanked for their participation. Recent research has been more successful in inducing blushing by arranging circumstances to elicit embarrassment. As we have seen, asking someone to sing a children's song, perhaps accompanied by making appropriate noises and gestures, can induce a blush in most adults, as can having participants watch a videotape recording of their performance in the company of others, in some cases members of the opposite sex. Responses in these conditions can be compared with baseline measures or with circumstances that are emotionally arousing but presumed not to be embarrassing (for example, Shearn *et al.*, 1990 and Mulkens *et al.*, 1997, had their participants watch the shower murder scene from Alfred Hitchcock's movie, *Psycho*, which most viewers find frightening).

Self-report measures

It may not be productive to ask people to report on their blushing since they may not always be sure whether they are doing so. For example, Mulkens *et al.* (1997) reported little association between self-ratings of blushing intensity and physiological indicators of blushing during an embarrassing incident. However, the appropriateness of a measure depends on the research question that is addressed. Asking people is informative about the subjective experience of blushing. For example, Simon and Shields (1996) and Crozier and Russell (1992) asked university students directly about their blushing and participants in both studies reported the blush was of short latency to onset (1 to 10 seconds) and of brief duration (less than one minute).

This approach yields valuable information about individual variation in blushing that could not readily be elicited by other means. Simon and Shields compared four American groups, Asian, Black, Hispanic and White. Those with a lighter complexion were more likely to cite visible colour change as well as increase in facial warmth as evidence that they were blushing whereas those with darker complexion gave change in temperature as the evidence. Those with light complexion were more likely to report that they tried to stop blushing once it had started and were also more likely to claim that the change in skin colour influenced others' reactions. Drummond and Lim (2000) reported differences between Caucasian and Indian participants in self-ratings of blushing intensity (greater among the lighter complexion participants), yet found no difference between the groups in measures of blood flow and cheek temperature. Our study (Crozier and Russell, 1992) formed three groups of participants – blushers, intermediate, or non-blushers – on the basis of their scores on a short questionnaire. Participants were asked to describe their complexion as either 'very fair', 'fair', 'natural tan', 'dark' or 'very dark'. Blushers were more likely to report their complexion as 'very fair' or 'fair' skin whereas non-blushers tended to reported that they had 'natural tan' or 'dark' skin.

Shields *et al.* (1990) reported age differences in the experience of blushing among a sample of 32 women and 33 men aged from 13 to 55 years. Self-reported frequency of blushing decreased with age, and older participants believed they blush less often now that than they had done in the past. In themselves, these self-reports do not prove that the frequency of blushing declines with age. Nevertheless they are consistent with physiological evidence that the neurochemical receptors that control the dilation of the facial veins become less numerous with age (Mellander *et al.*, 1982). It is also feasible that as one grows older the kinds of situations that evoke the blush are encountered less frequently and strategies for dealing with these encounters make blushing less likely. The average age of recalled onset of blushing is around 13 years (Edelmann, 1990b) and there is evidence that self-consciousness peaks at about this age too. This age coincides with early puberty and with growing sexual awareness and interest in sexual relationships.

Physiological measures

Research increasingly involves physiological recording at the skin. We have noted Drummond's (1997) use of a flowmeter to measure subcutaneous blood flow. Other techniques are measures of cheek temperature, where thermal measures (thermistors) are attached to the skin, and photoplethysmograph probes. A photoplethysmograph is an optical device that detects changes in volume in the blood vessels by measuring changes in the light that is transmitted through the capillary bed. The transmission of light is modified by variation in the pulse wave in the arteries.

Are these valid measures of blushing? The first requirement is reliability, that is they should give similar results in similar circumstances on different occasions, should be inter-correlated, that is, would increase together in blush-inducing circumstances but not increase during other circumstances. They should have construct validity, that is, be influenced by events in theoretically meaningful ways. Shearn *et al.* (1990) reported that four physiological measures – cheek temperature, cheek photoplethysmograph, ear photoplethysmograph and finger skin conductance (intended as an index of general arousal) – increased significantly while participants watched a videotape of their singing relative to measures while they were watching the excerpt from *Psycho*. Finger conductance increased while watching both videotapes but significantly more so for the embarrassing tape. Mulkens *et al.* (1999) reported that peak level measures of coloration and temperature were significantly higher during an embarrassing incident than when watching a neutral videotape in the presence of others. Mulkens *et al.* (1997) reported a parallel difference between watching the embarrassing videotape and the excerpt from *Psycho*.

However, although the measures were significantly greater during the embarrassing event in Shearn *et al.*'s study and were inter-correlated while participants were watching the scene from *Psycho*, the indices of cheek colour and temperature and of cheek colour and skin conductance were uncorrelated during the embarrassing event. Shearn *et al.* (1990, p. 690) interpreted this decoupling as indicating that blood flow and temperature increases are activated by different control mechanisms. They also found differences in the latencies to peak increases in the measures, with latencies to change in colour coming much sooner (average latency 18 seconds) than the latency for temperature change (92 seconds). Interestingly, this implies that a blush is visible to others before it is experienced by the blusher via a detectable increase in the warmth of the face. Other people know you are blushing before you know. Whether this difference in the time course of reactions is a factor in the absence of correlation between measures in Shearn *et al.*'s study is not known.

The latency data can be compared with the self-report information collected by Shields *et al.* (1990). The majority of participants (71%) who were interviewed claimed that the latency to the onset of the blush was short, within 2 seconds of the precipitating event, much shorter than the latencies obtained in the laboratory. It is difficult to know what information the self-reported blush is based on; perhaps participants are drawing upon output from early stages of processing information about the precipitating circumstances. It is possible, of course, that we are not very accurate in reporting very short time intervals from memory when the prompt is quite general: asking for characteristics of 'the typical blush' (Shields *et al.*, 1990, p. 176).

It is worth drawing attention to one consistent finding from these studies, the implications of which will be discussed again in Chapter 11 when we come to consider those individuals for whom blushing is problematic. Although the participants in Drummond's (1997) study were selected to represent extremes on the self-report measure of blushing propensity, the physiological differences between the two groups were small. Blushing of comparable intensity was found in both groups, implying that subjective blushing propensity might be independent of the objective frequency or intensity of blushing. Research conducted by Mulkens and her colleagues presents a similar picture. Participants with high scores on the blushing questionnaire reported greater fear of blushing and a higher intensity of blushing, particularly during the embarrassing task, but self-rated intensity did not correlate with any of the physiological indices. Nor was there any difference in these indices between participants with high and low scores in blushing fears. Fear of blushing may lead individuals to believe they are blushing when they are not and to believe that others perceive them as blushing when they have in fact little grounds for believing so. An alternative explanation is that their fear might make them more sensitive to physiological cues so that a lesser intensity of facial temperature increase is needed to generate awareness of a blush. More research is needed here.

Finally, limitations of these studies are their reliance on staged events for inducing blushing and the restrictions imposed by the recording devices on participants, for example, having probes attached and having to remain still while recording is made. Such restrictions are necessary for physiological recording. There is no doubt that these studies have provided valuable information about blushing and will continue to do so in the future. Indeed, they have the potential to transform our understanding of the blush. Nevertheless, there is a risk that the concentration on inducing embarrassment overemphasises the connection between embarrassment and the blush, whereas more naturalistic studies would provide insight into those situations, embarrassing or otherwise, where blushing occurs, and this could enable researchers to return to physiological measurement with greater knowledge of the precipitating factors and thereby reduce some of the uncertainties entailed in the interpretation of current findings.

Conclusion

It could have been concluded as recently as ten years ago that little more was known about the blush than Darwin had described in 1872 but the research reviewed in this chapter suggests that the picture is rapidly changing. Researchers have devised techniques to study physiological reactions 'on-line' and this method promises much for the future.

The onset of the 'classic' blush is rapid, implying that it is under neural control, and research has suggested the role of sympathetically innervated β-adrenoceptors. Other mechanisms seem to be involved as well and it is possible that the creeping blush is produced by different, possibly endocrine factors. The change in facial colour is associated with an increase in skin temperature, indeed that is an important cue for our awareness of our own blushing and is a particularly important cue for those whose complexion renders the blush less visible. The temperature control centre in the hypothalamus connects with the medulla and with other components of the emotion-regulation system, including the amygdala. However, it is not clear whether the vasodilation that produces the blush is in response to a temperature increase that has been triggered by an emotional stimulus or whether it is triggered directly by the stimulus. Drummond (1997, p. 163) takes the latter position, arguing that 'an increase in facial temperature might intensify blushing but does not explain the onset of the blush'. Drummond's study showed that whereas pharmaceutical blockade of β-adrenoceptors produced some diminution of increase in forehead blood flow during an embarrassing task, it had no effect on blood flow during physical exercise or when the body was heated by being wrapped in a blanket with hot air blown under the blanket by a fan heater. The nature of the relation between the emotional blush and the temperature-regulation system is a significant issue for research.

The hypothalamus and the thermoregulation system are involved in another uncontrollable autonomic response, namely, shivering; constriction of the skeletal muscles is not only a response to low temperature but is involved in heightened emotional states. We shiver when certain pieces of music move us, when we are in love, when we are afraid. We talk of our hair standing on end, of goose bumps, of shivers down our spine. Research into the blush has tended to focus on its appearance rather than on temperature; a reorientation to think of the relation between reddening and a sudden rise in temperature might have some value.

4
Reasons to Blush

True and false blushes

Undoubtedly investigation of the physiological mechanisms involved in facial flushing and increased skin temperature will make a significant contribution to understanding the blush yet it cannot provide the whole story. One obvious consideration is that the blush is, as far as is known, a uniquely human response (as Mark Twain wrote in *Following the Equator*, 1897, 'Man is the only animal that blushes. Or needs to') and explanations have to take this into account. What is it about being human that makes us prone to blush? Answers to this question refer to a unique moral sensibility or to an advanced degree of self-consciousness, and transcend the physiological level of explanation.

Moreover, the occasion of a blush is a social event and explaining it requires locating it in its social context. The blush has psychological meanings and implications and these have to be explained. There is ambivalence towards it: it can be attractive or an unwelcome intrusion. The art critic Ruskin wrote in 1858, 'A blush rose (or better still, a blush itself,) is the type of rightness in arrangement of pure hue'.[1] Make-up can be applied to the face to give the complexion the semblance of a blush. A British marketing survey undertaken in 2000 reported that blushers are worn by 42 per cent of women over the age of 15, and 20 per cent apply it on a daily basis. A recent advertisement for a blusher product claimed that it makes you look 'fresher' and 'prettier'. Yet a blush does more than contribute to physical attractiveness. It can be a sign of positive qualities of modesty and charm and reveal sensibility and sensitivity to the feelings of others.

In contrast, many people dislike their blushing intensely and describe it in entirely negative terms. Cosmetics are marketed to hide the blush;

a woman might try to mask the redness by applying a green colour corrective cream under her foundation. Some individuals avoid situations that they anticipate will make them colour or rely on alcohol or tranquillizers to cope with the anxiety produced. Others are prepared to undergo surgery to prevent blushing.

Burgess's book on the blush, introduced in Chapter 1, appeared in a medical series; nevertheless he expressed doubts that an explanation of the causes of blushing could be obtained through scientific research since the question of its cause belonged to the 'mysteries' of 'the higher attributes of man'. Notwithstanding his reservations, Burgess distinguished two reasons for blushing. The 'true blush' represents human innate conscience and is evident in all human 'races', even those alleged to be 'savage' and intellectually inferior, since all humans possess a moral instinct. The blush is involuntary and its 'break through' to visible expression provides evidence of the powerlessness of the will to override the dictates of conscience. While most of his book is taken up with discussion of shame, Burgess provides examples of other emotions breaking through. He writes of a 60-year-old man showing his collection of drawings who, when asked who drew a particular one, blushed as he replied that it was the work of his son who was now dead: 'Here the irrepressible blush revealed the hidden anguish of the bereaved parent, and clearly demonstrates the impossibility of the *will* ever being able to overcome or subdue the *genuine* emotions of the *soul*' (Burgess, 1839, p. 53; emphasis in original).

The 'true' blush is to be contrasted with the 'false' or 'uncalled-for' blush, which results from morbid over-sensitiveness: 'Blushing in its diseased form is evidently the result of an over-refined sense of *sensibility*' (ibid., p. 11; emphasis in original). Burgess regards this 'disease' as a defect of character, partly a product of civilisation, partly due to lack of moral education and partly influenced by individual temperament. He bemoans the distortion of the passions brought about by over-refinement – 'Whoever heard of an American savage blushing from morbid sensibility?' he asks (ibid., p. 26) – and its implications for the blush, namely that it can no longer be taken as unambiguous evidence of good character. Burgess's description of over-sensitiveness relates it to shyness, fear of failure and lack of self-esteem. He writes about young men who are timid in society, and gives an example of a young man who enters a room where there are people he doesn't know, and who blushes without good cause and is abashed and embarrassed.

Burgess provided no evidence in support of his distinction between true and false blushes but it corresponds to contemporary observations that the blush is a sign of shame or guilt, that some individuals are more prone to blushing than others are, and that shyness, social anxiety and over-sensitivity to the opinions of others are predisposing factors. The relation of the blush to shame, guilt and shyness is discussed in Part III of this volume. Whenever contemporary theorists have proffered specific explanations of the circumstances of blushing they have made two claims: (i) blushing is a reaction to being the centre of attention; (ii) the blush is a signal. This chapter reviews each claim in turn.

The self unmasked

Unwanted social attention

Leary's self-presentational account (Leary *et al.*, 1992; Cutlip and Leary, 1993) follows Darwin in proposing that blushing is a response to unwanted social attention. It is worthwhile quoting this thesis (Cutlip and Leary, 1993, p. 183) since it represents one of the few explicit expositions of the causes of blushing.

> The necessary and sufficient cause of social blushing is undesired social attention. Put simply, people blush when they receive attention from others that they do not desire and cannot escape. Often, people receive undesired social attention after they have behaved improperly, thereby accounting for the link between embarrassing events and blushing. However, any undesired attention – even that directed at one's positive attributes or behavior – will result in blushing, thereby accounting for the effects of both positive attention and staring.

Several points can be made about this position. First, the blush is regarded as a *consequence* of attention from others, presumably contingent on the blusher's sense that he or she is the object of that attention, since you can be the object of attention without being aware of it or can mistakenly believe that you are under scrutiny.

Second, it addresses the question why someone might blush when being the object of positive attention. Some authors have tried to account for the blush in these circumstances by suggesting that praise or a compliment can lead to an undesirable state of affairs. Buss (1980, pp. 138–9) argued and presented empirical evidence for the position that it is over-praise (unmerited or exaggerated) rather than praise *per se* that produces the blush. Leary suggests that the key issue is whether the attention is *undesired* and there are different reasons why this might be so: attention might be unwelcome because the blusher believes that the praise is undeserved or is not sure how to respond appropriately or is apprehensive about being able to cope with the attention that has been attracted.

Third, Leary outlines the circumstances in which blushing occurs in the absence of embarrassment. An incident that attracts undesired attention without creating a self-presentational predicament would produce blushing but not embarrassment. Conversely, a predicament that is unaccompanied by undesired attention would result in embarrassment but not a blush. Unfortunately, there is as yet no evidence to test this claim.

Fourth, it can be asked whether this account can generate a classification scheme to capture the range of social situations that elicit a blush. Leary *et al.* (1992) propose that four classes of situation do so: threats to public identity; praise and positive attention; conspicuousness; accusations of blushing. Threats to public identity include violation of social norms; inept performances, loss of control and behaving out-of-role (circumstances that typically give rise to embarrassment). People blush when they are the focus of positive attention, when they are singled out for praise, compliments or thanks. Conspicuousness is a cause of blushing such that people colour simply because they are the centre of attention, for example, being asked a question in class or entering a crowded room. Finally, being told that you are blushing can induce it, and awareness of your blushing can intensify it. It is an empirical matter whether this set of classes of situations is necessary and sufficient to account for, say, recollections of occasions for blushing, and I return to this issue in Chapter 5.

Exposure

Examination of numerous descriptions of episodes where someone is said to blush suggests a common pattern, which can be characterised as follows. If an event X brings into the open (or threatens to do so) a topic Y, and Y is something that the individual wishes to keep hidden or believes ought to be kept hidden, X will elicit a blush. Often where blushing occurs, personal information has been disclosed, a secret is alluded to, something private is made public, or someone is teased about a personal or intimate matter. A blush can be elicited by allusion to hidden feelings, when a memory is triggered of a past incident that only the blusher knows about, or by the implications of a remark that would only be recognised by the blusher. A blush can also be a reaction to exposure of topics that are sensitive for all members of a particular cultural group, not just to an individual, for example references to bodily functions or sexual behaviour. In our culture this includes sexual acts, references to genitals and other body parts, certain body functions like menstruation, elimination, belching and flatulence, as well as swear words, which themselves often derive from sexual references.

The novelist Glenn Patterson (2005, p. 146) provides an example of a woman describing her husband's improvement in hospital to Avery, a clergyman.

> He's able to hold his own knife and fork and, ah, everything.
> Her face flared in a sudden blush.
> Oh, right enough, Avery said, as his own face came out in sympathy.

The choice of topics that ought not to be aired is influenced by cultural considerations and social conditions such as gender and social status. Historically, in British society at least, women have been expected to be more modest than men and it would be as necessary for a 'lady' to blush to hear a coarse remark or an improper suggestion as it would be unthinkable for a 'gentleman' to utter them. Topics can be gendered: a man blushes when a woman replies to his compliment that she owes her slim appearance to her girdle. That the patient's wife blushes owes something to her consciousness of Avery's social status: the topic is unmentionable in the presence of a clergyman.

The 'secret' need not be something that the blusher is ashamed of, and also someone can blush at the exposure of qualities and actions that would deserve public approval. An example is this memorial to a Reverend John Andros, who died in 1842, that I saw in Malmesbury Abbey, in England.[2]

> Zealous in the discharge of his pastoral duties,
> Kind and liberal to the distresses of others,
> To the poor
> Charitable even to munificence,
> He did good by stealth
> And blushed to have it known.

The connection between the blush and the exposure of something that ought not to be revealed has implications for people's estimation of the blusher. For example, someone who colours hearing a lewd remark or a salacious joke reveals him or herself to be one type of person, whereas one who fails to do so shows himself to be another type. A blush can show modesty, propriety, chastity and innocence; failure to do so can indicate the absence of these qualities: unblushing and shameless are synonyms.

Exposure has been identified as a factor in several accounts of blushing and embarrassment. Simon and Shields (1996, p. 177) wrote that, 'blushing, though a fleeting episode, is experienced as an unwelcome public revelation of one's most private thoughts'. Buss (1980) regarded breaches of privacy by casual acquaintances and strangers as a cause of embarrassment. He identified three types of intrusions: exposure of parts of the body that should not be seen; being touched in parts of the body that ought not to be touched or an invasion of the intimate zone of personal space; the revelation of private cognitions and feelings that we would not want others to know. Cupach and Metts (1990) also identified privacy violations as a cause of embarrassment, relating these specifically to those predicaments brought about by someone other than the embarrassed person.

These accounts seem to exclude those infringements of privacy brought about by the self, occasions when one 'gives oneself away'. In this respect they contrast with Miller's (1992) classification scheme for circumstances that produce embarrassment, in which *failures of privacy regulation* are classified as a type of normative public deficiency, where actors are responsible since they have 'insufficiently protected private thoughts and actions from public view' (ibid., p. 193). Miller's example is of a man who comes into a room in his underwear unaware that women visitors are present. For Miller, it is the man's ineptitude that provides the basis for assigning this incident to this category. If someone else had engineered these circumstances, it would be classified as an instance of *audience provocation*. If no one were at fault, the man's predicament would be classified as an instance of yet another category, *conspicuousness*. Thus, in Miller's scheme breaches of privacy are not assigned to a single category. Audience provocations also include those occasions where other people fail to keep a secret or they reveal information about the embarrassed person; this can be done intentionally, by teasing, for example, or else occur by accident. Miller distinguishes categories on the basis of whether or not the event involves an actual transgression by the embarrassed person. However, the source of responsibility for a breach of privacy might not be the key issue. You may be embarrassed when no matter whoever accidentally discloses personal information about you or whatever circumstances have brought about an invasion of your personal space.

The blush as communication

As described earlier, Burgess (1839) regarded the blush as the involuntary expression of conscience. It allows others to know that an individual has infringed some rule and serves as 'a moral atonement for his culpable transgression'. Its visibility provides a valuable social function in acting as a constraint and in helping to sustain social relations. Contemporary theorists have taken up this theme. Castelfranchi and Poggi (1990) argue that the blush serves as an act of appeasement or submission, intended to inhibit the aggression of another. Those who blush are performing an acknowledgement, a confession and an apology aimed at inhibiting others' aggression or avoiding social ostracism. In *The Dying Animal*, Roth (2001, pp. 137–8) provides a subtle illustration of the blush serving as an apology.

> 'I was buying flowers in Madison Avenue with my mother last Saturday,' she told me, and the florist said, 'what a nice hat you're wearing,' and I said, 'It's there for a purpose,' and he understood and he blushed and apologized and gave me a dozen roses for free. So there you see how people respond to a human being in distress. They don't know what to do. Nobody knows what to say or do.

Here, the florist blushes when he realises the nature of the topic that he has inadvertently raised even though the topic remains unsaid – that the customer (who is undergoing chemotherapy) is wearing a hat because of the hair loss brought about by the treatment – and his blush augments his verbal apology for having touched on the matter. Nothing explicit has been said about her illness but his blush communicates acknowledgement of his unintentional wrongdoing.

Halberstadt and Green (1993) tease out three versions of the appeasement-submission hypothesis. First, the blush serves to conciliate, to placate a more powerful other. Second, it is an apology, an admission of blame and an expression of regret. Third, it functions as remediation, helping to restore social relationships after a predicament. Writers on the blush tend not to distinguish among these three versions of the hypothesis even though they have different emphases. Halberstadt and Green suggest that they vary along three dimensions, which they label process, power and relationships. Thus, conciliation emphasises the restoration of relationships without implying submissiveness; appeasement implies a power differential; remediation carries no message of inequality or admission of blame. These distinctions are valuable and should contribute to better understanding of the communicative significance of the blush.

Halberstadt and Green compared the appeasement and remediation accounts by having participants complete a number of paper-and-pencil measures. Blushing propensity was significantly correlated with embarrassability and interaction anxiousness. However, its correlations with submissiveness, abasement and apology were weak and even weaker when the influence of embarrassability and anxiousness was statistically controlled. Nevertheless, as the researchers admit, a research strategy that is based on assessments of individual differences cannot rule out the possibility that in any given situation a blush can serve to appease or apologise. Indeed, this is surely more plausible than the expectation that people who are submissive in social relationships should be more prone to blush, particularly if the statistical analysis assumes that this relation should be linear and hold across all values of the dominance-submissiveness dimension.

The signal account is most convincing in those cases where the actor is responsible, directly or indirectly, for creating the social predicament and hence an apology or act of appeasement is called for. It is less plausible in those cases where the actor is simply conspicuous or is the recipient of praise or a compliment. There is also the issue of the involuntary nature of this particular signal since it cannot be 'sent' deliberately even though its appearance might be timely (Castelfranchi and Poggi, 1990, p. 240, acknowledge that it can be non-intentional or even 'counter-voluntary'). Also, there are cases where a blush is akin to a 'leakage'. For example, a young woman who is keeping her pregnancy to herself gives it away by blushing when someone else's expectancy is mentioned. In cases like this, a blush can create a predicament where none would otherwise exist. It is possible that the trigger (the reference to pregnancy) creates apprehension that a predicament might ensue and thus the blush serves as a kind of apology in anticipation – it is simply unfortunate that the involuntary reaction actually brings about the predicament. However, it is not obvious that this explanation is compatible with what is known about the temporal sequence of the embarrassment display, nor does it seem a particularly parsimonious account.

That a blush can serve a useful purpose is not itself grounds for concluding that this is its primary function. A parallel point can be made about the expression of fear. Pallor or trembling shows that someone is frightened and this can be a useful signal, for example in bringing a mother's support to a frightened child. On other occasions, when it is important for someone to appear strong or brave, it is an unwanted signal. In *Grace Abounding to the Chief of Sinners* written in 1666 while he was imprisoned for preaching without a licence and fearing, with good reason, that he might be executed, John Bunyan was troubled that he,

> should either with quaking or other symptoms of faintings, give occasion to the enemy to reproach the way of God and his people, for their timorousness: this therefore lay with great trouble upon me, for methought I was ashamed to die with a pale face, and tottering knees, for such a cause as this.

The corollary of the involuntary nature of the blush – that it cannot be feigned – introduces an alternative approach to the study of facial expressions, one that suggests that the costs that accrue to the mother-to-be are worth paying because of other benefits that a blush can bring. The sincerity of expressions – the honesty or reliability of signals – is of interest not only to researchers into blushing but is an issue for theorists in several disciplines: biology, evolutionary psychology and microeconomics.

The nature of signals

Throughout the natural world organisms send signals to fellow members of their species. These assert claim to a territory, a mate or their position in a dominance hierarchy, display their strength and sexual prowess, indicate their sexual availability, and communicate where a supply of food is to be found and the presence of predators. Signals are adaptive in increasing the likelihood of finding food and escaping danger. Animals that threaten each other until one of them submits can resolve their conflict without the heavy costs that a fight entails: fighting is exhausting, is likely to lead to injury and takes up time that could be used to search for food or a mate. But why don't organisms cheat when there is an obvious incentive for them to do so? If your signal about the whereabouts of food sends your conspecifics rushing off in the wrong direction or you can induce them to flee from an imaginary predator, you can help yourself to rich pickings of food or mates in their absence. Why doesn't this confer an evolutionary advantage on organisms that cheat since, in the circumstances described above, it increases their chances of surviving to reproduce and pass on genes for cheating to their offspring? Furthermore, if organisms lack the cognitive capacity to memorise incidents of deceit they will not be able to identify those individuals with a proclivity to cheat and would be at their mercy over and over again. Indeed, what would be the value of signals for a species if they were invariably accompanied by uncertainty? Yet signalling is characteristic of very many species and must, in Maynard Smith's terminology, constitute an evolutionary stable strategy.

Costs and benefits

Zahavi (1975) introduced the 'handicap principle', suggesting that signals are guaranteed to be reliable when they are costly to produce. Costs accrue when the organism uses up vital energy in making the signal or exposes itself to risk, increasing its vulnerability to attack by getting too close to an opponent or eliciting an aggressive response. Zahavi illustrates this with the case of the peacock and the extravagant display of tail plumes that it makes to peahens. The display has evolved because it confers an advantage on the peacock despite its disadvantages: it is highly visible and likely to attract the attention of predators, and is cumbersome, making it difficult to carry out routine activities and, in particular, making it difficult to escape from predators. Its evolution can be explained in terms of sexual display and the peacock's ability to attract females, assuming that the reproductive success that is gained from it outweighs its disadvantages. However, this raises the question why the female should find the display attractive. This would be understandable if the more extravagant display were a marker of greater quality (and hence desirability) of the male, but how does the peacock's tail, with all its costs, indicate this? Zahavi argued that it does so *because* of the costs or 'handicap' involved – only males of highest quality would be able to sustain the extravagance.

Frank (2000) and Maynard Smith and Harper (2003) have applied game theory to systematic analysis of the potential net payoffs – the benefits minus the costs – of alternative courses of action available to the signaller and the recipient of the signal. The analysis showed that equilibrium points could be identified, that is a signal can be reliable and become a stable feature of a species. These analyses alert researchers to questions about the blush that are important to address if its function in communication is to be understood. It can be analysed in terms of its benefits and costs. The blush has positive outcomes for the group. First, it helps its members deal with the predicament that is created by the circumstances that cause one of them to blush and enables the group to resolve any conflict that would arise and that would disrupt its activities. Second, it stabilises the group by confirming that the errant member belongs to it, and avoids the difficulties inherent in censuring one of its members. Third, it strengthens the group by re-affirming its values and showing that these are recognised and shared.

A blush has several costs. It interferes with cognitive processes: blushers say that their blushing flusters them and makes it difficult for them to think clearly. It adds to their embarrassment and produces its own problems. It affects the self-image of the blusher; as we have seen, people dislike their blushing and for many it is a serious problem. It influences observers; as we report below, empirical studies show that observers can take a negative view of blushers in circumstances where there has been an infringement of social rules and there is ambiguity about the motives of the person who has brought this about (de Jong *et al.*, 2003). Nevertheless, Frank (1988) pointed out that whether or not the blush of guilt has costs to the blusher in the short term as his or her guilt is revealed to others, it may have long-term benefits if he or she gains the reputation of being a trustworthy member of the community.

Sincerity

Another issue in the study of signals is their reliability, or sincerity. Maynard Smith suggests that a guarantee of reliability is a type of signal he defines as an 'index' – a signal that cannot be faked. He provides the example of the Red Deer; the pitch of its roar is an index of its body size and is correlated with its reproductive success. It makes sense to be wary of the loud roar since it cannot be produced by a weak deer 'pretending' to be a strong one. Frank takes a similar approach to the analysis of emotions, recognising that the sincerity of signals is a crucial issue in human social encounters, particularly when the interests of protagonists are in conflict. How do we know that an adversary is sincere and can be trusted? Frank (1988, p. 99) writes of guarantees of signals that include the costs of faking signals (his analysis of the loudness of a toad's croak is similar to that of the roar of a deer). There are advantages in appearing honest and being trusted and a signal of honesty ought to be costly to fake.

Frank argues that emotional expressions fulfil this role because they are difficult to feign. If they were under conscious control and thus an individual could pretend to have an emotion, then they could be routinely used to convey false information and would lose their value as signals. It is important for honest dealers to be able to detect cheating and, more generally, to be able to identify the intentions behind another's actions. According to Frank, the facial expression of emotion may be one medium for achieving this because it appears spontaneously, is easy to recognise but difficult to simulate. Those who don't want their motives to be read by others, poker players, for example, work hard to mask their facial expressions. But this can be difficult and the emotion can 'leak'. Pavlidis *et al.* (2002) reported evidence of slight but discern-able increases in facial temperature in the region around the eyes when the participants in their research attempted to deceive the researcher.

A blush makes a useful signal because knowing that the blush reveals guilt and that you cannot control it deters people from cheating. If people did not redden or could control their blushing there would be more incentive to cheat: as Burgess asked, 'how can those be trusted who know not how to blush?' Frank argues that the blush serves as a sign of trustworthiness, and that a reputation for honesty is beneficial even if sometimes it has costs, for example, a blush can give you away when you want to keep a secret or when you are telling a lie. The blush would seem to make a particularly effective guarantor since it is difficult to feign. While Frank argues that all emotions are difficult to simulate, we can make a better effort at pretending to smile, laugh, look sad or sur-prised, or lower the eyes coyly than we could at attempting to blush. As we have noted, it is also difficult to terminate a blush, and awareness that you are reddening can lead you to do so even more intensely.

Nevertheless, this account is not without problems. For example, as we discuss below, de Jong *et al.* (2003) have shown that a blush means different things to observers, depending on the context. It seems to be more closely associated with embarrassment than with guilt and this will affect interpretations that are made. Frank's account draws heavily on the notion of the spontaneous, uncontrolled expression of emotion, but spontaneous expressions are relatively rare and expression is typically governed by display rules. Even 'fake' expressions of emotion serve valu-able social functions and there may be a 'currency' of insincere emotions. While Pinker is correct (1997, p. 415) to point out that we are not taken in by a flight attendant's smile, we don't believe that the smile represents her delight in greeting us, and we are aware that the atten-dant may put on the smile along with her uniform, we realise that this display is serving a particular function (as does the uniform). She aims to establish an atmosphere that is conducive to the smooth running of the flight, tries to appear at ease and thereby reassure the more nervous passengers and so on. Indeed, attendants would be disconcerted if we were to take their smiles as a sincere indication of their feelings to us as individuals.

Visibility

This explanation relies on the visibility of the blush but not all ethnic groups have skin pigmentation that enables the blush to be readily detected. Yet members of these groups do blush. This implies that the origins of the blush do not lie in its communicative function, however it has subsequently come to be used. Frank addressed this problem for signals and emotional expressions more generally, with his concept of passive signals. Passive signals, those that are not under voluntary control, do not usually originate for a communicative function, since it would be difficult to see how they could have evolved to do so. Whatever their origins, signals can be subject to the process of natural selection as they fulfil their function as a signal:

> If, for example, trustworthiness and a tendency to blush go together, and if being known to be trustworthy is advantageous, selection pressures can clearly affect both the tendency to blush and the emotion that triggers it (Frank, 1988, p. 133).

Casimir and Schnegg (2002) propose that blushing is part of a 'social fearfulness complex' where reddening has its origins in the increase in blood flow in the skin that is produced by heightened arousal associated with anticipation of punishment for the infraction of a social rule. This anticipation is learnt: because others react negatively to an infraction we come to expect that future infractions will elicit a negative reaction. When the capacity for self-reflection evolved in higher primates self-evaluation would produce feelings of shame and embarrassment and these would be accompanied by heightened arousal and increased blood flow. Casimir and Schnegg argue that if early hominoids were dark skinned, the increase in blood flow would not be visible to others. Therefore the blush would only become available as a sign of shame and embarrassment for those groups whose skin pigmentation would permit the subcutaneous blood to become visible. They argue that this implies that the blush was a developed reaction before the evolution of self-consciousness and the emergence of complex social structures with their prescriptions for role performance.

Their research asked participants from countries throughout the world about the colours they associated with particular emotions. Participants from 98 of the 135 languages and dialects studied made an association between emotions and colour terms. Shame (standing for the self-conscious emotions) was associated with the colour red in 78 of the 98. Casimir and Schnegg analysed the geographical distribution of associations between shame and colour, and they provided a graphical illustration of the trends in distribution by superimposing the statistical data of the frequency of this association upon a map of the world. It is evident that the distribution varies considerably across the world, and the tendency is for populations with fair complexions to associate reddening with shame. In some cases where complexions were 'relatively dark', shame was associated with the colour black, implying a darkening of the skin due to blushing, whereas other populations, where complexions were 'very dark', made no association between shame and any colour term.

This raises a question about the significance of the blush for individuals and populations who have dark complexions and hence no visible change in demeanour. We noted in Chapter 3 Simon and Shields' (1996) report that participants with darker complexion described the experienced change in facial temperature as constituting the evidence that they are blushing whereas those with light complexions refer to the visibility of the blush as well as temperature. No explanations of the blush have focused on change in facial temperature, nor has this figured much in theories of the emotions more generally.[3] Nor have explanations considered that the blush is a signal to the self as well as to others. It can warn the person that he or she faces a threat, specifically a threat to acceptance by the group. This would be analogous to the early processing of incoming stimuli relevant to potential threat that triggers a startle; in this instance the threat is specific to social standing. I return to this in Chapter 7 when shame is examined.

The following section considers whether there is evidence to support the hypothesis that the blush serves a communicative function. Research into this issue suffers because it is difficult to elicit or measure the blush in natural settings, and studies have depended on ratings of hypothetical incidents.

Empirical studies

Semin and Manstead (1982) devised vignettes portraying incidents, for example where someone knocked over a stack of cans in a supermarket, and manipulated the description of the person who was responsible for this (the 'actor') in order to test whether research participants who read the vignettes formed different impressions of the actor depending on the content of the description. Actors who were described as embarrassed were regarded in a more positive light than those who were not. de Jong (1999) adapted these vignettes to study blushing. Blushers were rated more positively than shamefaced actors, and their misdemeanours were judged to be less serious when the actor blushed or looked shamefaced than when the actor left without reaction. A second study addressed more directly Castelfranchi and Poggi's explanation of the blush in terms of shared values. Actors who blushed were judged to be more likely to adhere to shared values than were those who were shamefaced or who simply left.

A third study manipulated the extent to which actors and observers in the vignettes shared values. The vignettes described breaches of rules in settings where the rules are important, but only to a particular section of the population, for example, vegetarians' rules about eating meat, and asked participants to identify with the actor in situations where his or her behaviour infringed the rule. Participants responded that they would be more likely to blush (mean probability, $p = 0.85$) if both actor and observer endorsed the infringed rule than if the rule was held only by the actor ($p = 0.50$) or only by the observer ($p = 0.43$). Blushing was thought unlikely ($p = 0.15$) if neither party adhered to the rule. The findings provide only partial support for the proposal in Castelfranchi and Poggi's claim about the importance of shared values for the blush since a moderate likelihood of blushing was reported in conditions where the actor and observer did not share values, whereas their claim is that shared values are a precondition for the blush.

de Jong *et al.* (2002) investigated blushing during social interaction and included a plethysmograph measure of cheek coloration. Participants acted as protagonists in a version of the prisoner's dilemma game, where the players choose whether to cooperate with their opponent or 'defect' in order to pursue their own 'selfish' ends. The researchers asked one protagonist in each game to 'defect' on a nominated trial. Defectors evidenced a higher peak measure of cheek coloration during the trial on which they 'cheated' in comparison with the measure on the immediately preceding trial, and they reported blushing more intensely and were perceived by their opponent to blush more intensely on this trial. The more intense the blush the less trustworthy the defector was rated.

In these circumstances a blusher was not seen in a more positive light. A possible explanation is that, in the context of the game, the defector has chosen to act in an unacceptable way, and de Jong and co-authors suggest that the blush might be seen, not as a sign of contrition, but as evidence of the intention to defect. However, this interpretation assumes that a player would not blush if she accidentally defected on the critical trial. According to Castelfranchi and Poggi, shame can be experienced before the other even if the actor is aware that she is innocent: it is the actor's awareness of how the behaviour looks to the other that instigates the blush. Furthermore, the situation is quite complex as the player has been asked by the researcher to behave in a way that is inconsistent with her values, and it is possible that this has created a degree of conflict about her own motivation that conceivably is picked up by the observer. Finally, the design of the experiment needs the inclusion of a control or comparison group where the players do not share values, in order to reach unambiguous conclusions about the role of shared values.

de Jong *et al.* (2003) revisited the question of intent. Vignettes were manipulated to produce three conditions varying in degree of intent: descriptions of mishaps, intended moral transgressions, and ambiguous situations that could have come about either by accident or intention. 'Actors' were described as blushing in half of the vignettes. Participants rated the actor on a set of personality traits, the seriousness of the infringement and the extent to which it was brought about by accident. It was found that whether the blush elicited a positive or a negative response depended on the context, and the perceived intention of the actor seems to be the crucial factor. There were no main effects of the blush manipulation, showing that the blush does not influence responses uniformly; specifically the blush does not invariably lead to a more favourable evaluation of the actor's conduct. If it seems that the infringement was deliberate, the blush results in the actor being viewed less negatively and the transgression is judged to be less serious. However, when the available information is ambiguous about the actor's intention, the blush leads to the actor being perceived more negatively and the infringement is rated as more serious. If the actor has infringed some rule but it is evident that she has done so accidentally, the blush tends not to influence the reaction. (This last finding is inconsistent with other studies reported by de Jong and his team and may reflect the particular choice of vignette in this experiment.)

In these vignettes the actor is described as either blushing or not. Some writers have made the point that in order to deflect negative reactions it is not enough to blush: the blush has to be seen and interpreted as such by others. In his novel, *The History of Tom Jones*, Henry Fielding draws attention to the fact that where a blush is called for, it has to be seen: 'When a woman is not seen to blush, she doth not blush at all'. Similarly, Harré (1990) has argued that when our appearance breaches standards of modesty it is not sufficient to take corrective action, we have to show embarrassment as well in order to avoid being thought shameless.

It is important that the blush is not interpreted as something else. For example, if reddening of the face is interpreted as a flush induced by alcohol rather than as a blush, a person's misdemeanour is not excused but is likely to be regarded as even more reprehensible. Leary *et al.* (1996; Experiment 2) found support for the hypothesis that a blush serves as a remedial device only if others notice it and interpret it as a blush rather than as flushing due to physical exercise. Participants in the condition where temperature increase was attributed to exercise rated their self-presentations more positively than did those in the condition where the researcher commented on their blush. The self-ratings of the latter group did not differ from those in the control condition; the researchers interpret this as evidence that the blush helps to resolve the self-presentation predicament faced by the participants, so that they have no more need than the control group does to enhance their self-presentations in order to save face.

The dependent variable in this study is not the degree of embarrassment or difficulty experienced but how positive are participants' self-descriptions: scale items refer to cheerful, friendly, honest and (not) conceited. The researchers interpret positive self-descriptions as participants' attempts to convey more favourable impressions. It would be valuable to tease out the various meanings these responses might have, for example distinguishing strategic behaviour from, say, changes in mood. Although couched in terms of embarrassment and a self-presentational model, the argument is similar to that proposed by Harré: if you are embarrassed it is important that others know you are. However, as Leary *et al.* acknowledge, it is not always the case that we want others to know we are embarrassed and often we want to hide it by escaping the situation or by trying to cover our blushes. Presumably this is because embarrassment will create a further predicament, but this explanation does not suggest what the conditions might be that encourage the person to blush or hide their blushes. In any given situation the individual has many goals, which presumably form a hierarchy. It can make sense to forego one identity in order to shore up another: acting silly or appearing foolish is much more costly on some occasions or in front of certain people than it is at other places or times.

Conclusion

The 'signal' account of the blush has generated empirical research that yields considerable insight into the circumstances of blushing. Castelfranchi and Poggi's characterisation of the blush has had considerable heuristic value. To be sure, the research has relied heavily on vignettes, but it identifies factors that provide a basis for future investigations, for example into the circumstances where the blush leads to either a more or less favourable perception of the blusher. The studies have focused on mishaps, errors, failed public performances, infringements of rules, moral transgressions and so on, and have neglected circumstances where the blusher has nothing to apologise for. We do not know what a blush would communicate in these circumstances and what inferences would be made about the blusher's character.

Do explanations in terms of self-attention, exposure and signal provide a convincing account of the circumstances that give rise to a blush? Clearly it would be desirable to analyse situations where someone actually blushes in order to test whether some accounts fit better than others and whether some fit better than others in some circumstances than in others. As reported in Chapter 3, methods have been developed so that it is possible to induce blushing in particular conditions, and the research reported in this chapter has examined the likelihood that people will react with a blush to a variety of incidents (typically embarrassing ones); nevertheless, and despite these welcome developments, we lack an overview of the kinds of situations that cause people to blush. The next chapter reviews existing research into this issue and presents findings from a study where participants recall occasions when they blushed.

5
Occasion to Blush

Classifying episodes

There have been scarcely any systematic attempts to classify situations that elicit blushing. This contrasts with research into embarrassment where there exist several schemes for categorising incidents (Miller, 1996; see also Chapter 6). The dearth of taxonomies presumably reflects the widespread assumption that blushing is simply an expression of embarrassment and hence no specific analysis of eliciting circumstances is required.

One approach to classifying situations is based on statistical analysis of the Blushing Propensity Scale (Leary and Meadows, 1991), which has respondents rate how likely it is that they would blush in a prescribed set of circumstances. The scale does not invite nominations of situations that elicit a blush, and thus is unlike classification schemes for embarrassment, which are based on participants' nominations. Application of factor analysis to responses to the scale items by Leary and Meadows (1991), Edelmann and Skov (1993) and Bögels *et al.* (1996) has consistently identified two factors and these are broadly similar across the studies. The first factor involves items where the individual is the centre of others' attention, whether this is in positive, neutral or negative ways (being praised, conspicuous or criticised). Items with highest loadings on this factor refer to 'being the centre of attention' and 'looking stupid or incompetent in front of others', and Leary and Meadows interpret it in terms of situations that pose immediate threats to the blusher's social identity. It has proved difficult to discern a theme underlying the second factor and there is no consensus on naming it. Its items refer to interactions between individuals rather than to behaving in the public eye; inspection of the items suggests two possible groupings. Some refer to talking about a personal matter or a sexual topic of conversation and are compatible with the proposal that a blush is a reaction to exposure of a sensitive or private topic, and indeed Edelmann and Skov (1993, p. 496) label it a 'personal exposure' factor. Other items refer to meeting someone for the first time and talking to a member of the other sex; it cannot be resolved from these items whether the factor reflects the characteristics of the other person present or the blusher's shyness. Whatever the nature of the second factor, its existence implies that blushing is not a response to public attention alone.

The psychometric approach to the classification of situations has limitations. It depends crucially on the selection of items. The researchers select items and response scales and there is no input from participants. If the choice is guided by theoretical considerations then the results will tend to be biased to the theory. If the researcher has omitted blush-inducing situations they cannot be retrieved from the analysis, however sophisticated it might be. Furthermore, the items are standard for all participants and this loses information about situations that are likely to elicit a blush in some participants but not in others. Finally, the questionnaire layout and 'tick box' response format can encourage 'top of the head' or stereotypical responding where participants draw upon conventional notions of the blush rather than consider at any length how likely it is that they would blush in each of the situations.

Inviting participants to nominate situations is a strategy that has been widely used in the study of embarrassment. This approach too has its disadvantages. As Miller (1996) has argued, it may elicit more vivid and dramatic examples than those routinely encountered so that there may be over-representation of situations that were problematic or which the individual was unable to resolve. Responses may be guided by participants' 'lay theories' of blushing. The method relies upon what they understand by blushing – they might take the word to be a synonym of embarrassment and provide instances of the latter, whether or not they blushed on those occasions. It also assumes that people have insight into the circumstances of their blushing, which is not necessarily the case.

Shields *et al.* (1990, p. 175) provided participants in their study with a definition of blushing: 'A blush involves a feeling of warmth on the face and/or reddening of the face in response to being made the center of attention, embarrassing situations, or similar circumstances'. In the course of individual interviews the researchers asked participants about the situations that evoke a blush. Situations were coded into three categories: others present doing something unintentionally to elicit the blush (55% of situations mentioned were placed in this category); making a faux pas (15%); one's own actions other than a faux pas (24%). These are rather broad categories, and the instances produced may have been influenced by references in the definition to being the centre of attention and embarrassing situations. The inclusion in the study of equal numbers of (self-described) frequent and infrequent blushers affects the representativeness of the sample of situations. Nevertheless, inviting nomination of situations represents a promising approach.

Recalling blushes: method

Nomination is the method adopted in the study reported here, with the modification that participants were asked to report on blushing incidents that took place because of something that was said. It was thought that this would elicit more mundane examples, omitting the major faux pas or loss of physical control that are memorable but (thankfully) rare. A brief questionnaire was constructed specifically for the study. It was introduced as follows:

> Everybody must blush at some time or another. Often, one blushes because of something one has done or something that happens, but one can also blush because of something that is said. The latter is the focus of this brief questionnaire, and it would be very helpful if you would recall and briefly describe an occasion when you blushed at something somebody said.

The definition made no reference to embarrassment or to any specific eliciting factors such as being the centre of attention. The first two items were 'What was said to cause you to blush?' and 'Why do you think this made you blush?' Each was followed by space for respondents to write their answers in their own words. Responses were submitted to content analysis. Subsequent items comprised various rating scales applied to the nominated situation. A sample of 101 students enrolled in courses in education, social studies and occupational therapy completed the questionnaires in classroom settings. The sample was predominantly female, reflecting the gender distribution of the population of students taking the courses. Two participants wrote that they could not recall an incident, one adding that she rarely blushed, and the remaining 99 responses formed the basis of analysis.

The circumstances that were reported by this sample of participants can be compared with a second source of blushing occasions. This comprises a sample of episodes drawn from works of fiction by women and men writers and covering contemporary fiction as well as the nineteenth-century novel (Crozier, 2004, provides a list of the sources). Works by ten writers were searched for references to words with the root *blush* and related root words, *colour, pink, red*, and 164 extracts were identified referring to blushing or its synonyms

Why examine fictional accounts? The blush has attracted the attention of literary critics and inspection of these sources suggests that it has a range of meanings. In the introduction to her book, *Telling Complexions: The Nineteenth-Century English Novel and the Blush*, O'Farrell (1997) associates the blush in successive paragraphs with pleasure, grace, moral obligation, manners and authenticity, as well as eroticism and embodiment. Ricks (1976) also identifies a connection between the blush and embarrassment, itself, he suggests (ibid., p. 5), 'not only a nineteenth-century sentiment but a narrowly English one'.[1] He points to the blush's various associations with sexual attraction and modest innocence. Both critics emphasise the involuntary nature of the blush; as O'Farrell writes, it is an involuntary intrusion of the body into the social order of civility and manners and thus is revealing in diverse ways of character (and of the social order).

Ricks and O'Farrell regard the blush as a key device in nineteenth-century novelists' treatment of courtship and the 'marriage plot'. They draw upon the writings of Darwin and, in Ricks's case, Goffman, to analyse the blush, embarrassment, mortification and manners. It is useful to sample literary texts more widely than the nineteenth-century novel to see if the use of the blush is restricted to these devices. Also, a comparison of literary episodes with responses to the questionnaires could prove of value in identifying themes common to the different sources. Finally, drawing upon two sources would possibly yield a broader range of situations and permit consideration of instances that were specific to one source.

Content analysis of questionnaire responses and literary excerpts proceeded as follows. They were coded in terms of three categories of causes of the blush: Being the centre of attention; the topic of conversation; the characteristics or role of the person with whom you were interacting. Table 5.1 presents the coding scheme. Episodes assigned to the 'centre of attention' category were further classified as positive (the person is praised, congratulated or thanked), neutral (speak up in front of others, be conspicuous) or negative (criticised, accused or make a public faux pas). The transcripts were also coded according to whether the blusher or another person had made the remark that elicited the blush and also

Table 5.1 Blushing coding scheme

Category	Examples
Being centre of attention; singled out; in the spotlight	• Thanked/applauded/praised/complimented • Speak up in front of others • Say/ do something that makes you conspicuous/ be object of attention • Unspecified comment is made about you • Teased/ribbed/mocked/made fun of/ laughed at/criticised/ corrected/ reprimanded/accused/challenged • Say/do something foolish in front of others
Something about the person you are interacting with	• Boss, teacher, authority figure • Person of opposite sex • Sexual attraction
The topic of conversation	• Personal or sensitive topic • Recognise sexual allusion/reference/implication/ connotation in what is said/done • Expose more of private affairs than you would want known; • Divulge secret/ alludes/refer to something you think is personal/want to keep hidden; past embarrassing event; • Refer to topic that is culturally sanctioned/ taboo/ought to be kept hidden for a given audience • Say something that would cause offence to/embarrass another if recognised

in terms of the numbers of people present (one item asked participants to report on this).

There are quantifiable differences between the questionnaire responses and the fictional source. Authors of fiction are more likely to describe episodes where two people are present, where something the other person says gives rise to a blush and where what is said concerns relationships between the sexes or a sexual theme more generally. This pattern contrasts with that found in the questionnaire data, where substantial numbers of people were said to be present, and in the majority of episodes the blusher finds herself or himself the centre of attention. Furthermore, a substantial proportion of these incidents involve receiving positive attention, being complimented (the most common instance in this category) or praised, whereas receiving positive attention is much less frequent in the fictional episodes. Another difference between the two sources is that embarrassment is commonly mentioned in the questionnaire responses when participants explain why they blush but is rarely present in fiction episodes, where a variety of words refer more generally to the social emotions: shame, humiliation, shyness, bashfulness, awkwardness, timidity, modesty, consciousness, self-consciousness, sensibility and guilt.

The next section identifies and illustrates recurrent themes across the two sources and compares these with examples from other sources of information about the circumstances of the blush.

Recalling blushes: themes

The object of attention

Positive attention

This represents the largest category in the analysis of responses to the questionnaire. Participants recalled blushing when a compliment was paid, whether this took place in front of other people or when only the person making the complimentary remark was present:

> When someone praised me – in public – at a school where I had worked. [Why blush?] Because everyone looked at me and I knew that I was getting flushed which made me feel worse.

> My boss told me he valued my work. [Why blush?] Embarrassed, didn't know how to respond.

In these instances, the participant draws explicit attention to the public nature of the compliment and also hints at the predicament this can cause: the blusher does not know how to respond. Compliments are present in the fiction episodes, albeit less frequently. In *The Country Girls*, O'Brien (1963) describes 'Caithleen' blushing in school when she realises that the teacher is about to draw to the class's attention that she has won a scholarship. In *Lorna Doone* Blackmore (1999) portrays a compliment intensifying an existing blush.

> Ruth herself came and let me in, blushing very heartily; for which colour I praised her health, and my praises heightened it.

Negative attention

Unwanted attention, making a faux pas or having attention drawn to a mistake also calls forth a blush. Again, these frequently but not necessarily occur in front of a substantial audience:

> In a lecture, I asked a question that the lecturer had only just covered and everybody laughed. [Why blush?] Because it was obvious that I hadn't been listening properly, but I really hadn't heard it.

> I was with friends and the boy I was going out with arrived with a bouquet. I thanked him, assuming it was for me but he was taking it to his mum for her birthday! [Why blush?] Everyone was totally embarrassed, I felt such a fool.

In *The Country Girls*, O'Brien (1963) describes a scene where two school-girls are meant to be singing a duet on stage. In fact, one of the girls is only pretending to sing and when her partner stops singing her mime is suddenly exposed to the audience, and she blushes. Being the recipient of 'negative' remarks – being criticised, challenged or accused – also elicit a blush, and these too can take place whether a large group or only a small number are present.

> Customer complaint at work [Why blush?] Because a number of people were waiting to be served and were listening.

> A comment was made about me. [Why blush?] I was embarrassed as I was surrounded by people and friends.

The truth of accusations does not seem to be the crucial factor. People blush when they are accused of something they did not do, and even when they do not know what it is that they are accused of.

> Being accused as a group member of dropping paint – no one owned up and I blushed – and I got the blame though it was someone else.

Conspicuousness

Being conspicuous without explicit reference to whether the attention is positive or negative also elicits a blush. In questionnaire protocols, this occurs, for example, when the person is asked a question in class by the tutor or is called upon to speak in class, when it is her birthday and the others sing 'Happy Birthday', or when she is publicly nominated for a place on a committee. In these instances the person who will blush is singled out for attention, but this is not a necessary condition. Students blush when they walk across the front of the lecture room to reach a vacant seat and when they enter the room after the lecture has started – they feel conspicuous even though no one may be paying any attention to them. People blush when the speaker mentions their name even though no one present would recognise them. There are instances in fiction. A character is expressing an opinion at a dinner party and when the others stop their conversations in order to listen, with the result that she is the only one speaking, she blushes (Updike, 2000).

Being conspicuous can shade into finding yourself in the wrong place. In the example below, Blackmore (1999) depicts a scene where the character is ordered to be less conspicuous while a crowd is waiting for a royal procession to pass.

> Being frightened to find myself among so many people of great rank and gorgeous apparel, I blushed at the notice drawn upon me by this uncourteous fellow; and silently fell back into the corner.

Sexual attention

One class of episodes refers to being the object of sexual attention, whether this is being complimented on one's appearance by a member of the opposite sex, hearing a comment on one's appearance or attracting a sexual approach.

> My friends told me I had a good cleavage. [Why blush?] Embarrassing.

> A very effective chat up line. [Why blush?] I was unsure how to respond to the person who I was very attracted to.

In these instances the respondents blush because they have been made conspicuous by the attention drawn to them. They are conscious of being the object of attention and they often find it difficult to know what to say or do in the circumstances in which they find themselves. Yet some of these examples shade into another category, where the person blushes simply because a particular topic has been raised: here the person does not have to be the object of attention in order to blush.

Topics

Being the object of public attention cannot explain all occasions since a blush can be elicited when a sensitive or personal topic is raised during a conversation such that you may colour whether or not you are the centre of attention. In Chapter 4 it was proposed that the blush accompanies the exposure of something that (according to the blusher's values) ought to be hidden. This can be physical exposure of the body, the airing of a topic that is taboo or the disclosure of confidential information about the self. As we have seen, sexual topics frequently induce blushing, and these often relate to these kinds of exposure. This account has affinities with interpretations of the blush in terms of modesty since it too is concerned with what ought and ought not to be revealed.

A topic can trigger a blush because it involves the exposure of something private that the person does not want others to know about or prefers not to be discussed. The person blushes when she realises that something that she assumes was not known to others, or does not want divulged, is indeed known.

> Something personal was told to a lecturer by a friend. [Why blush]
> I was embarrassed that he knew about my personal life.

This occasion to blush also appears in fiction. Eliot provides an example in *Mill on the Floss*, depicting a scene where 'Maggie' admits to 'Stephen' that the high quality of her sewing is due to a time when the family was poor and she needed to take in sewing work:

> Lucy, good and simple, as she was, could not help blushing a little: she did not quite like that Stephen should know that – Maggie need not have mentioned that.

In another set of episodes there is reference to a previous embarrassing incident. In the first example below, one person is embarrassed when the topic is raised and hence she might become the object of attention. In the second example, however, it is not stated whether the strangers present are aware of what the incident entails. I suggest that their awareness is not required for a blush and hence there would be no need for her to become the object of their attention unless, of course, the blush drew attention to her.

> Friends were talking about events of a night out that we had all gone on. [Why blush?] Embarrassment.

> A reminder of a previous embarrassing incident. [Why blush?] Because I remembered the incident and I was with strangers.

Indeed, a blush does not require actual disclosure; it can also ensue when there is a risk of revelation, when a topic is alluded to or even if it is brought to mind without being drawn to anyone else's attention. This is illustrated in Jane Austen's *Emma*. 'Jane Fairfax' has a secret involving a visit to Weymouth, a 'Colonel Campbell', 'Mr. Dixon', and 'Frank Churchill'. Allusions to Jane's time in Weymouth or to any of these characters make her blush, which arouses Emma's suspicion that Jane has a secret. Emma (Austen, 1966, p. 229) sees the 'blush of consciousness with which congratulations were received, the blush of guilt which accompanied the name of "my excellent friend Colonel Campbell" '.

> When on glancing her eye towards Jane Fairfax she [Emma] caught the remains of a smile, when she saw that with all the deep blush of consciousness, there had been a smile of secret delight, she had less scruple in the amusement, and much less compunction with respect to her. – This amiable, upright, perfect Jane Fairfax was apparently cherishing very reprehensible feelings.

When a tune that Jane is playing on the piano is recognised as one she had played at Weymouth, 'She looked up at him [Churchill] for a moment, coloured deeply, and played something else' (ibid., p. 249). When Churchill accidentally almost lets the secret out, he conveys this to her indirectly during a game where the players have to guess a word (ibid., p. 344):

> The word was blunder; and as Harriet exultingly proclaimed it, there was a blush on Jane's cheek which gave it a meaning not otherwise ostensible.

Jane has no reason to believe that these allusions will be understood by anyone else yet she blushes on each occasion and runs the risk of others guessing the truth. Indeed, Emma does guess that there is a secret although she gets it wrong, believing there to be an attraction between Jane and Dixon. Subsequently (ibid., p. 458), she blushes when the truth is revealed and Emma realises how wrong her interpretation had been:

> He named the name of Dixon – Emma blushed and forbade its being pronounced in her hearing. 'I can never think of it,' she cried, 'without extreme shame.'

I have summarised this series of episodes at some length because they draw attention to interesting aspects of the blush as represented by Austen. She makes use of a discrepancy in perspectives on Jane Fairfax's blush, between the reader's perspective and that of the character as portrayed by the author. Austen describes the character's blush and informs the reader that it has been noticed and interpreted. At this point the reader does not yet know the reason for the blush but guesses that the topic that elicits the blush has some special significance for Jane. Austen judges the blush to be the appropriate response by Jane whenever there is some allusion to a topic which Jane is keeping secret. Author and reader share this assumption. But the author has Emma place a particular interpretation on this blush, which guides her subsequent behaviour and which turns out to be erroneous and, indeed, causes her eventually to blush at the recollection. Austen implies that Emma shares this assumption about the meaning of a blush. I think this illustrates nicely the social nature of the blush and indicates its potential for communication and its role in social affairs. Yet, although the blush tells the other characters something, it is not something that Jane Fairfax wants them to know. The blush is a 'leakage'. Furthermore, it has its social function without anyone (other than the blusher) being aware of the nature of the secret that is the source of the blush. It also tells us about character. Although Emma is critical of Jane for the behaviour she is keeping secret, it is to Jane's credit that she sees fit to blush about it: not to have blushed and have the facts revealed would have led to severe disapproval of the kind of person she is.

Sexual topics

We have noted that being the object of sexual attention is a reason to blush and sexual topics are also a reason. People blush when they think about someone to whom they are attracted, hear his name mentioned or are teased about him. They redden when they hear that someone is attracted to them or when they learn that other people believe there is an attraction. They colour at hearing explicit mention of a sexual topic, whether or not it directly involves them, or when they realise that a remark has a possible sexual connotation.

> That I fancied a particular bloke. [Why blush?] Because I didn't know anybody else had realized this! [What, if anything, happened next?] Someone said, 'you're going red'. Which obviously made it worse.

There are frequent examples in fiction and this represents one of the most common reasons to blush found in this source. In *Mill on the Floss* Eliot presents a scene similar to that involving Jane Fairfax described above. The character in the following excerpt has a secret relationship with Philip and they have their trysts at a place called [ironically] 'Red

Deeps'. She is at the dinner table when Philip's name and this place are mentioned:

> At Philip's name she blushed, and the blush deepened every instant from consciousness, until the mention of the Red Deeps made her feel as if the whole secret were betrayed.

There are very many examples in twentieth-century fiction as well. In Updike's *Bech: A Book* (1970) Bech is teaching English and when a student asks him for an example of the point he is making, he replies 'lovemaking' and sees her blush intensely. In Barstow's novel, *A Kind of Loving* (1982), 'Ingrid' finds a book of 'pin-ups' in her boyfriend's pocket and her discovery makes him go red. As Ingrid looks through the pictures praising the figures of the models, he compliments her on her figure and he blushes as he does so. When he falteringly compliments her on her breasts, she tells him not to say so, that he will make her blush, and indeed she does.

Persons

In this category, the blush is elicited by the role or qualities of the person involved rather than the topic aired or being the centre of attention. However, there were only four instances of this category in either questionnaire responses or fiction, two of which appear below. Nevertheless, there are instances in other studies. Shields *et al.* (1990, p. 179) report an interviewee stating 'I always blush when talking to a boss, teacher, or authority figure'.

> When I had to speak to my tutor on the phone to explain something. Generally the fact that I had to speak to him, regardless of what he said. [Why blush?] Because he is a professor, and I didn't <u>expect</u> to speak to him.

> I walked past the window of a person I like and he happened to look out of the window and saw me. [Why blush?] Because it was unexpected and I hadn't prepared myself for seeing him

Embarrassment and self-consciousness

It has already been noted that a number of questionnaires made explicit reference to embarrassment. Transcripts included references to aspects of embarrassment, for example, humour, mentioned by 28 per cent of participants. One item asked respondents 'what, if anything, happened next'. Twenty-five per cent mentioned laughter as a sequel to the embarrassing remark; of these, 13 per cent mentioned the blusher laughing ('laughing it off'), four mentioned the other people laughing, and eight both the blusher and others laughing. Responses to this item also mentioned other physiological reactions, including 'felt hot and sweaty'; 'felt aware of the blush – felt anxious'; 'speech affected, feel uncomfortable, hot, breathless'; 'slight palpitation'. The reactions included typical embarrassment displays – 'I hid my face behind my hand and pulled my hair across my face.' There was mention of the blush producing further blushing or aggravating the predicament.

> The blushing was pointed out giving more attention to me making me blush more and longer.

> I could feel the colour rising in my cheeks and my heart was beating rapidly. I was saying to myself 'Stop blushing', but that just made it worse because I was thinking about it.

There were references to attempts to cope with the predicament. These included trying to ignore the remark and escaping or withdrawing from the situation.

> I just ignored their teasing.
> I walked away.
> I apologised and had to walk away.
> I didn't say anything for the rest of the class.

One frequent response was to attempt to change the subject or to combine this with laughter.

> Tried to laugh it off. Topic of conversation was quickly changed by myself.

> Tried to redirect conversation away from the subject as I was embarrassed.

This was not necessarily effective:

> I tried to change the subject (unsuccessfully) and made it more obvious that I was embarrassed.

The questionnaire in Crozier and Russell's study included items referring to coping with blushing. Responses were submitted to factor analysis and two factors were extracted. Items with high loadings on the first factor included, 'If I feel I should be blushing I begin to blush' and 'When I try to stop myself blushing I blush even more', and the factor seems to refer to lack of control over blushing. The second factor items included, 'When I feel myself blushing I try to relax', and 'When I feel myself blushing I concentrate on something else'. There were significant differences among blushers, non-blushers and an intermediate group on factor scores for the first factor: blushers reported less control than either the intermediate group or the non-blushers (these two did not differ). Frequent blushers claimed to have less control over their blushing in comparison with those who blush less often. The issue of control is discussed again when we consider individual differences in blushing problems (Chapter 11). There was no significant difference between groups in scores on the second factor.

Finally, a common theme throughout the responses was self-consciousness, being the focus of attention, and being aware of being observed. In some cases there is simply reference to the group size or the numbers present, and this was sometimes described as an 'audience':

> Because there was an audience.
> Embarrassment. Being in the presence of others while it [compliment] was being said.

In other cases there is reference to being observed:

> Everybody then looks at you at the same time.
> Because I was embarrassed by everyone looking at me.
> Drew attention to me.
> It put me on the spot a bit.
> Became very aware that I was being watched.
> Recognising the fact that I was being closely observed.

This could include being listened to rather than being observed:

> People were looking at me and listening to what I was saying. I don't usually mind people looking at me, it was more listening to what I was saying.

Discussion and Conclusion

The variety of circumstances described in both sources can be classified into a relatively small number of categories. People blush when they

become the centre of attention. They do so when they are complimented or criticised, and when they succeed or do something foolish in
front of other people. When explaining this participants refer to the
number of people present, to being conscious of being looked at and of
drawing attention to themselves. They frequently mention feeling
embarrassed and not knowing what to say or do. There are invariably
others present and the explanations of the blush often refer to the presence of the audience or onlookers. Often, too, there is a predicament
that has been brought about by the circumstances and the blush can
contribute to this, and make the predicament more difficult to manage.
This pattern is consistent with explanations of the blush that emphasise
self-attention. It is also consistent with the findings from factor analysis
of the Blushing Propensity Questionnaire and with research that man-
ages to induce a blush by having participants perform in front of others,
particularly an action that is embarrassing.

Yet this does not seem to be the whole story, as is also implied by the
difficulties of interpreting the factors that emerge from the factor
analytic studies. In many cases of blushing there is no apparent public
attention, at least prior to the blush, and there need not be a predicament,
unless the blush brings this about. Many of the instances classified as
belonging to the 'topic' category are difficult to interpret as due to being
the focus of attention. Also, many instances of being the object of attention involve some exposure of the self. A feasible interpretation of these
instances is that the blush is an anticipation of being the focus of attention. In many cases the topic has the potential to draw attention to the
self and to produce a predicament even if this potential is not realised
on this occasion. This 'premature' reaction is often counter-productive
and can bring about the feared circumstances, as illustrated in the
excerpts from Austen's *Emma*.

An alternative way to think about these findings is to regard the exposure of some aspect of the self as the key to the blush. Specifically, a
blush occurs whenever there is a breach – or the threat of a breach – of
the boundary between self and other. Such a breach can take different
forms. When the person is the centre of attention the private self is
suddenly thrust into the 'spotlight'. This is an aversive experience if
the person has revealed him or herself to be foolish or to lack poise.
Nevertheless, this is not essential, and the blush can ensue simply
because the preferred role of being anonymous or inconspicuous is no
longer sustainable, for example, 'asked to read out something in front of
others'; 'standing up in class and speaking out'. Conversely, if someone
seeks a conspicuous role being the centre of attention produces no

breach unless that role is threatened in some way or the person loses confidence in the ability to sustain it.

A particularly striking example of a blush where there has been no predicament or attention from other people occurs in an episode in *Mill on the Floss*. Here there is a shift in the character's awareness that is sufficient to make her blush.

> But they had reached the end of the conservatory, and were obliged to pause and turn. The change of movement brought a new consciousness to Maggie: she blushed deeply, turned away her head, and drew her arm from Stephen's.

Here, the blusher is not exposed to a specific audience but, we might say, her shift in awareness leads her to see herself through the eyes of a generalised other, that is, her blush is contingent on awareness of how her behaviour would look from another perspective. It is difficult to elicit subtle instances like this relying upon research methods that ask for recollections of blushing since no 'trigger' is salient. The episode resembles Taylor's example (1985, p. 61) of an artist's model who has been relaxed for some time posing nude until a shift in her awareness leads her to think that the artist no longer sees her as a model but as a woman. The shift from being at ease in the situation to being ashamed does not have to involve any change in either person's behaviour but only a change in the ashamed person's perception of her situation. Taylor argues that the model does not have to see herself from the artist's point of view but only has to realise how she could be seen. The episode resembles Castelfranchi and Poggi's 'good Samaritan' example where a man giving a woman mouth-to-mouth resuscitation need only imagine how his action could look to an observer in order to experience shame before the other: no actual audience is required. Common to these examples is the ashamed person's recognition that being seen like this is a plausible interpretation of his or her behaviour, together with an acknowledgement that it is wrong or inappropriate to be seen in this way. Furthermore, the view need not be that of anyone present (the model or the artist; the good Samaritan or a passer-by) or of any specific observer. While public exposure of some moral infraction or shortcoming is fundamental to theories of shame (see Chapter 7) it is a moot point whether it is necessary for a blush: perhaps awareness that the self is exposed to the view of another is sufficient to induce a blush.

How do the two accounts – being the object of attention and exposure – relate to one another? Do they represent separate causes of the blush, or does one subsume the other? We don't know enough about the circumstances to answer this question at present, and our only evidence comprises recollections of episodes, ratings of hypothetical occasions and fictional accounts. We are far from being able to observe the blush 'live' or 'on-line' across a range of situations and we are not in a position to manipulate properties of situations to see how they affect the likelihood or intensity of a blush.

Finally, a distinction has to be kept in mind between the circumstances that are likely to provide the occasion for a blush and the cause of a blush. The circumstances provide clues as to its causes but it is associated with a psychological state not directly brought about by external factors. Being conspicuous is different from being self-conscious. One participant wrote, after describing her blush while giving a speech to a group of about eight people: 'I nearly always blush when I consciously realise that everyone's attention is on me' [emphases in original].

The substantial number of instances where positive attention elicits a blush is worthy of comment. Are these occasions of blushing with pride? There are few references in the psychological literature to blushing with pride although we sometimes hear it said in everyday conversation that someone flushes or is flushed with pride. We also say that someone walks tall or swells with pride, which contrasts with the shrinking and hiding associated with shame, but colour seems to play a smaller part in descriptions of pride than it does in shame. Indeed, in the instances of receiving positive attention reported in this study the participant's explanation of his or her blush refers not to pride but to being looked at or to embarrassment about how to respond to what has been said in the hearing of others. This is true of all four examples presented above.

Other examples refer to the surprise that the remark occasioned. While Buss (1980) had suggested that overpraise rather than praise causes someone to blush, the element of surprise seems important and this may trigger embarrassment in the sense of causing fluster and uncertainty on how to behave.

Compliment in the presence of others, possibly because it was unexpected and surprising. [Why blush?] Embarrassment. Being in the presence of others while it was being said.

A compliment – someone thought I was seven years younger [Why blush?] Shock! Surprise! Total amazement!

I was praised for organising a client's party by a senior member of staff. [Why blush?] It was unexpected. I didn't feel it was that well done.

A recurrent theme across the examples is that the blush is elicited by awareness of the presence of others and of being the centre of attention rather than evoked by any feelings of pride. There seems to be little evidence to suggest that people would blush because of their achievements if they were not observed, believed that they might be observed or if the reactions of others were not salient in their imagination. Nor do we know whether the focus on the self that is entailed in pride is the same state that we commonly call self-consciousness, whether this is characterised as Harris's ANPS-A or Tomkins's shame affect. The next set of chapters examines the blush in the context of the social emotions.

III
The Social Emotions

6
Embarrassment

Embarrassment and the blush

Blushing has been regarded as the 'hallmark' of embarrassment (Buss, 1980, p. 129), and Miller (1996, p. 137) concludes that, 'on the whole, blushing is a reliable sign of embarrassment'. Evidence reviewed in this volume confirms that embarrassment and blushing are indeed closely associated. The situations that are contrived to elicit a blush in the measurement studies described in Chapter 3 certainly seem to be embarrassing: singing children's songs, dancing in front of an audience or watching a videotape of yourself carrying out these activities while you are in the presence of others would surely be embarrassing for most of us. Observations of blushing provide another form of evidence. Asendorpf (1990b) reported an experiment where the frequency of participants' blushing as rated by observers was greater in an embarrassing situation (when asked to make an evaluative comment about another person in that person's presence) than when participants were interacting with a stranger or during a baseline condition (conversing 'outside the experiment' with the researcher).

Findings also come from questionnaire studies. The item 'red in the face' is a central element in one of the clusters of prototypical features of embarrassment derived from cluster analysis of ratings of typical incidents by Parrott and Smith (1991), who concluded (ibid., p. 478) that 'most accounts mentioned blushing as a sign of embarrassment'. Ratings of blushing as a characteristic reaction of embarrassment were high for both actual and typical incidents (respective means of 7.55 and 7.96 on 9-point scales).

The connection is apparent when people describe events that caused them to blush. There are many spontaneous references to embarrassment in the study described in Chapter 5, where participants recalled an occasion when they had blushed, and being embarrassed is a frequent explanation for blushing in these accounts. Another illustration is provided by analysis of a web site (www.thatsembarrassing.com) that elicits accounts of embarrassing incidents.[1] A very high proportion of the submitted episodes refer to blushing; specifically, a word search located 730 episodes that mentioned blushing or being red faced, approximating the 745 episodes mentioning being embarrassed. Of course, we don't know the provenance of these submissions and they do portray highly dramatic, and often (at least in retrospect) humorous social predicaments: the incidents in the education section are reminiscent of comic scenes in American movies set on college campuses. Nevertheless, while these incidents may not be representative of everyday instances of embarrassment there is no reason to expect that submissions would be biased with regard to prevalence of references to blushing.

However, the claim that the blush is a straightforward expression of embarrassment has been disputed. It is less securely located in accounts of embarrassment than are other elements of the display. Keltner and Buswell (1997) do not consider it as integral to the display arguing, first, that reddening of the face is not specific to embarrassment but is present in other emotions, and, second, that its onset occurs significantly later than the other elements of the display. Ekman (2003) argues that the blush does not qualify as a sign of embarrassment because it is not visible in people with dark complexion.

Despite the many spontaneous references to embarrassment in recollections of blushing episodes there are reasons to be cautious about identifying it with blushing. Only two mentions of embarrassment were found in the text adjacent to fictional episodes of blushing that were analysed. This difference between sources perhaps reflects the semantic connections that exist between embarrassment and blushing and many respondents to the questionnaire would perhaps recall embarrassing incidents when cued by the word 'blush'. On the other hand, writers of fiction may feel that they have provided a sufficient portrayal of the character's emotion by referring to the blush – mention of embarrassment is superfluous. Yet there were emotion words adjacent to blushing in the fiction, referring to the self-conscious emotions more generally. This raises a more fundamental objection to the embarrassment account, namely that blushing is associated with other emotions, notably shame; I consider this in Chapter 7.

There is evidence that blushing may not be an inevitable response to embarrassing incidents, for example, it is not mentioned in all self-descriptions of embarrassment. Only 50 per cent of mothers mentioned blushing in a survey of their descriptions of their children's embarrassment (Buss *et al.*, 1979). Just over half (58%) of respondents to a survey who were invited to recall an embarrassing incident reported that the incident caused them to blush (Parrott and Smith, 1991). Edelmann (1990a) presented findings from a cross-cultural survey indicating that the incidence of blushing as a reported symptom of embarrassment varied across the participating societies. The proportion ranged from 21 per cent of respondents (Spanish) to 55 per cent (British). Such findings have led Edelmann (1987) and Leary *et al.* (1992) to conclude that one can be embarrassed without blushing and blush without being embarrassed. Admittedly this constitutes only indirect evidence. It is entirely possible that a measurable increase in skin temperature always accompanies embarrassment but is not necessarily of sufficient magnitude to be noticed by the embarrassed person. People are not always good judges of whether or not they are blushing in any given situation, and the correspondence between physiological changes and observer reports of blushing is modest. It may be difficult for people to answer questions about how frequently they blush.

A blush is not only an embarrassed reaction, it can itself cause embarrassment and this can give rise to a vicious circle where the embarrassment produced by the blush intensifies the blush and so on. The blush projects an image of the self into the social encounter and this can be an unwanted image. One chronic blusher with whom I spoke about his blushing was distressed that he was unable to form a romantic relationship and believed that this was because he blushed whenever he interacted with a woman and he believed that women would regard this as unacceptable in a man. For him this was not an idiosyncratic standard that he was failing to meet but, he was convinced, a normative one.

Signs of embarrassment

Embarrassed smiles

Embarrassment does seem to have a distinctive emotional display, involving a pattern of gaze aversion, head movements, touching or covering the face, smiling and a stiff posture. The prototype of embarrassment derived from ratings of typical incidents reported by Parrott and Smith (1991) includes redness of the face, perspiration, gaze aversion, hiding the face, lowering of the head, a nervous laugh or smile, and fidgeting. The frequencies of various signs of embarrassment mentioned by the British respondents in Edelmann's (1990a) survey were: blushing (55%), averting their gaze (41%), smiling (37%) laughing (19%), and touching the face (16%).

Keltner (1995) undertook a detailed analysis of somatic responses to embarrassment using Ekman's Facial Action Coding System. The typical display is not represented by a fixed expression but is characterised by a rapid sequence of movements and postural changes that overlap in time and which lasts for some five seconds following the event that triggers the embarrassment. The initial stage in the display is gaze aversion, which begins about one second after the precipitating event and persists throughout the sequence. Between one and two seconds after the event there is an attempt at controlling an emerging smile – biting the lip or pressing the lips together – that lasts for about one second before it gives way to a smile of a type identified as a non-Duchenne smile. This is not the 'full smile' of genuine amusement but one that involves only the major muscle action that pulls the corners of the lips upwards.[2] Following the smile there begins in rapid succession a further head movement, downwards and to the left, a shift in gaze, a second attempt at smile control and another shift in gaze.

Close analysis has thus uncovered a distinctive display that unfolds over time. People seem to be able to tell from live observation, still photographs and videotapes when someone is embarrassed. They can reliably discriminate embarrassed smiles from smiles of amusement. Keltner and Buswell (1997) report a degree of consensus in judgments of spontaneous expressions and photographs in studies carried out in the United States and India, although there were some cultural differences. Indian participants attributed both shame and embarrassment to someone who covers the eyes with his or her hand. Biting the tongue, which is, Keltner and Buswell report, an appeasement gesture throughout Southeast Asia, was frequently judged as embarrassment in India (53% of participants) but rarely in the United States (10% of participants).

The display has components that are not under full control: although there are attempts to inhibit a smile, it breaks through. This resembles the blush, which is also involuntary and beyond control. It was argued in Chapter 4 that the blush makes an effective signal of apology because it is not in the blusher's command and cannot be feigned. It seems that other elements of the display of embarrassment are also difficult to control and perhaps to simulate, although evidence is needed on the latter point. The involuntary nature of the display is surely significant for social encounters since the display can provide an additional source of embarrassment and deny the person the opportunity to exhibit poise or pretend ignorance of the predicament. Silver *et al.* (1987) provide an example of a man who makes an advance on a woman and who is rebuffed, and they suggest that he would find it more difficult to pretend that his approach was other than it was, were he to show signs of emotion following the rejection. Exhibiting embarrassment makes it difficult to act as if the advance were quite innocent.

There seems to be a connection at the level of the display between embarrassment and humour since smiling plays a part in both, even if a smile of embarrassment does not seem to be quite the same as a smile of amusement. Observing an embarrassing incident (someone slipping on a banana skin) makes people laugh, often involuntarily. As mentioned at the beginning of this chapter, the embarrassing episodes documented in a web site were frequently narrated as humorous incidents, and the audience was almost invariably described as laughing. This implies that there is something inherently funny about embarrassing events even though those present often recognise that humour is out of place and try to suppress it. In a study of descriptions of experiences of shame, guilt and embarrassment undertaken by Tangney *et al.* (1996a), embarrassment was distinguished clearly from shame and guilt on items that referred to other people being amused at the time, such as 'hurts now/can laugh at it now'. Of course, embarrassment isn't always a matter of humour. People often fail to see the funny side of their predicament and are hurt by it, for example in cases of malicious teasing. Situations can be both painful and embarrassing, for example, bringing bad news to someone.

The blush in the display

Keltner's analysis excludes the blush and does not regard it as intrinsic to the display of embarrassment; it is not known where the blush fits into the sequence that comprises the display. Keltner and Anderson (2000) suggest that there are many unanswered questions about the blush, including whether it is unique to embarrassment, whether it is universal, and whether it serves as a signal of appeasement or is a derivative of other responses. Blushing is thus in the paradoxical position of being part of the prototypical embarrassment response in research into lay descriptions, whereas researchers assign it a subsidiary role as a by-product or auxiliary response. In part, this might be explained in terms of the ambition of some psychologists to identify unique distinguishing features of embarrassment. Keltner and Buswell (1997) dispute that the blush is the primary non-verbal signal of embarrassment, arguing that it is not seen in young children, in contrast with other components of the embarrassment display, and that it comes later in the display sequence than the other components, some 18 seconds after the trigger event.

In response to the first point, there exists little evidence on the development of embarrassment. Indeed, as discussed in Chapter 2, Lewis has distinguished two forms of embarrassment, one form appearing in the middle of the second year along with the capacity for self-referential behaviour and is evident, for example, in the child acting coy or 'silly' when seeing his or her reflection in a mirror. The second 'evaluative' form emerges in the third year when the child is aware of standards for social behaviour, and embarrassment is related to awareness of failure to meet normative expectations. It is feasible that blushing accompanies the second form and would not be evident at 18 months even though the child shows other signs of embarrassment at that age. The distinction made by Lewis raises questions: Does the distinctive display apply to one form or both? Are some aspects of the expression of emotion characteristic of exposure embarrassment and others of evaluative embarrassment? Unfortunately, there has been little research into these matters.

Second, the time difference between the onset and offset of the patterned display and the onset of blushing is only relevant if the duration of the experience of embarrassment is restricted to the initial five seconds or so of the display. If it is considered that the experience is extended in time then the sequence will continue to unfold over what would still be a relatively short period of time. If the social predicament that triggers the response persists beyond 20 seconds or so and if, as researchers have argued, some elements of the display amplify other elements, such that awareness of blushing intensifies it and awareness of embarrassment is a source of further embarrassment, then it is likely that the display will endure. Goffman (1972) suggested that some occasions of embarrassment are short-lived moments within an encounter whereas other occasions are sustained over long periods of time until the whole encounter comprises an embarrassing situation. Furthermore, there exists little evidence on the time course of the blush. In the study by Shearn *et al.* (1990) that is cited by Keltner as identifying the timing of peak blush (mean 18.7 seconds, standard deviation 12.7) the increase in measured cheek blood flow was specific to the embarrassing stimulus and was not evident in the scene from *Psycho*, suggesting that it is a specific response to embarrassment. Also, the measure is of greatest change in flow relative to the pre-stimulus value; we do not know how changes in flow relate to the visibility of the blush.

Finally, the distinctiveness of the embarrassment display resides in the patterning of elements rather than in the involvement of elements in themselves, for example gaze avoidance and lowering of the head also accompany shame and shyness. The analysis of embarrassing situations undertaken by Parrott and Smith (1991) identified a cluster of reactions involving blushing, temperature change and rapid heartbeat, a nervous laugh or smile, as well as the elements isolated by Keltner (1995): gaze aversion, head down and hiding the face. It would be useful to study the relation of blushing to these elements in different kinds of social situations and predicaments.

A question that has not been addressed is whether the display makes an effective communication simply because it shows that the individual is embarrassed, giving rise to one interpretation of her action and ruling out other possible interpretations, or whether it is effective because it goes beyond serving as a marker for this emotion to convey an apology or gesture of appeasement. If you display embarrassment you show you are discomfited or 'thrown'. What others make of this depends on the circumstances. In some cases the discomfort has been engineered – if you are teasing someone, the blush and the embarrassed smile provide a reward for your tease since they show that it has been effective. Similarly, it is rewarding to see that you have produced an effect on someone who you perceive to be haughty or with whom you are flirting. In other cases, when someone is publicly praised or complimented, the signs show that he or she is unused to this kind of situation and uncertain how to behave, and this is rewarding in its own way to the audience as it proves the recipient to be appropriately modest. No one likes graceless winners.

In the scenarios described in empirical studies, the actor has behaved badly or inappropriately in some way, and observers take a more positive view of the actor if he or she shows signs of embarrassment. If people display embarrassment when they have behaved badly they show that they are conscious that expectations about their moral obligations have not been fulfilled. If they fail to do so, it may be because they remain ignorant of their wrongdoing (the actor has to know that he has knocked over the stack of cans in the supermarket – he might not have noticed the trail of damage he left behind). If, however, the observer has reason to believe that the person is aware of the consequences of his action then the failure to display embarrassment is evidence that he is indifferent to what people in such situations can reasonably expect of one another.

Is the display of embarrassment effective because it shows that the person is aware of their social obligations or is there more to it than this, that the person is offering an apology or enacting appeasement?

A problem with this position is how to account for embarrassment when we are praised, complimented, thanked or honoured, and perhaps also when we are teased. Nevertheless, following Castelfranchi and Poggi's influential analysis of blushing and shame, and Keltner's analysis of the embarrassment display, the view that the actor is signalling apology or appeasement has become accepted. One of the arguments for appeasement is the apparent similarity between the embarrassment (and shame and shyness) display and signs of submission in humans and other species. Gilbert (2002, p. 14) argues that 'the pattern of *behaviours* noted in shame are submissive, associated with desires to conceal the self, hide, escape, avoid eye gaze and inhibition of confident display behaviour and outputs'. Keltner and Buswell (1997) analyse appeasement in terms of a sequence of submissive and affiliative actions intended to pacify an aggressor. It is a response to social threat and is evident in other species that live in groups. Keltner and Buswell have provided a detailed review of appeasement behaviours in different species and have identified elements that are found in the human display of embarrassment, including gaze avoidance, turning and lowering the head, self-touching and submissive posture. Smile-like grimaces involving baring the teeth and retraction of the lips are seen in several species of primates. Other species also take actions to try to restore good relations, for example in making bodily contact such as grooming.

Yet, while some elements of the embarrassment display do resemble submissive behaviours, the blush does not and is not found in other species (although Keltner and Buswell speculate that it might be similar to the reddening of the skin, which is a sexual cue in some species, and that presenting a red bottom is an appeasement gesture in certain primate species). The blush makes the person more conspicuous rather than less visible. This account of the display of embarrassment in terms of appeasement seems to offer another reason not to identify the blush too closely with embarrassment. Castelfranchi and Poggi offered a convincing account of the blush as a non-verbal form of apology but it does leave the question why their account focuses on the blush rather than, say, on gaze aversion or smile control. What is it about the blush, other than it being a sign of embarrassment or shame, that conveys an apology?

The causes of embarrassment

What is embarrassment and why might it produce a blush? Embarrassment is triggered when some event – often, but not necessarily, a flawed public performance – creates a predicament for the individual by putting his or her social identity at risk, either by threatening loss of public esteem or 'face', or by giving rise to uncertainty about how to behave. Favoured explanations are that either it is triggered by loss of esteem in the eyes of others or that it represents fluster and awkwardness brought about by an interruption of the social encounter and the individual's inability to play a part in it. The latter, following Goffman (see later) is labelled the dramaturgical perspective: the actor has mislaid her script and is at a loss to know what happens next. The etymology of embarrassment is the French *embarrasser*, meaning to block or to obstruct, and the notion of events coming to a stop and needing to be restarted is common to accounts of the experience. Various approaches have been taken to its analysis. Some take the social encounter as the unit of analysis and conceive of embarrassment as a disruption of the smooth running of an encounter, while others focus on the experience and behaviour of the embarrassed person.

Embarrassing encounters

Embarrassment occurs when a social encounter comes to a stop and at least some of those present are uncertain how to proceed. There might be attempts to change the topic or to alter the mood by introducing humour but perhaps this is not possible and the topic 'hangs in the air'. Those who created the embarrassment may be quite ignorant of what they have brought about and remain unperturbed, or they might glean from others' reactions that their action is somehow inappropriate and become embarrassed. Ideally they would take steps to put matters right. (Billig, 2001, characterises these hopes in terms of a 'nice guy' theory of social relations, which holds that people are motivated to take remedial action and to heal whereas, he argues, a common reaction to predicaments is to find them funny at the perpetrator's expense.)

Goffman provided an influential analysis of embarrassment in terms of the management of social encounters. He argued that embarrassment represents a breakdown in an encounter and occurs when a definition of the situation that participants have constructed cannot be sustained:

> Embarrassment has to do with unfulfilled expectations ... the elements of a social encounter consist of effectively projected claims to an acceptable self and the confirmation of like claims on the part of others. When an event throws doubt upon or discredits these claims, then the encounter finds itself lodged in assumptions which no longer hold. (Goffman, 1972, p. 105)

Goffman discussed embarrassment in terms of its function in facilitating the smooth running of encounters and he explained its causes in terms of a breakdown in the presentation and acceptance of social identities which, he argued, are essential for successful social interaction. Thus, from this perspective, embarrassment is not merely an unpleasant experience to be avoided: it serves essential social functions. It provides a means for stopping and re-starting a social encounter before any problems that have arisen bring it to a complete halt and impede future interactions. The penalty it provides for untoward behaviour is severe enough to restrain behaviour but not so harsh that it permanently incapacitates the person for future involvement. A society where embarrassment was unknown would be a harsh place with few restraints on aggression; likewise, an individual who lacks the capacity for embarrassment would be unpleasant to know. Embarrassment permits flexibility in social interactions since it enables individuals to move beyond rigid social categories and allows them to test the boundaries of acceptable behaviour without excessive risks. This provides one explanation of the link between embarrassment and humour, which also brings together incongruous categories and the testing of boundaries.

Since an embarrassing incident brings matters to a halt, the encounter will have to be reconstructed in some way if it is to continue. The situation calls for someone who can behave with tact and find a way out of the impasse. Those present draw upon 'corrective practices' in order to bring about this reconstruction. Of course, situations cannot necessarily be rescued and some things cannot be unsaid, nevertheless it might be possible to 'paper over the cracks' and to provide a temporary respite so that nothing worse will be said, the situation will not deteriorate, and the participants will save face and be in a position to reconstruct identities for future interactions, if not for the current one.

One advantage of construing embarrassment at the level of the social encounter is that it acknowledges that people feel embarrassed even when they are not responsible for bringing about the predicament. Silver *et al.* (1987, p. 58) propose that 'embarrassment is the flustering caused by the perception that a flubbed (botched, fumbled) performance, a working consensus of identities, cannot, or in any event will not, be repaired in time'. It does not require that the botched performance has been produced by the individual who is embarrassed; indeed it is not necessarily the responsibility of anyone present, since the disruptive event can be entirely accidental. Silver *et al.* (1987) describe an incident where a woman is embarrassed at a formal dinner when a waiter spills borscht on her white dress. She is not responsible for the stain that causes her embarrassment, but as the authors point out, her self-presentation is now flawed and it is difficult for her to continue to act naturally and with poise, thus she is responsible in that sense. Many embarrassing incidents occur by accident but this does not make them any less personal – 'this could only have happened to me!'

Embarrassment has also been studied in terms of individual emotional experience, and one line of argument is that it is due to the individual's loss of esteem. There is debate whether this is loss of self-esteem or of esteem in the eyes of others, that is whether the behaviour is judged against personal standards or involves negative evaluation by others. Leary *et al.* (1996, p. 620) claim that 'specifically, embarrassment occurs when people experience a self-presentational predicament in which they think that others have formed undesired impressions of them'. Miller (1996, p. 129) defines embarrassment in terms of the fluster that is brought about by events that 'increase the threat of unwanted evaluations from real or imagined audiences'. For example, a candidate attending an interview is embarrassed when she realises that there is a huge ladder in her tights that is visible to those interviewing her. She is aware of the flaw in her appearance, but she relates her embarrassment to being seen, implying that it is what she believes the flaw reveals about her to the interviewers that gives rise to her embarrassment.

A problem with esteem accounts is that we can be embarrassed by and for others, even when our involvement with them is slight. Consider the example of a comedian hosting a television programme who delivers weak jokes that 'fall flat', evoking little laughter from the studio audience. It is possible to be embarrassed *by* him (and also feel embarrassment *for* him) though he may be oblivious of the audience's unresponsiveness or its embarrassment. It can be argued that the audience is party to his predicament in that they are partners in a 'contract' between performer and spectators where certain expectations hold about the appropriate behaviour of all participants, and thus the programme is their joint construction; also, audience members are in his presence and are faced with the difficulty of knowing how to behave correctly. Nevertheless, it is possible to feel embarrassment watching his performance even when you are remote from it in time and space, for example watching a pre-recorded programme on television in your own home.

The phenomena of vicarious and empathic embarrassment provide a valuable reminder that this emotion is experienced not only by those who make a faux pas or are otherwise to blame for the predicament in which they find themselves. It cautions us against defining the experience solely in terms of loss of esteem or attracting the negative evaluation of others. Miller (1987) submitted empathic embarrassment to empirical investigation, finding that observers were more embarrassed watching an actor's predicament than were those in a control group who observed an actor performing innocuous tasks. However, although observers rated themselves as embarrassed, they tended to be less embarrassed than the actors themselves, implying that empathic embarrassment is a milder form than that occasioned by performing the activity oneself.

Embarrassing circumstances

There has been substantial research into the circumstances that elicit embarrassment and several typologies of situations have been proposed. In a recent comprehensive study Miller (1996) classified over 750 episodes derived from diaries that participants, high school and college students, kept over a period of weeks, recording weekly any instances of embarrassment that had occurred during the week and reporting their most recent embarrassment. He assigned episodes to four broad categories on the basis of whose behaviour was responsible for the social predicament that was brought about.

(i) The largest category, comprising 64 per cent of episodes, incorporated situations where the individual's own conduct caused the embarrassment. This was subdivided into several sub-categories: physical 'pratfalls' and clumsy and inept performances; 'cognitive errors' – various kinds of mistakes such as forgetting someone's name, making slips of the tongue or getting words confused, loss of control over one's body or possessions; failures of privacy regulation (most of the instances involve unintentional nakedness); harming others. Other divisions of this category were embarrassment brought about by conspicuousness and over-sensitivity in situations that are only moderately awkward.

(ii) The next largest category, comprising 14 per cent of episodes, was labelled 'audience provocations' and brought together circumstances where embarrassment was caused by the conduct of other people, for example, having borscht spilled on your dress.

(iii) The category of 'awkward interactions' (9% of episodes) includes situations where embarrassment is brought about by the joint behaviour of two or more people and the blusher is not personally to blame: had different people been present, the predicament might not have arisen.

(iv) The episodes in the final category, 'bystander behavior', are instances where the individual's embarrassment is caused by witnessing others' embarrassing actions, including the actions of people with whom the embarrassed person is associated (10%), and empathic embarrassment (3%).

Two of these sub-categories are of particular relevance to our account in Chapter 4 of the causes of the blush – failures of privacy regulation and conspicuousness – since these resemble the exposure category described in that chapter. More generally, it is instructive to compare in broad terms the set of instances generated by the recall of blushing incidents with the reports of embarrassing situations classified by Miller (1996). In Miller's study, making errors and faux pas of various kinds and loss of control accounted for nearly half of the incidents but there were relatively few references to simple conspicuousness or to compliments or similar remarks. This is the opposite pattern to that found in the study of blushing. Admittedly we are not comparing like with like, yet the difference in pattern of responses is suggestive. In principle it would be useful to compare recollections of embarrassing incidents where people also report whether or not they blushed at the time with incidents of blushing where they are asked to report whether or not they had been embarrassed at the time. However, the questions posed to participants would have to be phrased carefully because of the difficulty of distinguishing embarrassment and blushing in ordinary discourse.

Cataloguing circumstances in an inductive or 'bottom up' fashion is a useful step towards understanding the causes of this reaction. In itself, however, it does not inform about the processes that give rise to embarrassment nor does it permit any tests of hypotheses about its causes or consequences. In seeking to identify what it is about situations that makes them embarrassing Sabini *et al.* (2000) took a 'top down' approach, drawing upon two theoretical positions on embarrassment – that it is brought about by loss of esteem in the eyes of others and that is occurs when social interaction is disrupted or threatened with disruption. They propose three classes of situations:

(i) where the individual makes a faux pas, either in front of friends or relatives or in front of strangers;
(ii) 'sticky' situations, defined as those where the actor does something that threatens the identity of someone else present.
(iii) When people are the centre of attention but for reasons other than having made a faux pas.

Sabini *et al.* constructed scales comprising items representing these classes of circumstances. Respective examples of the three types of scenarios are failing to cook the meal properly for parents and in-laws whom you have invited to dinner; having to ask someone to repay a loan; being called upon to read aloud in front of the class. Participants rated each scenario in terms of how embarrassed they would be in that situation. Embarrassment was rated highest on average for faux pas, followed by sticky situations and being the centre of attention, although none of the scales seemed very embarrassing in that only the mean rating on the Faux Pas scale was above the mid-point of the scale. Women reported more embarrassment than males on the Faux Pas scale, and their mean rating was close to 5 (where 7 is the maximum), implying that they found these types of situations particularly embarrassing. There was no gender difference on the other two scales. Ratings on the three scales were inter-correlated, suggesting that they shared a common factor, nevertheless the correlation coefficients were modest and an oblique factor analysis identified three factors corresponding to the three scales.

The finding that situations where you are the centre of attention without having committed a faux pas is embarrassing, and is significantly more embarrassing than finding yourself in a sticky situation, is of considerable interest in the context of blushing. Items in the scale refer to receiving awards in front of the class, speaking up in front of others and having 'Happy Birthday' sung to you, situations that feature in recollections of blush-inducing episodes. It is not clear why being the centre of attention in these ways is embarrassing in itself. Sabini and co-authors allude to evidence that simply being the centre of attention is arousing but arousal in itself does not necessarily take the form of embarrassment.

Self-consciousness and embarrassment

Perhaps being the centre of attention combines with some other elements to create embarrassment. Our account of blushing has suggested the role of being conscious that you are seen or might be seen in a particular way, and this makes you uncomfortable. There are examples of this in instances of blushing. To begin with a personal anecdote, I was watching a school play and during a brief interval to allow the scene to be changed a student appeared and proceeded to move the props around the stage – the lights were still on. He seemed to be doing this quite naturally but he blushed when he became aware that the audience (bored, perhaps, and not able to do anything else in the short interval) was following his movements. When he had completed his task and started to leave the stage the audience applauded humorously and he blushed more intensely. When he had begun his activities he was surely aware that he was undertaking them in front of a large number of people but he was not necessarily conscious of being the focus of attention. When the scene mover realises that he *is* the focus of attention he blushes. If, say, the audience were not attending to him but he believed that it was doing so, I predict that he would also blush. Similarly he would blush, I imagine, if he were to drop a prop, to make a loud noise or otherwise catch the attention of the audience. The change is between being the centre of attention unconsciously and being aware of being the centre of attention. A respondent to the blushing questionnaire alludes to this distinction when she writes, 'I nearly always blush when I <u>consciously</u> realise that everyone's attention is on <u>me</u>' (the underlining is hers and she had added the words 'nearly' and 'consciously' to the original sentence).

Self-consciousness is prominent in Parrott and Smith's (1991) study of recalled and typical embarrassing incidents, at least on rating scales. Mean ratings for the self-consciousness item (on a 9-point scale) were 7.89 for an actual embarrassing incident and 8.57 for a typical incident. Mean ratings were also high (6.47 and 7.70 respectively) for the item referring to feeling conspicuous. Self-consciousness was also apparent in hierarchical cluster analysis applied to judgments of similarities between features emerging from content analysis of participants' written descriptions of the incidents. The items on one cluster referred to 'feel self-conscious, feel exposed and vulnerable, feel center of attention, everyone noticed, desire less attention, wish to leave, hide, or escape'. Although a relatively small proportion of written accounts spontaneously mention feeling self-conscious or feeling exposed (the proportion of each is 19%), a larger proportion mention feeling the centre of attention (43%) and wishing to hide, leave or escape (35%).

More generally, participants in the study are much more likely to report that self-consciousness (and blushing) are elements in embarrassment when they are presented with these as items on a ratings scale than they are to spontaneously mention them in written accounts. Presumably, this discrepancy reflects the difference in response format and is partly due to a difference between recognition and recall of events – participants completed the written descriptions before responding to the items. There may also be bias in coding the accounts, in that self-consciousness does not have many synonyms. Nevertheless, self-consciousness is less salient in the unprompted recall of embarrassment relative to other components of embarrassment, and this is worthy of further study.

Surprise and uncertainty

The analysis of circumstances conducted by Sabini and his colleagues distinguish three sets of triggers of embarrassment and treat being the centre of attention as a distinct category that excludes situations where the person is the centre of attention because he or she has made a faux pas. Thus, for example, the item referring to finding yourself in the wrong classroom and having to get up and walk out is included in the Faux Pas rather than the Centre of Attention scale. This approach is consistent with the aims of their project – to identify triggers of embarrassment – but it could be misleading if it was thought to be representative of the actual situations that cause people to be embarrassed or to blush since particular situations can have elements of one or more triggers. A recurrent theme in instances of blushing is that the blusher is conscious of being seen or of the possibility of being seen; sometimes this is because of a faux pas (you arrive to dinner and suddenly realise that you have put on a dress that is stained) and on other occasions it can be accidental (the waiter spills the borscht) or engineered by someone else (you are teased that your dress is stained when it isn't). These circumstances do create predicaments that fluster and leave the blusher uncertain on how to carry on.

A sense of uncertainty is evident in episodes that were recalled in the questionnaire study presented in Chapter 5. A young woman blushes when her former schoolteacher calls out to her in a busy shopping mall and initiates a conversation with her: 'I just wanted to escape from the situation as my embarrassment was evident due to my face being bright red'. The awkwardness of the encounter creates an element of uncertainty.

Another source of uncertainty is that many embarrassing incidents happen quickly and by surprise and they provide little time for the victim to gather his or her thoughts or to react appropriately: a sudden gust of wind can dislodge a toupee or blow a paper plate of food off the picnic table onto your lap. It is difficult to carry on with dignity in any of these circumstances. The surprise element is presumably a factor in the fluster and confusion that frequently accompany embarrassment and the blush (and in the sudden laughter that such situations can evoke). If embarrassing events were more predictable the actor would have more time to initiate 'facework' or to adopt a protective self-presentation strategy. Surprise and uncertainty what to do next are common in embarrassment. I can vouch for this from personal experience when I was at the (now closed) Granada Tours in Manchester and came to the exterior of the mock 10 Downing Street, with an actor playing the role of policeman guarding the door. Through the window I could see activity in the set backing onto this one. I was trying to make out what was going on when the policeman said, 'Make a habit of looking through people's windows, do we sir?' I couldn't think of a retort and just stood there, blushing furiously. My inability to think of an appropriate reply played a large part in my embarrassment and this was due to the fluster brought about by the policeman's unexpected yet plausible interpretation of my behaviour.[3] Darwin devoted a section of his chapter to the mental confusion that accompanies the blush, proposing that it is a consequence of the physiological changes:

> if then, there exists, as cannot be doubted, an intimate sympathy between the capillary circulation in that part of the brain on which our mental powers depend, and the skin of the face, it is not surprising that the moral causes which induce intense blushing should likewise induce, independently of their own disturbing influence, much confusion of mind. (Darwin, 1872, p. 325)

Conclusion

It is a truism that blushing accompanies embarrassment and this is confirmed by surveys and the small number of measurement studies that has been conducted. Critics argue that the blush is not invariably triggered in embarrassing circumstances and that it is not peculiar to embarrassment but accompanies other emotional states as well. The next chapter considers whether we also blush with shame, which raises another question, whether embarrassment and shame are distinct emotional states. Embarrassment seems to have a distinctive and uncontrollable display where smiling and attempts to suppress the smile play a significant role. However, Keltner, who has done much to identify this display, is reluctant to admit the blush as a component because it does not always accompany other elements of the display and because its onset is discrepant from these elements.

Studies of circumstances that elicit embarrassment present a somewhat different picture from those that trigger the blush. There is greater emphasis on faux pas and errors of various kinds, and less emphasis on conspicuousness and receiving positive attention. Nevertheless, there exists little systematic research into the circumstances of blushing. Why might a blush accompany embarrassment? One answer is that it is a visual ingredient of the corrective practices that are required to manage the social predicament that has been created. Since it signals embarrassment and possibly an apology it can play a useful role. As discussed in Chapter 4 it can help others interpret the actor's motives and forestall their anger. A blush can contribute effectively even if the blusher is not responsible for the incident since it helps all present identify and label the predicament and it may suggest some corrective action that might be taken. An alternative view is that it accompanies the self-consciousness that embarrassment induces. Surveys, for example that undertaken by Parrott and Smith (1991), report that blushing, self-consciousness and feeling the centre of attention are common experiences in embarrassing situations. Themes of self-consciousness and exposure are explored in the next chapter in the context of shame.

7
Shame

Blushing with shame

The idea that we blush with shame is an old one. References are found in the King James Version of the Bible, published in 1611, for example:

> And he said, O my God, I am ashamed and blush to lift up my face to thee, my God: for our iniquities are increased over our head, and our trespass is grown up unto the heavens. (Ezra 9: 6)

In the following excerpt from Shakespeare's *Richard III* (Act I, Scene II) Lady Anne addresses Gloucester, who has murdered her father and her husband, and demands that he blushes for his actions. The blood in the blusher's face is linked with the references to spilt blood and she claims that the presence of the murderer causes the corpse to bleed again.

> If thou delight to view thy heinous deeds,
> Behold this pattern of thy butcheries.
> O, gentlemen, see, see! Dead Harry's wounds
> Open their congeal'd mouths and bleed afresh.
> Blush, blush, thou lump of foul deformity,
> For 'tis thy presence that exhales this blood
> From cold and empty veins where no blood dwells;

Anthropological research provides evidence of the association of the blush with shame in cultures remote from our own. Strathern (1977) analyses a public performance of a song by women in Papua New Guinea during a dance ceremony celebrating the hoped-for arrival of money for the community. The ceremony was important and poor performance would reflect badly on the members of the group and lead to loss of standing in the eyes of other groups. The song includes the line 'there is shame on our skins', and Strathern considers why shame should be on the skin. He suggests (ibid., p. 101):

> The women who sang the song were exposed to the collective scrutiny of groups in the surrounding community. The skin, their outer self, is the immediate point of contact with the physical world outside them and can also conveniently symbolise the point of contact between them and social forces that surround them.

Interviews established that shame on the skin is experienced when people are the object of others' attention, when they are found out or exposed. Examples included saying something in public that is wrong while other people are listening and are aware that it is wrong, or being seen defecating or urinating when it is believed that no one is around. In English there are many expressions describing emotion that refer to the skin: those who are over-sensitive or insufficiently sensitive to the opinion of others are either thin-skinned or thick-skinned; matters get under our skin or are superficial and only skin deep.

Yet despite such examples, there is no conviction among psychologists that people blush with shame, and the predominant view has been that it is an expression of embarrassment. For example, Buss (1980, p. 148) was explicit that shame does not involve blushing, and argued that if ashamed people did so it must be because they were experiencing shame and embarrassment simultaneously. However, given the enormity of Gloucester's crimes it is improbable that Lady Anne believes that he ought to be embarrassed about his deeds, and she is surely calling upon him to feel shame or guilt. Embarrassment seems too slight an emotion for the circumstances.

Why should shame be neglected as a cause of the blush? H. B. Lewis (1971) and Scheff and Retzinger (2001) would interpret this neglect as evidence of the invisibility of shame in contemporary Western society. They argue that because of its aversiveness and intensity shame is rarely acknowledged at the individual or societal level even though it exerts a powerful influence at both levels. An alternative, though not unrelated explanation, is that contemporary social science attaches greater significance to embarrassment than to shame. This reflects the influence of Goffman, who concentrated on the uncertain encounters between people that characterise societies where distinctions of class and status are not clearly drawn. This emphasis may reflect and contribute to the invisibility of shame. The relation between embarrassment and shame is considered below. First, this chapter considers some theories of shame and their treatment of the blush.

Theories of shame

When I embarked on a survey of psychological theories of blushing I imagined that a likely place to find a detailed account would be Sylvan Tomkins' theory of the affects. This seemed a good starting point for several reasons. First, Tomkins devoted his academic career to producing a comprehensive theory of affect that encompasses the whole range of emotions. Second, he wrote extensively on shame affect, and shame and embarrassment are given considerable attention in his theory. Third, the face and facial expression are fundamental to Tomkins's account. According to his theory, the affects are primarily facial responses and only secondarily visceral responses, and awareness of emotion is based on awareness of facial responses; hence we might expect the theory to pay particular attention to the blush. Moreover, although the face is involved in all affects, it is particularly salient in shame. He wrote (Tomkins, 1963, p. 136):

> The experiential salience of the face in shame is a partial answer to the question why shame is so central a human motive insomuch as the salience of the face involves the salience of the self and exaggerated self-consciousness.

Tomkins regards shame as an auxiliary affect, auxiliary because he does not class it as one of a small number of primary affects; it is, he argues, produced by the sudden and incomplete reduction of either of two primary affects, interest or joy. For example, a young child who experiences pleasure in playing with his or her genitals is shamed by the sudden and unexpected reprimand by the parent. A child who eagerly expects to welcome a parent after a period of separation is suddenly confronted by a stranger and becomes overcome with shyness.

Shame is displayed by lowering of the head, averting the eyes and blushing. Despite the important part that the face plays in his theory Tomkins has surprisingly little to say about the blush and he shares with other theorists uncertainty about its role. He defined it as a 'response auxiliary to the shame complex' since it increases the visibility of the face whereas the 'shame response proper' reduces facial communication (ibid., pp. 120–1). Unfortunately, Tomkins is not explicit about the grounds for concluding that the blush is not an integral part of the proper response, particularly as he makes the point elsewhere that while the shame response serves to bring facial communication to a halt, this interruption itself is communicated by the response: 'one has communicated one's shame and both the face and the self unwittingly become more visible, to the self and others' (ibid., p. 136). This effect is augmented when the blush accompanies gaze aversion, with the face turned away and the head lowered. Indeed, the blush can increase shame because it is so visible and communicates to others that the person is ashamed. Tomkins notes its 'self-defeating' nature, that is, the person draws attention to his shame at the very moment when he seeks to hide from others, and the awareness that others know his shame is itself cause for further shame. Tomkins suggested that the blush might be a reaction to heightened self-consciousness rather than part of an innately patterned response. He argues that the reason why self-consciousness and shame are so closely connected is that the shame response draws attention to the face. 'It is not possible to be ashamed or humiliated ... without self-consciousness. The self is completely salient in the face that blushes or hangs down' (ibid., p. 135).

Although the theory does not lend itself readily to predictions (as opposed to post hoc interpretation) it claims that blushing is more likely when levels of interest and enjoyment are high but something 'shaming' happens to interrupt positive affect. However, this proposition has not attracted empirical attention. Despite the central role that the face plays in the theory, the blush is seldom addressed.

Tomkins distinguishes between affect and emotional experience and argues that shame, shyness, embarrassment, guilt and humiliation are identical at the level of affect even though they are experienced differently. They share a common response pattern involving blushing and lowered eyes and head. Thus the question whether the blush is an expression of shame or embarrassment is not an issue since these are identical at the level of affect. The circumstances in which the reaction is evoked and the intensity of the reaction will produce different experiences and will be labelled in different ways.

The master emotion

Shame, like embarrassment, is often discussed in terms of its role in the social regulation of conduct as well as in terms of individual experience. Indeed, it has been characterised as *the* social emotion or 'master emotion' (Scheff and Retzinger, 2001) because of its profound social significance. From the perspective of evolutionary psychology, the human is inherently a social species, evolved to live in organised groups. Belonging to the group is adaptive in the sense of increasing reproductive success whereas social exclusion is maladaptive and makes it less likely that excluded individuals will survive and pass on their genes. From this perspective shame is a reaction to the threat of banishment by the social group. Gilbert (2002) interprets it as a reaction to the threat of social rejection or devaluation because the individual's action has diminished his or her attractiveness to the group: attractiveness is a key element in securing access to essential resources. Members of groups have appraisal systems that enable them to be alert to threats of attack, exclusion, rejection and loss of status, and have developed competencies for selecting appropriate responses. Shame has evolved as a mechanism for detecting threat and responding to it with suitable defensive behaviours, including escape, hiding and making submissive gestures.

It is widely accepted in developmental psychology that the establishment of bonds with the mother figure is crucial for the infant's healthy development. The quality of the early attachment relationship exerts an influence on social relationships and adjustment throughout life through 'mental models' or expectancies that the individual develops and which shape his or her interactions with others. Shame is experienced when bonds are threatened because the ashamed person has transgressed in some way. Significant others can use shame as a means of socialisation, to ensure that the individual conforms to social norms and values. Shame is an intense emotion because of its crucial role in the maintenance of bonds in social life. Its intensity is evident in the language associated with shame: degradation, disgrace, dishonour, humiliation and ignominy. Shame originates in the infant and young child's helplessness and dependence on the adult and the threat to his or her survival that would ensue from the adult's rejection.

As individuals mature and become active participants in society shame comes to play a key role in the regulation of conduct: its control ranges from the mundane – our fear of what others will think of us guides our choice of what to say, do or wear on social occasions – to the profound, where someone is prepared to give up his or her life rather than endure public shame or humiliation. Shame can be a short-lived experience that has benefits for the ashamed person: it alerts him or her to the threat to the bond and motivates actions to repair the damage. Instances of transient embarrassment take this form. However, shame can be enduring and can exert a powerful influence on the individual's sense of self and his or her well-being. This dimension of shame has been explored by H. B. Lewis (1971). She argued that it is not necessary for the individual to be conscious of shame for its effect to be exerted. In post-Freudian psychology it is accepted that early traumatic events and reactions to them can have long-term effects, although for a short-term emotion to have an enduring effect requires that it is internalised and maintained in some way, for example by means of the formation of 'mental models', 'scripts', or what Lewis terms 'feeling traps', where the individual feels ashamed of his or her shame.

Lewis (1971) investigated shame by means of systematic content analysis of patients' talk during therapy sessions. She coded transcripts of their talk for the presence of keywords that are indicators of shame, for example phrases that refer to deficiencies of the self and criticism or ridicule by others. These indicators were found to be extremely common in these transcripts and were much more frequent than indicators of fear and guilt. However, explicit mention of shame or its synonyms was rarely present, even when the context referred to situations where the individual was criticised or made to look foolish by others. Shame was unacknowledged by both patient and therapist.

Lewis distinguishes two kinds of shame. The first is overt, undifferentiated shame, awareness of a painful emotional experience that is evident in physical symptoms such as blushing and sweating, but one that is not identified as shame. Instead, the patient might attribute the emotional disturbance to someone else's behaviour or to the difficulties inherent in a situation. For example, she might attribute blushing to her skin complexion or to a medical condition rather than perceive it as a manifestation of shame. In the second kind, which Lewis calls unacknowledged or bypassed shame, the person has the negative thoughts characteristic of shame but does not experience the intense emotion, only a 'peripheral, non-specific disturbance in awareness' that might be felt as a 'wince', 'bolt' or 'jolt' (Lewis, 1971, p. 197). The emotional state is not overt but is inferred by the researcher or therapist. For example, a patient might appear indifferent and this lack of emotion can be interpreted as her attempt to ward off feelings of shame and prevent others from discovering the shameful fact about her. The denial of shame contrasts with the ready use of embarrassment to label everyday experiences. The tendency to associate the blush with embarrassment rather than shame might reflect the inaccessibility of shame rather than the frequency with which blushing accompanies it.

Distinguishing embarrassment and shame

There have been several attempts to distinguish shame and embarrassment. Suggestions are that shame is the more 'serious' emotion, involving major transgressions and a deficiency of the self whereas embarrassment involves minor flaws and errors, a deficiency of the socially presented self. Shame belongs to the moral sphere and embarrassment to the realm of social standards, manners and etiquette. Shame involves a serious moral transgression whereas embarrassment is a matter of a breach of convention. Shame involves a negative evaluation of the 'core' self whereas embarrassment involves evaluation of more transient, less central aspects. The experience is more intense in shame because it involves the whole self. It is described as an extremely unpleasant experience, one that is painful, a torment or a sickness; the ashamed person feels ridiculous and small. Izard (1977, p. 391) wrote of the phenomenology of shame: 'the self is seen as small, helpless, frozen, emotionally hurt. The self is seen as foolish, inept, out-of-place'. Yet, this description of shame can also describe the phenomenology of embarrassment and shyness, and it is not obvious that these necessarily differ in terms of how small or helpless the individual feels. Moreover, embarrassment can be an intense experience and its anticipation can, for example, prevent someone from seeking medical advice even though he or she is extremely anxious about a possible illness and is aware that the longer the consultation is postponed the more serious the condition may become.

Miller and Tangney (1994) adopted an empirical approach to the distinction, asking people to sort a set of cards, each carrying a description of an emotional experience, into either a Shame pile or an Embarrassment pile. Cards most frequently assigned to the shame pile referred to feeling a bad person, where the feeling was caused by a deep-seated flaw: 'I felt that other people were disgusted with me'. In contrast, embarrassment cards referred to a temporary error, an accident and 'other people laughing at me'.

Some writers have suggested that the emotions may be distinguished on the basis of the presence of an audience and perhaps its composition. Does an audience have to be present, or can shame and embarrassment be experienced while we are alone, imagining or remembering the reaction of the other? Sabini and Silver (1997) propose that an audience is required for embarrassment, but not for shame. Tangney *et al.* (1996a) reported that recollections of episodes of shame were significantly more likely than episodes of embarrassment to refer to occasions when the individual was alone; also, shame was more likely than embarrassment to be experienced in the presence of those who were close rather than acquaintances or strangers. Conversely, embarrassment elicited higher ratings on a scale that assessed the extent to which participants felt that others were looking. Nevertheless, it does seem that we can be embarrassed when we are alone, for example, while recalling an event, perhaps realising for the first time its embarrassing nature:

> I was with a colleague and I read out and mocked a point that a student had made in an essay. Afterwards I discovered that the student had been quoting my colleague and I felt really embarrassed.

Yet the embarrassment resulted from thinking what the colleague must have thought at the time even though he did not say anything. The embarrassed person sees himself through the eyes of the other even though the other is not present. The journalist Lezard[1] describes his reaction to hearing his name mentioned on the radio: 'for some reason made me blush extravagantly and go all hot and cold'. Again, I suspect that the audience is salient and he imagines other people hearing about him.

Other attempts to distinguish shame and embarrassment have focused on physiological reactions and bodily changes. The blush has also been argued to distinguish them, but here there is considerable disagreement over whether it occurs in both embarrassment and shame (Keltner and Harker, 1998) or only in embarrassment (Edelmann, 1987; Miller, 1996). Shame involves a distinctive display involving slumped posture, head and eyes lowered, the corners of the mouth turned down and the lower lip tucked between the teeth. Embarrassment involves smiling and attempts at smile control, gaze aversion and nervous touching of the face. It was noted in Chapter 6 that smiling and smile control are sufficiently common in embarrassment to comprise part of its prototypical display. Feeling foolish commonly accompanies embarrassment, whereas shame is accompanied by feelings of inadequacy, regret and distress. In Miller and Tangney's study, the cards most frequently assigned to embarrassment referred to humour, jokes, smiling and laughter. Shame cards referred to not smiling, to the incident not being an accident, and to feeling a bad person and angry with self.

Research has related differences between shame and embarrassment to physiological measures. Shame and social-evaluative threats are associated with elevated levels of cortisol (Dickerson and Kemeny, 2004). In a study of four-year-old children, Lewis and Ramsay (2002) identified a correlation between increases in salivary cortisol levels and shame and evaluative embarrassment following failure at a task. However there was no change in cortisol level after success. In episodes intended to induce exposure embarrassment (children were conspicuous or complimented or they looked at their reflection in a mirror) there was a slight and non-significant association between *reduced* cortisol levels and embarrassment. The difference in pattern between evaluation and exposure forms of embarrassment seems clear. However, the numbers of children who displayed shame were small (eight out of 60 participants) and only a minority of children (15) showed embarrassment after success or failure at the task, and this may well have influenced the results.

In summary, there are measurable physiological changes and observable patterns of gestures and postures that can be identified when participants in studies undertake tasks that have implications for self-evaluation. In Lewis and Ramsay's study, different psychophysiological patterns of reactions accompany emotional experiences that ensue from success and failure outcomes. Nevertheless, it can be difficult to map the ordinary English language terms shame and embarrassment onto these patterns, and it seems likely that different languages and dialects will have different mappings and will associate success and failure outcomes with emotional reactions in distinctive ways.

Sabini and Silver (1997) propose that shame and embarrassment (and, as we see in Chapter 8, guilt) should be distinguished not in terms of differences in the experience of emotion but in terms of alternative descriptions of the experience. They suggest that these share a common hypothetical state x (little x), which they define (ibid., p. 3) as:

> the state of believing that one's self has been exposed, and that the self is (in mild cases of x) unappealing, flawed, scarred, in extreme cases the self is seen as vile, revolting, disgusting. Along with these beliefs in state x is a desire in mild cases to leave, to disappear, to hide, to retreat from the world, in extreme cases to cease to be. At the same time in state x one feels frozen, unable to get away.

State x resembles Tomkins' shame affect and can be labelled either embarrassment or shame. It is called shame if a flaw that has been revealed and which has brought about state x is a flaw in character whereas calling it embarrassment refers to an apparent rather than an actual flaw. The evidence may suggest to onlookers that an action has revealed a flaw – and this judgment may be a reasonable one on their part – but the person who is embarrassed does not believe that the action reveals a flaw. Sabini *et al.* (2001) explored some implications of this analysis by asking participants to conjecture which of a set of six emotions they would experience in a range of scenarios and to rate the intensity of the emotion. The scenarios were designed to reveal either a real flaw or a failing that was not a real flaw. For example, the protagonist was caught leaving a shop taking a CD that had not been paid for, and this action was described as either intentional (and predicted to be seen as cause for shame) or accidental (predicted to be seen as embarrassment). In another example, 'Alice' and 'Bill' (the boyfriend of Alice's friend 'Carol') kiss and decide to keep it a secret; Carol finds out what has happened and accuses Alice of betraying her. In the alternative (embarrassing) version Carol arrives just as Alice is unexpectedly kissed by Bill and accuses Alice of betraying her.

The findings lend support to Sabini and Silver's account. When the scenario could be interpreted in terms of a flaw in the protagonist's character – stealing, or betraying a friend – ratings of shame and embarrassment were similar, but when it implied an apparent flaw it was more likely to be described as embarrassment. In addition, ratings of intensity of embarrassment correlated substantially with ratings of the intensity of shame, casting doubt on the thesis that the two emotional reactions can be distinguished on the basis of intensity of reaction.

The self in shame

Shame involves a negative evaluation of the self (or the prospect of such evaluation) by other people, and it serves as a deterrent or negative reinforcer: there is a strong motive to avoid shame. There is a dual role for the self, in that it is both the subject and object of shame. Tangney *et al.* (1996a, p. 1257) wrote: 'In shame, the self is both agent and object of observation and disapproval, as shortcomings of the defective self are exposed before an internalized observing "other" '.

One way of comparing alternative theoretical approaches to shame is to consider the emphasis they place upon self-evaluation relative to the individual's mental representation of others' evaluations. Some accounts focus on the individual's own evaluation of her behaviour and her judgment that it has fallen short of standards. For example, Scherer (1993) constructed a system for distinguishing among the fundamental emotions in terms of a series of 'stimulus evaluation checks'. Whether the self is judged to be the cause of a particular action and whether that action is compatible with the self-image are identified as two of the principal evaluation checks for shame. Gilbert (2002) distinguishes between external and internal shame: the 'self as seen and judged by others' versus 'self as judged by self'. External shame is associated with fear of exposure that will result in disapproval or rejection by others. Internal shame refers to negative self-evaluation. A problem with this approach is that it is difficult to distinguish between internal shame and depression or any kind of negative self-evaluation. An adverse self-evaluation gives rise to negative feelings, like regret, disappointment and depression. Furthermore, the account has difficulty in explaining cases of shame where there is no self-attribution of wrongdoing.

Accounts in terms of self-evaluation imply a unity of perspective that is disputed by those who argue the importance of the spectator-judge, whether this is Smith's 'impartial spectator' or Taylor's 'possible detached observer-description'. This assigns greater prominence to the person's evaluation of his or her behaviour as if seen through the eyes of another. Writers who adopt this position emphasise that the emotion arises because of a difference between the judgments made by the self and the other, for example Semin and Manstead (1981) write of a discrepancy between the self-image and the subjective public image.

Chapter 6 summarised evidence for two forms of embarrassment, and there have been claims in addition to that made by Gilbert that there is more than one form of shame. Castelfranchi and Poggi (1990) distinguish between shame before the self and shame before the other (Table 7.1 depicts the principal constructs of facts and values and their relations to the forms of shame). Their thesis shares features with Sabini and Silver's distinction between real and apparent flaws and Semin and Manstead's distinction between self-image and subjective public image. Each account assigns important roles to shared values and the information available to the ashamed person and observers of his or her behaviour. Alice knows that it is wrong to kiss Bill (the shared value) and appreciates what it must look like to Carol; she also knows, as Carol does not, that she has not done what she appears to have done. All the scenarios in Sabini *et al.*'s study involve situations where other people witness the apparent flaw – they are either present at the time or the behaviour becomes known later – and this creates a social predicament for the protagonist. Shame before the self is experienced when the

Table 7.1 Model of shame before the self and others (Castelfranchi and Poggi, 1990)

	Shame before others	Shame before both self and others	Shame before only the self
Values	Shared	Not shared	Not shared
Assumptions about facts and evaluation	Not shared	Shared	Not shared

individual is made aware of a flaw in his or her character, even if this is not known to anyone else.

Castelfranchi and Poggi give the example of a doctor who is asked by his patient about a new medicine and he does not know of it. If the patient is aware of the doctor's ignorance the doctor will feel shame before self and patient. If the doctor does know of it, but it has temporarily slipped his mind, he will feel shame before the other – the patient can reasonably assume that the doctor does not know and thus falls short as a doctor – but not before the self. However, if the patient is unaware of the doctor's ignorance, the doctor may still experience shame, before himself. Both doctor and patient share the value that the doctor ought to know about the medicine, but in this case the fact that the doctor does not know is not shared. Castelfranchi and Poggi label all these experiences forms of shame. Could they be described as embarrassment? If, as Sabini and Silver argue, the difference is a matter of the reality of the flaw then only instances where there is shame before the other without shame before the self could be embarrassment, since all cases of shame before the self and all those of shame before the other that also involve shame before the self entail acknowledgement of a real flaw. Castelfranchi and Poggi (ibid., p. 238) argue that a blush occurs only when shame before the other is felt, whether or not there is shame before the self, and it does not occur when only shame before the self is felt. The reality of the flaw is not the issue, but whether it might be visible.

Blushing, self-consciousness and shame

The conceptualisation of self as seen through the eyes of other suggests how someone might blush with shame. The blush might accompany the self-consciousness of shame before the other; alternatively, the circumstances that elicit the blush might be shaming in themselves. There is little evidence pertinent to either of these explanations. I explore the first explanation by means of examination of the link between shame and self-consciousness in a work of fiction before considering whether data on the circumstances that elicit a blush lend support to the second explanation.

Two fictional episodes

Elizabeth Gaskell's novel, *North and South* (1994) includes vivid descriptions of two episodes that cause her principal character Margaret Hale to experience intense shame. O'Farrell (1997) devotes a chapter to this novel in her book on the blush in nineteenth-century fiction, but she concentrates her attention on one of the other characters, Fanny Thornton. The analysis presented here differs from that applied to fiction in Chapter 5; the analysis there begins with the identification of passages that refer to blushing, whereas this analysis starts by identifying passages containing explicit mentions of shame and looks for references to the blush in these passages.

In the first incident Margaret Hale is recovering from an injury she sustained when she had come to the aid of the mill-owner Thornton during a strike at his factory when she overhears a servant talking to Fanny (Thornton's sister) about her action and realises that it is construed by Fanny, Thornton's mother and servants as her having made advances to Thornton. This forwardness is unbecoming to a woman of her social class, the more so as she is a clergyman's daughter. In the second incident, Thornton observes Margaret embracing a man (unknown to Thornton, the man is Margaret's brother, who is being sought by the police). She denies her presence there in a subsequent interview with the police, the lie is to protect her brother, but her falsehood is revealed to Thornton (in his position as a magistrate). She knows that Thornton knows she was there, despite her denial, but the circumstances prevent her from admitting the truth to him. Gaskell makes several explicit references to Margaret's experience of shame, associating it with her concern with what others will think, for example:

> a deep sense of shame that she could thus be the object of universal regard – a sense of shame so acute that it seemed as if she would fain have burrowed into the earth to hide herself, and yet she could not escape out of that unwinking glare of many eyes.

The second episode refers to shame in two senses. One is the emotion that Margaret experiences while the second is the shame of her position if her lie were publicly exposed in court. This would bring shame to Margaret and her family without Margaret necessarily feeling shame. The analysis here concentrates on the experience rather than on the position. It is noteworthy that Margaret is described as feeling shame not only at the time but on several occasions over a lengthy period whenever either incident is referred to, however obliquely. Indeed, the most intense shame is experienced as she recalls a past meeting with Thornton when, during an argument about honesty and deceit in business transactions, she had claimed the moral high ground. She compares her attitude on that occasion with her realisation that he now knows she has deceived the police for what must seem to him to be selfish reasons.

There are several references in the text to Margaret's shame in the eyes of other people. In the first episode, references to shame are invariably accompanied by reference to what other people thought – the servants and the Thornton family, in particular, but also 'other people' more generally and 'universal regard'. There are references to being talked about by others, to exposing herself to their comments. In the second episode, the focus of her shame is her standing in the eyes of Thornton. References to feeling shame are accompanied by references to being degraded, abased, disgraced and humiliated 'in his eyes' (five mentions), to his opinion (three mentions) and to being at his feet (one mention).

There are 12 references to colouring in passages relating to the first incident and eight in text relating to the second. The various colour terms seem to be used interchangeably. With regard to the first incident Margaret blushes when the topic of conversation reminds her of the incident, for example, when someone mentions the strike or people being present at the strike or, indirectly, when a friend asks if the strike had prevented her from keeping an appointment. She blushes when anyone draws attention to her injury. On two occasions she blushes when alone. On one of these she tries not to think of the Thornton family, but the effort to do so brings them to her mind's eye and she flushes. On the other she recalls her conduct and imagines how it looked to other people.

When Margaret meets Thornton for the first time after the incident that has caused her shame, she experiences indignation and shame in close proximity. First, she is angry at his expression of gratitude but blushes when this reminds her of the incident. On the second occasion, a few minutes later, she is offended by his declaration of love since she imagines that it has been triggered by her behaviour the previous day, but she blushes again when referring to the incident.

> In spite of herself – in defiance of her anger – the thick blushes came all over her face, and burnt into her very eyes.
> 'Yes!' said she, with revering dignity. 'I do feel offended; and, I think, justly. You seem to fancy that my conduct of yesterday' – again the deep carnation blush, but this time with eyes kindling with indignation rather than shame.

In the second episode, Margaret blushes when there is a reference to telling a lie, when she believes that Mrs Thornton is about to refer to the lie, and when she apologises to Mrs Thornton for not being in a position to justify her behaviour. She does so when there is a reference to Frederick as her lover ('she blushed as the word passed through her mind') and when discussing Thornton's inability to know that Frederick was not her young man. On one occasion she blushes when her father mentions the pleasure of Frederick's visit; she thinks that she has spoilt the visit by her behaviour and this reminds her of her lie.

The theme presented in Chapter 4, that a blush accompanies exposure or its threat, characterises the episodes in the novel. A blush is not restricted to the precipitating occasion but can arise when the character recalls the event, something reminds her of it or when she hears even an oblique reference to it. When other characters are described as blushing, the occasions are also consistent with the theme of exposure. Thornton reddens when his mother alludes to Margaret's feelings for him; Margaret's father 'almost blushed' when he asked Margaret if she was aware of Thornton having feelings for her.

What is the role of responsibility in Margaret's shame? Castelfranchi and Poggi's distinction between shame before the self and shame before the other implies that shame can arise from experiences that are connected with the self but for which the ashamed person's responsibility is slight. Shame can be experienced when there is no self-attribution of failure but there is acknowledgement that one's behaviour can be seen in a bad light. What is crucial is not one's personal responsibility for a breach or fault but the extent to which one concurs with the judgment that is made of it.

In neither episode is Margaret's shame contingent on a belief that she has behaved badly and she accepts responsibility for her actions. In the first episode she acted of her own volition and states that she would do the same again in similar circumstances; she is not responsible for the interpretation that has been placed upon it. She acknowledges the plausibility of this interpretation but regards it as unfair and thus can be said to experience shame before the other but not before the self. In the second episode Margaret has told a lie to protect someone, she acknowledges that her action was blameworthy and that she deserves to be condemned for it. Nevertheless, she is convinced of the integrity of her motive and she believes that her action was successful in enabling her brother to escape. While the blameworthiness of her action is cause for shame it is not in itself the cause of the shame that she experiences subsequent to this event; it is clear from the text that this is produced by her understanding of Thornton's perception of her actions. She accepts Thornton's right to judge her as she believes he does.

In each episode she is judged by others to have fallen short of standards and, although she believes in her own mind that her motives were not cause for shame, it is the perception of the others' interpretations and her recognition of the legitimacy of these interpretations that gives rise to the emotional state.

Shame and the blush

Are the circumstances that elicit a blush cause for shame? H. B. Lewis (1971) has argued that shame is an unacknowledged emotion that has to be sought in careful analysis of verbal and non-verbal behaviours. In *North and South* (Gaskell, 1994) the authorial voice is explicit that Margaret feels shame, yet shame was never mentioned in responses to descriptions of the two episodes made by participants in the study I now summarise. A sample of university students read paraphrased versions of the two incidents: 31 students read about the first incident, and 38 read about the second. These versions related the circumstances but omitted any reference to Margaret's reactions. Participants rated on a series of seven-point scales how likely they thought it would be that Margaret would experience each of a set of emotions: anger, anxiety, disgust, embarrassment, fear, grief, guilt, sadness and shame. Mean ratings of shame were close to the neutral point of the scale representing a judgment that it was neither likely nor unlikely. The students saw little reason for shame in either episode.

This does not reflect any insensitivity to the content as participants adjusted their ratings in the light of differences in content. For example they rated each episode for self-consciousness on Margaret's part: 'How conscious was she of how other people would think of her?', 'To what extent does she look at herself through the eyes of particular other people?' The second episode, where Thornton is aware of her lie, attracted significantly higher ratings than the first episode. The participants did not have access to the original text's repeated references to Thornton's eyes; nevertheless their higher ratings for this episode are consistent with his salient role as the one person who knows that Margaret has lied to the police.

Both incidents were rated as causing embarrassment, although this word is never mentioned in the text. Perhaps young people today see the episodes as occasioning embarrassment rather than shame because there have been marked changes since Gaskell's time in norms of propriety and physical contact between the sexes and a woman's role in initiating contact. It may also be the case that there has been a change in language and what used to be described as shame has come to be described as embarrassment. Finally, it is consistent with Lewis's argument that shame is a hidden, unacknowledged emotion that would not be spontaneously mentioned.

Lewis (1971) investigated shame by means of systematic content analysis of transcripts of patients' talk. She coded these for the presence of key words and phrases considered to be indicators of shame, drawing upon the Gottschalk–Gleser shame-anxiety content analysis scheme (Gottschalk and Gleser, 1969). This analyses the form and content of speech as a means of identifying emotional states. It provides an objective scale for assigning clauses in speech samples to thematic categories. Shame is indexed by phrases that refer to deficiencies of the self, to feeling inadequate, embarrassed, humiliated and exposed, and to being criticised or ridiculed by others. It is associated with hostility directed inwards, which is represented by thematic categories including self-blame, considering the self to be worthless, feeling depressed, self-critical, regretting, being sorry or ashamed for what one says or does, disappointment in oneself and unable to meet the expectations of self and others.

Descriptions of blushing episodes are replete with references to being exposed, embarrassed, ridiculed and criticised, particularly if mention of an audience and being looked at are coded as instances of exposure, on the grounds that the participant has specifically mentioned them in the brief description of the episode. This suggests that blushing may be elicited when the individual feels shame, even though this label is not one that the blusher attaches to the experience. As we have seen, blushers are likely to mention embarrassment or shyness while being looked at and feeling self-conscious.

The questionnaire responses analysed in Chapter 5 are much briefer and less detailed than the transcripts typically subjected to the Gottschalk–Gleser scheme. Nevertheless, it is of interest to apply it to these responses, albeit in a preliminary fashion. Four categories based on the scheme and Scheff and Retzinger's application of it to text analysis were drawn up and applied to the questionnaire responses. The categories, together with the percentages of responses assigned to each, are presented in Table 7.2. The procedure yielded 176 coded units – responses could be assigned to more than one category. The most common categories were *Exposure* and *Feelings of Inadequacy*. There were 89 instances where responses could be assigned to two codes, and the most common combinations were *Exposure and Feelings of Inadequacy* (27%) and *Praise and Feelings of Inadequacy*, each representing 27 per cent of the combinations. There were nine instances of a triple combination, the

Table 7.2 Blushing occasions categorised as shame episodes

Category	Indicators	Coded units (%)
Exposure	out of place; conspicuous; looked at; presence of audience	29
Criticism	accused, commented on; challenged; ridiculed; laughed at	22
Praised	complimented, praised	15
Feelings of Inadequacy	embarrassed; feel stupid; self-conscious; tongue-tied; uncomfortable; unsure how to respond	34

most common being *Exposure, Criticism and Feelings of Inadequacy* (six instances). An illustration of a triple coding is:

> Someone, my superior in work said something critical of me [why blush?] Because people were watching me and I felt embarrassed that I might not have done my job properly.

Perhaps the most significant finding is that all the participants' responses except for four could be readily assigned to these categories; the four exceptions are presented below. The first two are instances of the blushers' self-consciousness when the encounter makes them conscious of their feelings for the other person, although this is not self-consciousness in the sense of being aware of a personal deficiency. The second two are instances of the mention of a topic that is a 'secret' of the blusher. In neither case does it seem that the people making the remark are aware of the import of the remark for the blusher; if they were, this would have been coded as an instance of a comment addressed to the person.

> Said hello to next door neighbour [why blush?] Because of personal feelings toward him.
> Speaking to a boy I fancied [why blush?] Because I liked him.
> Friends talking in the pub about having sex in the open [why blush?] I did it once.
> When someone said the name of a bloke that I fancied [why blush?] Because I liked him.

Conceiving of the blushing as an instance of shame provides a parsimonious account of this set of episodes if we are prepared to define shame in the broader terms of H. B. Lewis to include feelings of embarrassment, being exposed to the comments of others and being aware of an audience for one's behaviour. Being the recipient of praise may be shaming because it creates awareness of a discrepancy between what is being publicly attributed to us and our private view of ourselves. As Poulson (2000, p. 14) wrote, 'even a "positive" global evaluation can be a trigger to a shame episode if the evaluation is incongruent with the individual's sense of self'. Perhaps, too, there is something inherently shaming about being self-consciously conspicuous, as in the example provided in Chapter 6 of the stagehand who is moving props on stage and blushes when he becomes conscious of the audience's attention.

This returns to the question whether shame and embarrassment should be considered distinct emotions. The conception of embarrassment as shame has a strong implication of self-deficiency as opposed to the notion of fluster that is emphasised in many accounts of embarrassment. As Sabini and Silver (1997) propose, the question might be better framed in terms of alternative descriptions of a common state, where the sense of an exposed and, in one way or another, deficient self is salient.

8
Shame, Guilt and Anger

Up to that moment he had only partly believed in her guilt, but he no longer had any doubt when he saw how she changed colour. It was partly anger, partly shame.

(O'Connor, 1973, p. 49)

The blush and the angry flush

Shame and anger

Redness of the face is characteristic of anger as well as of embarrassment although it is labelled a flush rather than a blush. Casimir and Schnegg (2002) found that the colour red was associated with shame in 78 of the 98 languages they surveyed; of the 78, 51 also associated red with anger and 48 associated it with rage. Correspondence analysis showed that shame, anger and rage clustered along with the colour red at one pole of a dimension, and at the other pole the colour white formed a cluster with shock, pain and fear. Of course, in English we do talk of blushing with shame, flushing with anger, and going pale or white with fright and shock ('his face was ashen'; 'she turned white as a ghost').

The relations among shame, guilt and anger have been analysed by H. B. Lewis (1971). Shame is frequently accompanied by anger as retaliatory rage is directed against the judging 'other'. However, the relation between the states is complex, because of the self's ambivalence towards the 'other' in shame, the ashamed person's sense of personal deficiency and his or her guilt at expressing anger. Lewis (1971, p. 87) analyses this relation as follows:

When humiliated fury is evoked, the self becomes the target of hostility since its deficiencies are the source of hostility. Expressing humiliated fury toward the apparent source of the humiliation is blocked by guilt for unjust anger; it is also blocked by positive feelings for the source of the humiliation, which co-exists along with the hostility. Humiliated fury or rage is thus likely to be diffuse and non-specific, except that it is evoked by indications that the 'other' does not value the self.

The angry reaction to the criticising 'other' is illustrated in *North and South*. When Mrs Thornton begins to comment on Margaret's indiscretion in being seen in public with a young man. Margaret initially blushes as she believes that the topic of her falsehood is about to be raised, but she becomes angry when Mrs Thornton begins to talk of Margaret's indiscretion: 'Margaret's eyes flashed fire. This was a new idea – this was too insulting' (ibid., p. 375). In the other episode Margaret considers the remarks she has overheard to be ' insolent words spoken about herself', but subsequently the sense of shame overwhelms the anger she feels. When she meets Thornton later, she is offended by his interpretation of her action; she feels indignation and is described as blushing. The participants who rated the likelihood of various emotions assigned high ratings of anger to this episode.

Although the interview schedule did not refer to anger several respondents mentioned it spontaneously. The most common response was that Margaret would be angry because she was the victim of injustice: she had acted for honourable reasons but her action had been seen in the worst light and her motives had been impugned. Some participants thought the anger would be directed at individuals, in particular the servants for making hasty assumptions, for not giving her an opportunity to tell her side of the story.

> She'd be angry because her actions were totally misunderstood.
> She's intervened and was trying to stop injustice.
> I'd be outraged that someone would think I had behaved in this way, go after a man and not be my own person. I'd be angry.
> She'd be angry at the woman – she should have her facts right. She was protecting him, not just throwing her arms around him.

Lewis found that indicators of anger were common in patients' transcripts, were frequently linked with shame indicators and were usually preceded by them. The combination of shame and anger provides an example of what Lewis calls a feeling trap, where the emotional states are prolonged because shame gives rise to anger which gives rise to shame and so on. Similarly, Scheff and Retzinger (2001) describe a shame-anger spiral, which leads to increasingly intense humiliated fury: quite trivial disagreements can escalate to end up as angry exchanges, fuelled by shame. Scheff and Retzinger applied the Gottschalk–Gleser shame content analysis scheme to episodes of conflict within marital relationships. They identified a shame-anger escalation. First, something that is said or implied poses a threat to the bond between partners and gives rise to unacknowledged shame. The perceived attack provokes anger as a defence. In response to the shaming entailed in this attack the partner feels shame and reacts with retaliatory anger, thus generating an escalating cycle of shame and anger. Scheff and Retzinger's content analysis showed that shame preceded every instance of shame-anger escalation.

Anger can lead to feelings of shame, guilt and remorse. Averill (1982) asked a sample of 160 respondents to report on a recent experience of anger, including its consequences, and found that there were frequent accounts of anger resulting in feelings of shame, embarrassment and guilt. Thus shame can lead to anger; anger can lead to shame. Tangney (2003) reviews several studies of the relation between anger and shame, both transient feelings of shame and inter-individual variation in pre-disposition to experiencing shame. She too found that someone who had been shamed by his or her partner in a romantic relationship was likely to become angry and to retaliate aggressively. She reports correlations between shame-related personality characteristics and feelings of anger and hostility. For example, a measure of proneness to shame was correlated with increased propensity to anger and aggression as assessed by a self-report questionnaire assessing anger arousal, anger intentions, responses to anger and judgment of the long-term consequences of anger (Tangney *et al.*, 1996b). The shame measure correlated significantly with all of these scales. Shame scores were associated with how angry participants imagined they would be in hypothetical situations described to them; they were associated with tendencies to have malevolent and fractious intentions ('getting back at someone'; 'letting off steam').

Studies of flushing

Burgess (1839, pp. 67–9) considered that the redness of the face was similar in anger and shame and that the difference between them was in the accompanying expressions: anger was accompanied by 'piercing, fire-flashing eye' whereas 'in the blush of shame every feature seems to be in a state of collapse'. Surveys have confirmed intuitions that flushing commonly accompanies anger, for example, flushing and a rise in temperature were mentioned by 63 per cent of participants in Averill's study. Little research has measured flushing and related it to anger and shame (or to embarrassment). An exception is a study by Drummond (1999) who took physiological measures of flushing in a sample of 38 women students, selected as either high or low scorers on a self-report measure of trait anger. An attempt was made to manipulate anger by having participants endeavour to solve a very difficult task while an observer made either derogatory comments about them or neutral comments on the difficulty of the task. Participants rated their anger and embarrassment at several points during the task. Physiological measures were taken prior to the task and at frequent intervals during it; they included forehead blood flow, finger blood flow, skin conductance, heart period and blood pressure. There were substantial individual differences in the measure of facial flushing; nevertheless trends were evident in the data and an increase in forehead blood flow was associated with the observer's derogatory comments. However, flushing did not correlate with scores on trait anger or with self-rated anger during the task; reported anger did increase during the task but only among participants high in trait anger.

There was evidence of short-term increases in forehead blood flow immediately following comments, whether or not these were derogatory, and, as Drummond points out, this could represent evidence of a blush associated with embarrassment: ratings of embarrassment increased for recipients of derogatory, but not neutral comments. It is difficult to distinguish a blush of embarrassment from a flush of anger on the basis of a physiological measure. Moreover, any situation can evoke a mixture of emotional responses. Not only is it embarrassing to hear comments on your performance (it draws attention to the public nature of your actions and it is difficult to know how to respond) it is also embarrassing (or shaming) for a student to have her performance at a cognitive task criticised, particularly if it is apparently a straightforward task.

Why should the heightened sympathetic arousal that is involved in anger result in reddening of the face? Anger mobilises resources for action and involves an increase in heart rate, diastolic blood pressure, blood flow to the muscles and to the hands, increased perspiration and electrodermal response at the skin. The pattern is similar to that of physical exercise. As the heat generated by increased muscle activity raises blood temperature this leads the thermoregulatory centre in the hypothalamus to initiate dilation of the skin blood vessels and sweating.

The process is reflected in everyday expressions: 'it made my blood boil'; 'she was steaming mad'; he's a hothead'. The clear connection between arousal, flushing and readiness for action in anger does not have an obvious counterpart in the facial flushing of shame, since this is associated with hiding and shrinking rather than with activity that demands great exertion, with 'collapse' rather than tension.

It may be that we are misinterpreting shame by conceiving of it as a passive state. Tomkins (1963) regards shame as an inhibitor of positive affect. Frijda (1986) made a similar point, speculating that the blush could be a response of sudden inhibition of an action tendency. It is arguable that embarrassment and shyness both involve the sudden inhibition of ongoing activity, which might have cardiovascular concomitants including vasodilation of facial blood vessels. Anger too can be interpreted in these terms since there are strong social pressures to curb it. The flush might reflect inhibition of arousal in both anger and embarrassment.

An alternative explanation to inhibition of action is that it is inhibition of arousal that has been generated by the threat-response system. Initiation of sympathetic arousal as preparation for fight or flight might be aborted when the threat-detection system registers that the threat is not a physical one and does not require offensive or defensive action: perhaps it is interrupted because the self becomes focal in awareness. Intrusion into our personal space produces arousal, but is interpreted differently according to the circumstances. In anger, attribution of the breach of a boundary is attributed to the other whereas in shame it is attributed to the self. Petronio (2000) construes personal space in terms of boundary regulation processes, and she extends this concept to argue that people erect an invisible boundary around themselves in order to make them less vulnerable to loss of face. Notions of penetration of a boundary and exposure are surely similar. H. B. Lewis (1971, pp. 31–2) argues that 'implicit in the concept of the self is the idea of the boundaries of the self' and asserts that 'shame involves more permeable self-boundaries than does guilt' and can involve closeness between the self and the evaluating 'other'. She writes of 'soft self-boundaries'. O'Farrell (1997, p. 10) also draws upon the notion of boundary in her account of the blush in the nineteenth-century English novel, writing of a 'recurrent fantasy that blushing effects a dissolution of boundaries and a confusion of bodies'.

Shame shares with anger and fear the registration of a threat but it is a specific social threat. Leary and Downs (1995) have hypothesised the existence of a sociometer, which monitors the degree to which we are accepted by other people and is alert to cues that we are at risk of rejection or devaluation. Although it is unsatisfactory to postulate a homunculus to explain what we don't understand, evidence does seem to point to the nervous system's capacity for rapid pre-conscious reaction to threat. In these terms the blush might accompany the emotional response to detected threat. This speculation immediately raises difficult questions. If there is a dedicated reaction to social threat why does it take this particular form? Of what relevance is the connection between increased blood flow and rise in body temperature, that is, does the reaction directly affect blood flow in tandem with facial skin temperature or are these merely by-products of sympathetically innervated heightened arousal? One point of view is that the blush is a dedicated reaction, arguing that a specific region is affected and the onset of the reaction is too rapid to be the product of blood temperature rise. Theorists who emphasise the communicative function of the blush would endorse this explanation. Admittedly it is entirely speculative. Even though research is beginning to clarify the specific mechanisms involved in the blush we don't have answers to quite fundamental questions about why the physiological states that accompany shame and embarrassment take the form that they do or why and how they differ from flushing in anger.

The flush as communication

Anger's characteristic facial expression – a glare accompanied by lowered and drawn-together eyebrows, clenched jaw, narrowing of the margins of the lips and lips pressed tightly together – signals intent: if anger is not restrained an attack is imminent. Although there are social pressures to inhibit the expression of anger, its display communicates the person's emotional state to others, and this can be effective in influencing their behaviour, for example inducing them to desist from some action. An angry stare can be enough to quieten a misbehaving child or cause someone to extinguish a cigarette in a no-smoking area.

Thus, the expression of anger can serve valuable social functions, and in this respect a flush is like a blush. However, it is not known whether the flush invariably accompanies anger, whether it serves as a means of communicating anger by itself or whether other, more controllable elements of the anger display are more effective in communication. Research using vignettes to describe hypothetical episodes suggests that reference to a blush can influence an observer's interpretation of an episode to take a different view of an actor's character, without any need for reference to any other elements of the actor's expressive display. While, to the best of my knowledge, the research has not been undertaken, I would think it unlikely that vignettes referring solely to an actor's flush in equivalent circumstances would yield unambiguous results, unless, of course, the reader of the vignette assumes that it refers to a blush.

Another difference is that the blush serves as a non-verbal apology, where the blusher is conscious of his or her own wrongdoing, whereas a flush, as an expression of anger, invites an apology from someone else. Thus the blush and the flush play different roles in social interaction. As noted above, anger and shame are often experienced in close proximity. This raises several questions about vasodilation of the facial blood vessels in these circumstances, whether different mechanisms are involved in shame and anger, whether any mechanisms are additive or interactive, and how reddening would be interpreted by the individual and others present.

Shame and guilt

Are shame and guilt different emotions?

Psychological theories emphasise the similarity between shame and guilt. Tomkins regards shame and guilt as identical at the level of affect. Cognitive theories locate guilt close to shame, for example in Ortony *et al.*'s (1988) cognitive model of emotion, guilt and shame (along with embarrassment) belong to the class of emotions they term 'attribution of responsibility' emotions, more specifically they are instances of self-reproach emotions that result from disapproval of one's own blameworthy action.

Nevertheless, shame and guilt have been distinguished in various ways. H. B. Lewis (1971) proposes several dimensions on which the two differ. Shame involves more self-consciousness and self-imaging than guilt. The self is the focus of negative evaluation, whereas in guilt it is what has been done that is focal in awareness. The self is passive in shame, but active in guilt, since the self has acted to cause harm to another. Tangney (2003) concludes that there is convincing evidence for the contention that shame involves negative evaluation of the global self whereas feeling guilty involves negative evaluation of a specific action of the self. This also implies that shame is the more intense experience since it entails a deficiency in the whole self. Tracy and Robins' (2004) model of the self-conscious emotions makes this distinction in terms of attribution theory constructs: shame involves attributions to stable, global aspects of the self while guilt involves attributions to unstable, specific aspects of the self. Thus a student who makes no contribution to a seminar discussion might feel ashamed if this is due to her shyness or ignorance of the topic but would feel guilty if she has been too lazy to prepare for the class.

Shame and guilt have been distinguished in terms of physiological measures of activity of the immune system. Dickerson *et al.* (2004) found that increases in proinflammatory cytokine activity were associated with heightened shame but not with guilt.

Guilt is more likely than shame to encourage the individual to apologise or to offer an excuse or justification for her behaviour or attempt to make amends for her wrongdoing, whereas the ashamed person tries to hide from others and to conceal what it is about herself that has given rise to this emotion. On the other hand, guilt may motivate the individual to cover up his actions and avoid detection, resulting in the stealthy look and avoidance of eye contact that are often taken as signs of guilt. A parent or teacher who wanted to establish if a child were guilty of some misdemeanour would try to maintain eye contact and interpret any evasion as an expression of feelings of guilt. This raises a question about the blush that has been posed elsewhere in this book, namely why does an emotion that is associated with hiding give rise to the visible reddening of the face. It introduces a further question: why don't we blush when we feel guilty rather than feel ashamed if the blush is a signal of appeasement or of apology, and guilt motivates us towards making reparation? (Though we have seen in Chapter 4 that evidence from a questionnaire study reported by Halberstadt and Green [1993] provided stronger support for an embarrassment account of the blush than for an explanation in terms of appeasement or apology.)

Does a sense of personal responsibility distinguish shame and guilt? According to H. B. Lewis (1971, p. 43) 'guilt is about things in the real world – acts or failures to act, events for which one bears responsibility'. Taylor (1985, p. 90) argued that responsibility is involved differentially in shame and guilt: 'Normally we are held responsible for what we do in a way that we are not for what we are'. Guilt follows some action (or failure to act) whereas shame may be experienced over events or personal characteristics that are beyond the individual's control and for which he or she can have little responsibility. There is nothing a man can do about his height but this will not prevent him from feeling ashamed of his perceived inadequacy. Attribution theorists might respond that while this is not a matter of responsibility in one sense, it does in another sense, that it 'has something to do with me'. However, it is not obvious that this will distinguish shame from guilt, or shame from disappointment or resentment, which the man might also feel. An appeal to relatedness to the self is not sufficient explanation.

Castelfranchi and Poggi (1990) propose that the individual's responsibility for his or her predicament is not the crucial issue in shame, illustrating this with their example of the 'good Samaritan' who blushes when he realises how his action might be misconstrued by an onlooker. He does so even though he knows he is acting in good faith; he only has to imagine how his behaviour would look to someone else – the source of his shame is his awareness that he is potentially the object of censure.

Sabini and Silver (1997) propose that shame and guilt are alternative terms for one experience, and that understanding the difference between these 'emotions' entails understanding the circumstances in which the terms are used. They suggest that someone who feels guilty about something accepts responsibility for it whereas this is not the case for someone who is ashamed of something. This seems a restatement of the distinctions between wrongdoing in guilt and deficiency in shame and between focus on the self and focus on an act carried out by the self. However, Lewis (1971) and Sabini and Silver (1997) point out that a guilty act can reveal a deficiency in character; we cannot always isolate our acts from our character. The greater the degree of responsibility for the action the more likely it is to reflect a deficiency in character.

If I pass on some unkind gossip about 'Asha' and she overhears or otherwise comes to know about this, I will feel guilty about having done this but may also feel ashamed to be shown to be the kind of person who would make a hurtful remark about a supposed friend. Even if she were not to find out I might still feel guilty and ashamed, aware of having said something potentially harmful to her and of having behaved in a way that is inconsistent with my values. Responsibility is a complex issue: I can feel guilty for having unintentionally harmed another person, for example saying something about Asha in all innocence only to discover that I have caused her offence or have stumbled upon a topic that is hurtful to her. Sabini and Silver (ibid., p. 4) discuss this in terms of not *being* guilty but having 'some of the reactions, beliefs and desires of a person who knows herself to be guilty', but innocence might not be enough to spare me from feeling guilty: I need not have said what I said about Asha. It is surely possible to blush immediately when you realise the import of what you have said prior to any reaction of the other. What is not clear is whether this would be a blush of guilt, shame, state x or exposure of the self. Nor would the blush require that Asha be harmed by what I have said. Ackroyd's novel, *Dan Leno and the Limehouse Golem* provides an example (1994, p. 75) where Leno asks Lizzie if she has a

'neat hand', intending to refer to her handwriting and he blushes immediately when he remembers that she has large, ugly hands. Lizzie might
have assumed Leno *was* referring to her handwriting or paid no attention to what he said; he blushed because he has said it and in advance of
any reaction. A plausible explanation is that he blushed with guilt but
there are other interpretations. He may blush with shame, because he
would be revealed to be an insensitive person, or with embarrassment
because he has brought about an awkward situation.

Cultural factors

The distinction between shame and guilt varies across cultures. In a
study undertaken by Li *et al.* (2004), a list of shame words was assembled
from dictionaries and interviews with native Chinese speakers. The 113
words generated by this procedure included 13 that referred to guilt.
Cluster analysis of judgments of the degree of similarity among words
yielded a 'basic level' category of guilt which, alongside other basic level
categories representing the loss of face and the fear of losing face, was
located within a superordinate category that the researchers labelled
'Shame State, Self-Focus'. The findings from this analysis – that many
Chinese speakers generated guilt words in response to the stimulus word
shame and rated them as related to shame – together with evidence that
some Chinese words combine shame and guilt imply that the distinction between shame and guilt is less sharp in Eastern than in Western
societies. Furthermore, shame and guilt in Chinese can be combined
within one compound word to label an emotion that is stronger than
either word in isolation (Li *et al.*, 2004, p. 788).

Harter and Whitesell (1988) investigated how children's understanding of pride and shame develops as they mature. They found that children below the age of eight years interpret these emotions in terms of
the reactions of significant others ('mother would be ashamed of me')
and do not talk of being proud or ashamed of themselves. Below the age
of six years children describe their reactions to the depicted events in
terms of happiness and anger. When they begin to talk of pride and
shame (at around five to six years) this is in terms of reactions of their
parents. In a further development children talk of experiencing these
emotions themselves but only while they are being observed. Finally, at
around seven to eight years they begin to refer to experiencing them in
the absence of significant others. However, evidence from studies of
Chinese children suggests that they understand shame terms much
sooner than the Western children studied by Harter and Whitesell, as
early as two to three years (Russell and Yik, 1996).

The large number of words for shame in Chinese, considered along-side evidence that children seem to understand the meaning of shame at an earlier age than do children in the Western world, implies that the concept of shame is more salient in China than in the West, and this relates to the distinction between shame and guilt cultures that has been emphasised by many anthropologists since Benedict (1946) pro-posed that Japanese society is a shame culture whereas Western soci-eties constitute a guilt culture. Shame is argued to be more common in collectivist societies whereas guilt is more frequent in individualist soci-eties. Behaviour in guilt cultures is controlled by the individual's inter-nalisation of norms whereas it is regulated in shame cultures by the individual's concern with what other people think of him or her. A detailed review of the extensive research generated by this proposal is beyond the scope of this book but it is worth drawing attention to recent psychological research that investigates representations of shame and guilt within different societies said to represent different cultures.

Fontaine *et al.* (2002) conducted research in Indonesia, held to be a shame culture, and the Netherlands, where guilt is apparently more prevalent than shame. The design of their study shared features with that of Li *et al.* (2004), in that emotion terms were collected from native speakers in each country and rated for typicality as an emotion. Another sample of participants sorted the terms into categories of their choosing and the groupings were submitted to cluster analysis of similarity between terms. Participants from the two countries represented shame and guilt somewhat differently in terms of their location in clusters and their distance from each other and from anger. In Indonesia shame (*malu*) appeared in the same cluster as fear and in the same sub-cluster as worry, confusion, uncertainty and embarrassment, while guilt (*bersalah*) and regret belonged to a separate cluster along with sadness. In the Netherlands both shame (*schaamte*) and guilt (*schuld*) appeared in the fear cluster and belonged to the same sub-cluster as regret, remorse and submission. Shame and guilt were closer to each other in the Netherlands than in Indonesia; they were located further from anger in Indonesia than they were in the Netherlands. Nevertheless, notwith-standing these findings, there was no evidence of a marked distinction between shame and guilt in either country. When participants rated the distance of shame and guilt from the remainder of the emotion terms the differences were of degree rather than categorical. Thus, guilt was located closer to anger than was shame in both countries even though the distances were marginally higher in the Indonesian sample than in the Dutch sample. More generally, the overall structure of emotion terms was similar in the two countries.

Both shame and guilt are distinct from anger in a study of maternal ratings of children's emotions reported by Zahn-Waxler and Robinson (1995). This study had a sample of mothers rate their children aged 14, 20, and 24 months on items referring to the prevalence over a period of one week of signs of shame/shyness, guilt, anger, fear and sadness. Anger was the most frequent and guilt the least frequent emotion at all three ages. The correlation between ratings of guilt and shame/shyness at each age was small. Shame/shyness, but not guilt, was significantly correlated with fear at each age (this may be mediated by the shyness items in the shame/shyness scale). Guilt was correlated with sadness, consistent with findings from studies of emotion words. The correlations between guilt and anger and shame/shyness and anger were modest. This study presumably reflects participants' 'common sense' understanding of these emotion terms as well as characteristics of the children, and hence may represent a study of emotion words, albeit of a different kind from the studies reviewed above.

Do we blush with guilt?

As is the case for shame, there are few references to blushing with guilt in the psychological literature, but many references elsewhere. The following excerpt from Shakespeare's *Macbeth* comes shortly after Macbeth has murdered King Duncan, and Lady Macbeth is telling her husband that she will smear the faces of Duncan's groomsmen with the king's blood in order to implicate them in the crime; presumably she gilds their faces rather than, say, smears their hands, as the red face would be interpreted as an expression of their guilt.

> If he do bleed,
> I'll gild the faces of the grooms withal;
> For it must seem their guilt.
>
> Macbeth, Act II, Scene II

Other literary examples have been presented in earlier chapters: Jane Austen writes in *Emma* of 'the blush of guilt'. In a contemporary novel, *The Spies*, Michael Frayn describes a young boy's blush when his father accuses him of a misdeed, even though the boy does not know what it is that he is supposed to have done (Frayn, 2001, p. 132). Another literary episode, this time from a 1950s novel, Roy Fuller's *Image of a Society*, portrays a woman travelling in a car with her husband who does not know that she is having an affair with one of his work colleagues (Fuller, 1956, p. 138).

> Before she could speak he took his left hand from the wheel and, with his eyes still on the headlight-pierced road, slid back the thin material of her dress until he found the bare flesh of her thigh. To her astonishment her body went rigid against the long-familiar caress and she felt a blush burning in her cheeks.

The sexual intimacy of the husband's action is a physical reminder of her wrongdoing and throws into sharp relief her sexual betrayal of him. While the touch is 'familiar' within marriage it is unacceptable outside it. Does she blush with guilt or with shame? While his action presumably triggers feelings of guilt in her, this can become shame if the behaviour she feels guilty about reflects badly on her character. As Lewis (1971, p. 197) writes, 'when guilty ideation and feeling are to the forefront of awareness, shame feeling may be high, but absorbed by guilt'. The excerpt indicates the woman's lack of control over her reactions and she is in effect the 'astonished' observer of her bodily response. The blush indicates that the self is the focus of her experience, and there are no references to other elements of the shame-variant embarrassment such as fluster or a social predicament – her husband cannot see her reaction because of the darkness inside the car.

Blushing seems to fit better with the view that shame is more likely than guilt to give rise to self-consciousness and a sense of being exposed because the self is central in awareness and there is a motive to hide from the eyes of others. This is the position adopted by Lewis. Shame involves a greater affective component than guilt and is more likely than guilt to be accompanied by heightened autonomic activity including the blush. It involves greater bodily awareness than does guilt, and Lewis goes on to associate this greater body awareness with 'visual and auditory (verbal) imaging of the "me" from the "other person's" point of view'.

Wicker *et al.* (1983) elicited ratings of shame and guilt on a series of nine-point scales including scales referring to self-consciousness and to the face being hot or flushed. One study found no difference in ratings on the flushing scale, with mean values for each emotion close to the mid-point of the scale; in a second study with a larger sample size the difference was statistically significant, with shame more likely than guilt to produce a hot and flushed face; nevertheless mean ratings were again close to the mid-point. On the other hand, in both studies shame was rated significantly higher than guilt on a scale related to feeling self-conscious and exposed, with mean ratings for the two studies of 7.6 and 6.6 on the nine-point scale (respective ratings for guilt were 6.3 and 5.8). In terms of absolute ratings both emotions were characterised by feeling tense, inferior in comparison with others and negative evaluation from self more than from others; shame was also characterised by feeling self-conscious and exposed and powerless; guilt by having done an unjust thing and feeling active. Flushing was not particularly characteristic of either emotion.

Conclusion

Shame is closely connected to anger and guilt and all are accompanied by facial flushing. In shame and guilt, but not anger, these are described as blushes, but research has not established whether the difference between blushing and angry flushing represents different processes. Drummond (1999) suggests that observers tell the two apart on the basis of the social context and other emotion cues rather than in terms of different mechanisms. Research into the blush has paid little attention to shame or guilt. There are close relations between the two. They are distinguished in that shame involves greater self-consciousness where the focus is on the self rather than on the action and this is the basis for H. B. Lewis's proposal that the blush is more likely to accompany shame rather than guilt. The self rather than the action is focal: there is greater self-consciousness and body awareness in shame. However, there exists no evidence that the blush is more frequent in shame, and research into this issue would be valuable.

As alternative to explaining the blush in terms of self-consciousness is that the blush is due to embarrassment in situations where attention is drawn to the self. Lewis regards embarrassment as a variant of shame and relates it to a loss of 'self-functioning', evident in hesitation and uncertainty how to act. It is feasible that shame (or guilt) experienced in the presence of others triggers a blush because of the uncertainties that the potential or actual social predicament creates. In some cases the blush of embarrassment is misperceived as guilt. The examples given below from recollections of blushing episodes are consistent with this interpretation.

Responses to my questionnaire study of recollections of blushing episodes (Chapter 5) include instances where the blushers believe they are being accused of something.

Being accused as a group member of dropping paint – no one owned up and I blushed – and I got the blame though it was someone else. [Why blush?] Because nobody else owned up I thought maybe I had done it. Even though I saw someone else drop the paint.

At work when all members of staff were told that somebody was stealing. [Why blush?] Because people would think it was me.

In practice, shame, guilt, embarrassment and anger can be experienced in close proximity, with one leading to the other, so that it is difficult to disentangle their influences on autonomic responses. Other influences come from social norms about the display and suppression of emotion. As has been noted on a number of occasions in this volume the display of emotion can be timely but it can also lead to unwanted consequences. While signs of anger can influence others without the need for recourse to aggressive action, there are pressures not to show anger and remain 'tight lipped' because of the consequences of its display for the social encounter, the potential for escalation and the implications for the perception of the angered person's character. Losing your temper is often regarded as a sign of immaturity or lack of control and in general people try to be assertive without doing so.

The next chapter looks at shyness. This is often regarded as a form of fear and is not always considered a self-conscious emotion – Tracy and Robins omit it from their model of these emotions. Nevertheless, it has much in common with shame and embarrassment and is frequently associated with blushing.

9
Shyness

Shyness and the blush

The study of shyness has shown it to be a complex experience involving cognitive, somatic and behavioral components. It is more likely to be elicited in some kinds of situations rather than others – when meeting someone for the first time, encountering the other sex and situations where the person perceives a greater likelihood of being evaluated by others. Accounts of shyness have appeared in the psychological litera-ture for many years. In his book on chronic blushing, Campbell (1890) proposed that three conditions are necessary for shyness. The individual is excessively self-conscious of his mental or bodily self; he has low self-esteem; he is sensitive to the opinion of others. Lewinsky (1941) defined shyness in terms of self-consciousness, feelings of inferiority and a state of inhibition accompanied by physical symptoms including blushing. Subsequent to Lewinsky's article psychologists paid little attention to shyness and it is only quite recently that there has emerged a sustained programme of research into shyness and related concepts of social anxiety, social withdrawal and behavioral inhibition. There have been seminal contributions on several fronts, including the publication of findings from the Stanford Shyness Survey (Zimbardo, 1977) which showed that the experience of shyness was widespread, the construction of the Cheek–Buss Shyness Scale (Cheek and Buss, 1981) for assessing individual differences in shyness, a growing interest in the clinical diag-nostic category of social phobia (discussed in Chapter 11) and Kagan's research into the temperament of behavioral inhibition (discussed later). Shyness is now extensively studied in children and adults.

Despite this accumulation of research little is known about the involvement of the blush in shyness and there is controversy over whether people do blush when they are shy. Several writers whose work has been discussed in earlier chapters maintain that people do so. Darwin identified shyness – along with shame and modesty – as one of the mental states that induce blushing, indeed he regarded it as 'one of the most efficient of all the causes of blushing' (Darwin, 1872, p. 329). Campbell regarded shyness, particularly about physical appearance, as the primary reason for blushing. Tomkins defined shyness and shame as the same affect, which has blushing as one of its expressions. There is evidence from self-report questionnaires that blushing is a symptom of shyness. One item in the Stanford Shyness Survey included blushing as a response option for describing possible reactions associated with shyness, and this item was endorsed by 53 per cent of respondents, a rate of endorsement similar to that found in surveys of self-reported embarrassment (Parrott and Smith, 1991). Ishiyama (1984) found that the majority of a sample of adolescents reported blushing when they felt shy; the frequency of reports was not very different among those who described themselves as dispositionally shy (71% of shy participants reported blushing when shy) from that among those who described themselves as not shy (reported by 61%). Descriptions of shyness commonly mention blushing, and this can be illustrated by examples from my own research. One respondent to the request to describe an incident where she felt shy listed her reactions: 'withdrawn, frustrated, scared; if I say anything then it's usually inappropriate; blushing, eyes look at ground; act withdrawn, keep quiet'.

Another described being overcome with shyness when, in the company of a (female) friend she unexpectedly met the boy she had been dating.

> I think I just mumbled a hello and see you tonight and walked off. I went bright red. I was thinking what he must think of me. I thought he might finish with me if he saw me not at my best. I would have usually taken ages getting ready before seeing him but didn't expect to see him that day so I didn't take the usual care in dressing ... My friend told me that I had gone bright red, which in turn made me feel even more embarrassed. Him seeing me bright red made it even worse.

Despite such evidence, contemporary accounts of shyness do not assign a prominent role to the blush. Buss (1980) maintained that it is associated with embarrassment but not with shyness. Admittedly there exists little evidence other than from self-report studies – few researchers have sought to collect the information. As discussed below, Buss modified his view of shyness to distinguish two forms: early-appearing or fearful shyness and late developing or self-conscious shyness. The latter form, he argued, is contingent on the acquisition of the capacity for public self-awareness. This distinction affords an opportunity to relate blushing to at least one aspect of shyness: the self-conscious form.

Most research into shyness has regarded it as a form of anxiety or fear, and this reflects the word's connotations of wariness and apprehension. The word is used in several ways in everyday talk. It describes a pattern of behaviour: 'he shied away'. It qualifies descriptions of behaviour: 'he entered the room shyly'; 'she gave me a shy glance'. It offers an explanation of behaviour: 'his quietness was due to his shyness at being introduced to her'. This explanation is extended to instances where the shyness seems divorced from observed behaviour: 'his bravado masked an underlying shyness'. It is used to describe either a transient state – 'I was suddenly overcome with shyness' – or a trait or predisposition: 'she is basically a shy person'; 'not many people realise how shy she is'. Given this diversity, it is not surprising that when the word is employed as a technical term in psychology it has generated confusion, arguments about definitions, even about the advisability of producing definitions, and has led some to reject the term as a useful scientific construct.

Our principal concern is with shyness as a transient state. Little research has addressed this directly with the exception of the theories of emotion developed by Tomkins and Izard. Both assign a role to the blush in shyness, although neither reports empirical findings specifically on blushing. There are other approaches to shyness which can be brought to bear on the question, albeit indirectly. One approach focuses on inhibited, reticent and socially withdrawn behaviour. Within this framework shyness is typically identified by observational methods, for example counting the frequency of attempts to initiate conversation or to join in social activities. The most consistent finding, among both children and adults, is that reticence is a common reaction in shyness and a common reason for attributing shyness to the self and others.

Another approach, as noted above, conceives of shyness as a form of fear or anxiety. The emphasis here has been on inter-individual differences on a temperament of behavioral inhibition and a trait variously labelled social anxiety, communication apprehension and shyness. Empirical studies of transient anxiety, whether using observational or self-report methods, tend to be conducted within the context of research into the trait. Little attention is paid to intra-individual differences, that is, comparisons of different occasions involving the same individual.

A third approach regards shyness as a member of the family of self-conscious emotions, closer to embarrassment and shame than it is to fear. This approach is the only one to routinely label shyness as an emotion; in contrast to the other approaches it has little to say about inter-individual differences.

Blushing plays little part in investigations of withdrawn behaviour since it is not usually included in observational measures, partly because of the technical problems of measuring it but also because there is no theory within this perspective to relate the categories of behaviour to blushing. Also, it is more difficult to see how blushing is related to fear rather than to, say, embarrassment, since vasodilation of facial blood vessels does not seem to be a characteristic fear reaction and does not figure in the extensive psychophysiological research that has been undertaken into fear – research that, as we discuss later, has links with research into behavioral inhibition and shyness.

Perspectives on shyness

Shyness as shame

Differential emotions theory (Izard, 1977) follows Tomkins in considering shame-shyness to be a fundamental emotion, which has a unique neurophysiological substrate, pattern of motor-expressive behaviour, including facial expression, and subjective-experiential or feeling state. Nevertheless, Izard and Hyson (1986) acknowledge that the evidence for these components is less robust for shame-shyness than is the case for other fundamental emotions. Ekman (2003) argues that shame-shyness does not have a distinctive and efficient signal that informs others what the individual is feeling, though he qualifies this assertion by arguing that embarrassment (which Izard regards as a variant of shame-shyness) is characterised by a distinctive sequence of expressions rather than a single momentary expression; however, shyness is not considered in these terms.

Izard proposed a characteristic expressive pattern involving gaze aversion, eyelids lowered, and turning away and lowering the head. My own investigation of the identification of facial expression of Izard's fundamental emotions (Crozier, 1981a) failed to find that shame-shyness could reliably be identified from a sample of still photographs including versions of those prepared by Izard for his research (Izard, 1971). Unlike previous research, participants provided their own words for the expression rather than be constrained to select from a prescribed list of words. Responses were scored as correct if the participants provided a word for one of the shame-shyness family of emotions or a synonym of any of these words. Compared to the other expressions, anger, fear, surprise and so on, where rates of correct identification of the emotions were high, rates were low for the shame-shyness faces and participants' rated confidence in their judgments was much lower for these photographs than for the other emotions.

This is not to conclude that there is not a characteristic expression of shyness identifiable by, say, videotape analysis, even though the other fundamental emotions identified by Izard can readily be identified in photographs. Reddy (2000) has reported that signs of coyness and shyness can be observed prior to 18 months; for example, even at two months infants show coy smiles that are accompanied by gaze and head aversion followed by return of gaze, smiles that are elicited by familiar adults as well as by strangers. At 9 to 12 months there is evidence of wariness to strangers expressed in wary brow, gaze aversion, coy looks and alternation of smiling and gaze aversion (Reddy, 2001). Unfortunately, little research has considered shyness in later childhood and adulthood as an emotional reaction other than anxiety and one consequence of this has been neglect of the roles of self-consciousness and blushing in shyness.

Shyness can be a private experience that is not noticed by others. Nevertheless, its display, like that of embarrassment, can influence the interpretations of behaviour that others make. It can lead people to conclude that an individual lacks interest in others, is self-centred, rude, conceited, untrustworthy and so on. Many shy individuals report being misjudged in this way. The lowered eyes and reluctance to make eye contact characteristic of shy people resemble a display of submission and this, together with reluctance to contribute to interaction, can constrain the social roles open to shy individuals. Respondents to shyness surveys, including the Stanford Shyness Survey, claim that their qualities are often underestimated by others, for example, by their university tutors and work superiors, such that they might be passed over when roles are allocated or when they wish to be considered for posts or promotions. This also has an impact on dating and finding romantic partners.

A blush would serve to augment these difficulties as it could be seen as further evidence of a lack of poise or control. It could also undermine the shy person's confidence in his or her self-presentation: a readily elicited blush would be something more to be shy about. On the other hand, it might encourage others to think the person was shy, which would help to deflect unwanted explanations of behaviour. Just as a blush influences observers to take a less negative view of the person who knocks over a pile of cans in the supermarket, it could forestall criticism or rejection of the individual who, when meeting someone, does not greet her or smile or ask her how she is, or who gives monosyllabic answers to friendly questions.

Before concluding consideration of this approach it is worth drawing attention to the ambivalence that Tomkins detects in shame affect. The ashamed or shy person wants to look and to be looked at, yet at the same time does not want to do so. Shyness is close to interest and enjoyment and can quickly turn into either of these; the shy person is reluctant to leave the situation because it can promise social rewards. This conflict between approach and avoidance is emphasised by all accounts of shyness, and is neatly captured in observations of children's 'wait and hover' behaviour, where the shy child lingers at the edge of a game, keen to join in but inhibited from doing so, at the same time unwilling to leave.

The combination of shyness and sociability – liking to be with people and welcoming the opportunity to mix with people – is associated with a distinctive pattern of anxious reactions and behaviours. Cheek and Buss (1981) surreptitiously videotaped women students differing in their patterns of scores on measures of shyness and sociability during the course of a conversation with a stranger. Shy women talked significantly less than non-shy women and they rated themselves as more tense and inhibited. Moreover, women who obtained high scores on both the shyness and sociability scales made more self-manipulative movements (touching the face or body with the hands) and spent less time looking at their partner relative to those who were not shy. Observers rated them as more tense and inhibited than the shy-less sociable women and the non-shy women. Schmidt and Fox (1994) reported that participants in their study who were high on both shyness and sociability had a significantly higher and more stable heart rate in anticipation of a novel social encounter than had participants who were shy and less sociable or who were not shy. The combination of shyness and sociability implies a greater degree of approach-avoidance conflict than is experienced by those individuals whose goals and preferences are inherently solitary. An influential account of shyness by Leary and his colleagues (e.g., Leary and Buckley, 2000) characterises this conflict in self-presentation terms, proposing that the shy person is motivated to create a desired impression in others but lacks confidence in the ability to do so. This conflict clearly resembles the ambivalence discussed by Tomkins, and seems to be a salient characteristic of at least one form of shyness.

Shyness as inhibition

The greatest impetus to the study of childhood shyness has been provided by Kagan's research programme, which has been developed within a biological framework (Kagan, 1994) and has identified a category of temperament that he has labelled *behavioral inhibition to the unfamiliar*. This is defined in terms of the child's initial reactions to a series of episodes involving unfamiliar people, objects and contexts, and challenging tasks. Kagan's research has several distinctive features. It emphasises behavioural and physiological measures and is wary of questionnaire methods. It argues for discrete types of temperament, in contrast to the predominant preference in individual difference research for continua and dimensions.

Kagan has developed an explanatory framework that postulates psychophysiological differences between inhibited and uninhibited children. This model assigns a central role to forebrain limbic regions, specifically the amygdala and its projections. Researchers have studied connections between forebrain limbic areas and the frontal cortex, structures that have been shown to be involved in negative emotional experiences and conditioned fear reactions. Indications of heightened activity in these structures and regions include measures of heart rate, heart rate variability, vagal tone, respiratory sinus arrhythmia (variation in heart rate associated with the respiratory cycle), eye blink startle, salivary cortisol and right frontal EEG activity. It has been found that inhibited children differ from uninhibited children on these measures, particularly when assessments are made during the early years (up to four years of age) and when children who are at the extremes of inhibition (as identified by behavioral measures) are assessed (Marshall and Stevenson-Hinde, 2005).

The programme design has been longitudinal and has addressed issues such as cross-situational consistency in behavioral inhibition, its stability over time, and the prediction of personality and behaviour in later childhood and adolescence. There is evidence of moderate temporal stability, particularly when groups with extreme scores are considered. This is an important finding given the reasons to expect instability over time. Observational measures or physiological recordings may be less sensitive to individual variation in emotional reaction later in childhood. The older child learns to regulate emotions and their overt expression, in part through increasing maturity, and in part because of processes of socialisation, where there are pressures to show emotional restraint. As children grow older they exercise greater choice over their activities and may be able to avoid sources of novelty and uncertainty.

The concept of behavioral inhibition is broader than shyness and encompasses individual differences in reactions to all forms of novel events and situations, not just social situations (Kagan, 1994). However, encounters with unfamiliar adults or children play a large part in the assessment of inhibition, and, as children grow up, measures of their inhibition draw increasingly on reactions to social situations, for example, latency of spontaneous speech or total number of utterances when meeting new people become significant markers of inhibition. Outcome measures in empirical studies include children's reticence and hesitation in making spontaneous contributions to conversation and their tendency to 'hover' at the edge of social situations, in addition to ratings of shyness made by parents and by observers of the child's behaviour.

Research within this paradigm explicitly links shyness to fear and anxiety and supports this with psychophysiological evidence. There is a substantial degree of similarity in structures, networks and processes in the model of inhibition described by Kagan (1994) and the model of fear set out, for example, by LeDoux and Phelps (2000). The models describe the same system and neither has a place for the blush. The next section considers a distinction between forms of shyness that would seem to create an opportunity to find a place for the blush in shyness.

Fearful and self-conscious shyness

The early signs of inhibition in social situations appear at an age before the infant or young child has acquired the capacity to reflect upon him or herself. Yet explanations of shyness in childhood and adulthood assign importance to the involvement of the self in shyness. The shy person lacks confidence in him or herself and does not expect to be successful in taking the initiative in social interaction. He or she is motivated to make an effective presentation of self but doubts the ability to do so and consequently adopts self-protective strategies in order to cope with these doubts. Shy people make stable, internal attributions for their social difficulties – they blame themselves for their predicaments. They report negative, self-deprecatory thoughts during social interaction.

What shyness shares with embarrassment and shame is the sense of an audience for one's behaviour and this requires a reflective self; one is aware of how one's behaviour will appear to others and specifically is aware that others can take an adverse view of that behaviour. As Miller (2001, pp. 293–4) writes, 'neither self-conscious shyness nor embarrassment would occur if people were genuinely heedless of the judgements of others, and it is this core characteristic that links the two states.'

The difference between fearful and self-conscious forms of shyness is illustrated by recollections of the problems faced at the end of the Second World War when fathers and husbands returned home after what could have been an absence of several years (Turner and Rennell, 1995). One woman recalled her shyness at the age of seven in the presence of the 'stranger' who had come to live with her and her mother. Another woman was shy about her husband seeing her in her tattered clothing, particularly her underwear.[1] Her shyness illustrates Campbell's thesis: she is conscious of her appearance; she believes it to be deficient; she fears negative evaluation. The instances are consistent with Asendorpf's (1989) thesis that shyness is associated with two kinds of concerns, fear of the unfamiliar and fear of being negatively evaluated by others, and that these concerns are triggered by two kinds of situations. The first kind entails interacting with strangers and adjusting to unfamiliar settings and novel situations. The second kind includes situations where evaluation by others is salient, such as speaking up in front of others, giving a speech, or attending interviews, but also routine or less public encounters, such as interacting with authority figures. It resembles H. B. Lewis's conception of shame; she regards shyness as a member of the shame family, characterised by 'fear of the "other" – either as a source of shame or as a source of some other specified danger' (Lewis, 1971, p. 75). It would make sense to say that the woman is ashamed of her appearance, even if the reasons for it are beyond her control; the returning husband is the specific 'other' whose deprecation she fears.

At what stage in the child's life does the self become involved in shyness and how does this involvement change through childhood? There have been two influential accounts of the development of shyness, embarrassment and self-consciousness that address this issue. Buss (1986) distinguishes between early-appearing fearful shyness and later-appearing self-conscious shyness. According to Buss, the first type is elicited by social novelty, breaches of personal space (intrusion) and social evaluation; the second is elicited by conspicuousness, receiving the attention of others, being noticeably distinctive from others and by breaches of privacy. As discussed in Chapter 6, M. Lewis (1992) distinguished between exposed emotions and self-conscious evaluative emotions. He focuses on embarrassment and shame rather than on shyness, and he has little to say directly on shyness, although he does argue that it is not an evaluative emotion because it appears early and 'does not involve an evaluative component in regard to one's action in terms of standards, rules, and goals' (ibid., p. 81).

Buss and M. Lewis regard the two forms of self-consciousness as emerging in sequence, with the emergence of each contingent upon cognitive developments. According to Buss, self-conscious shyness appears at four to five years and requires the acquisition of public self-awareness, which entails a sense of oneself as a social object and a focus on those aspects of the self that are observable and noticeable. These developments, in turn, are contingent upon the acquisition of a social self or 'advanced cognitive self' (Buss, 1986, p. 43).

In M. Lewis's theory, exposed emotions are contingent upon the acquisition of objective self-awareness, metarepresentation or 'idea of me', which occurs in the latter half of the second year, and is indexed by the child's capacity for visual self-recognition and self-referential behaviour, as evidenced on performance on the mirror self-recognition test and in the use of self-referential language (for example, personal pronouns). Exposed emotions precede evaluative emotions, since the latter require cognitive developments over and above the acquisition of a sense of self – the child must be able to absorb and possess a set of standards, rules and goals, and be able to evaluate his or her actions, thoughts and feelings in terms of these. The child must be able to determine success or failure in attaining these and attribute these outcomes to the self. M. Lewis does not provide details about the timing of the emergence of evaluative emotions, other than to suggest that they are acquired at around three years of age.

The two accounts differ in their treatment of self-evaluation. Buss identifies social evaluation with the earlier form of shyness, although he acknowledges that evaluation concerns are found only among older children and adults who have sufficient socialisation experience to be aware of a discrepancy between their behaviour and standards of evaluation. M. Lewis also maintains that concern with social evaluation comes when the child has internalised standards of evaluation but he identifies it with the later form of embarrassment. Asendorpf (1990a) has produced an account that is closer to Lewis's position, where he distinguishes between inhibition towards strangers (wariness) and social-evaluative inhibition, considering that the latter involves anticipation of negative evaluation by others and appears towards the end of the second year, contingent on cognitive developments. Asendorpf argues that the onset of public self-awareness is not sufficient for the later form of shyness since it is not inherently evaluative or aversive.

In summary, each theory proposes a form of shyness or wariness that appears early and resembles Kagan's construct of behavioral inhibition. Its emergence requires no awareness of self in the sense of consideration of the attitude of other people to the self. It only requires that infants have learnt to discriminate unfamiliar from familiar people; when this development is in place some infants will show greater wariness of the unfamiliar than will other infants.

To appreciate the different positions on shyness it is instructive to compare their conceptualisations of embarrassment. Buss's construct of self-conscious shyness resembles embarrassment, in that both are forms of self-consciousness elicited by conspicuousness and, according to Buss (1986), the affective reaction in self-conscious shyness *is*, at least in its extreme form, embarrassment, and is accompanied by blushing and heightened parasympathetic arousal. M. Lewis (2001) regards shyness as similar to exposure embarrassment in that both appear early and do not require evaluation but he makes a sharper distinction between shyness and evaluative embarrassment. According to Lewis, the later form of embarrassment results from the acquisition of standards and rules; for Buss, it only requires the capacity for public self-awareness.

In summary, Lewis claims that evaluative embarrassment requires self-awareness or self-reference, an appreciation of standards and the ability to evaluate one's behaviour relative to these standards – '*I* have done something bad or wrong.' Buss argues that self-conscious shyness requires public self-awareness, appreciation of oneself as a social object. Asendorpf argues that social-evaluative shyness requires the combination of public self-awareness and fear of negative evaluation; that others are viewing and evaluating the self – 'I have done something that *will be seen* as bad or wrong.'

There is evidence to suggest that the distinction between fearful and self-conscious shyness in childhood is a meaningful one. In a longitudinal study undertaken in Sweden by Kerr (2000), shyness was assessed by mothers' and psychologists' ratings during the period when participants were aged 18 months to 5 years and again when they were aged 6 to 11 years and 12 to 16 years. Early-developing shyness was not correlated with self-rated self-conscious worries (about appearance, getting on well with others, being made fun of by the opposite sex) but later-developing shyness was associated with these worries.

There are debates about the cognitive developments that have to be in place for the self-conscious form to emerge. Explanations have been framed in terms of the child's growing capacity to take other perspectives on the self and on the child's acquisition of a theory of mind. Yuill and Banerjee (2001) identify the acquisition of a theory of mind at around four years as the crucial development and propose that self-conscious shyness emerges around this age. In their interview study of children's conceptions of shyness, children were asked which of two hypothetical situations would make a child shy – singing alone in front of the class or meeting a stranger. Those who chose the former (the self-conscious option) were more likely to demonstrate understanding of self-presentational motives for behaviour, including the display of emotion. They were able to understand that a person might adapt his or her behaviour in order to impress someone. Banerjee and Yuill (1999) reported that children who were successful on a false-belief task[2] were more likely to identify self-presentational display rules correctly and provide appropriate justifications for their responses. Nevertheless, although these findings are suggestive, there exists little evidence that successful performance on a false-belief task is a pre-requisite for the emergence of a self-conscious conception of shyness. Furthermore, it has not been established that successful performance on these tasks reflects children's understanding that they might be the focus of others' evaluative attention.

The self-conscious form does not replace the fearful form, and both are evident in studies of the conceptions of shyness held by older children and adolescents. Fearful shyness is evident in adults, but the distinction between the two forms becomes blurred, at least in findings from an interview study that I undertook with Alison Garbert-Jones (Crozier and Garbert-Jones, 1996) and conducted with 21 'mature' university students, ages ranging from 24 to 59 years with an average of 40 years. They were not selected because of any shyness on their part but in order to explore their understanding of shyness, the role, if any, that it played in university life, and their means of coping. One participant said that she was very shy, three that they were shy and five that they were shy in certain situations; 12 said that they were not shy or not as shy as they had been in the past. The interviews were transcribed and responses to the question, 'Can you describe situations in which you felt shy' were coded for reference to fearful or self-conscious shyness drawing upon the descriptions of these provided by Buss (1986).

Assigning episodes to categories was not always straightforward. For example, according to the scheme, giving a public speech would be coded as fearful shyness whereas being scrutinised or being stared at represents self-conscious shyness. In practice, a participant's description of, say, making a presentation to the class can include mention of being scrutinised. Problems also arise because the forms of shyness are coded in terms of the eliciting circumstances as well as reactions. Thus both forms can co-occur in transcripts of individual episodes. A novel situation, like meeting someone for the first time creates uncertainties about how to behave and also social-evaluative concerns. Situations that are theorised to elicit fearful reactions – wariness, shrinking, an urge to escape – do have implications for the self; it could scarcely be otherwise since society expects adults to be poised, and the awareness that you find novel situations or meeting strangers difficult has implications for your view of yourself. Moreover, a novel situation's implications for self-presentation can be salient, as in this description of shyness:

> Generally when I'm meeting people that I know of but I haven't met them. Yet if it's just somebody that you meet on the street then I don't generally feel shy talking to people like that but if I know I'm going to meet say a friend's friend and I know they know somebody that I know I always feel like I've got to make an impression.

Unfamiliar situations can elicit embarrassment about feeling out of place and not knowing what to do:

> It's doing things like job interviews or going into situations where perhaps you're uncertain of what's happening. Starting university was an example. The first day nerves is absolutely horrendous turning up and queuing and being emb … I think embarrassment about am I in the right queue, should I be here in the first place.

Nevertheless, despite difficulties in allocating some of the episodes to categories, the eliciting circumstances could be placed into two categories that correspond to the distinction made by Buss. The first, larger category brings together new situations, meeting people for the first time, public presentations and speaking up in front of others. The second category includes situations where the individual is the object of attention (other than when speaking in public); is interacting with authority figures; is aware of being different from others.

The most common eliciting circumstances were (i) meeting someone that you don't know and whose impression of you is important (i.e., not a complete stranger), or (ii) having to speak up in front of other people, particularly people whom you don't know well, and this can be more difficult to do in a formal setting, or (iii) interacting with a specific person, who could be an authority figure or someone who overawes you or has a particular character ('this presence she had').

The most common reactions were not being yourself, unable to think of the right thing to say, not sure what to talk about, wariness or caution over what to say and concern that what you do say will appear foolish, uninteresting or inadequate. This can be accompanied by tension, nervousness, shaking, thumping heart, croaking voice, giggling and blushing. Being quiet, hanging back and tongue-tied (can't think what to say, inhibited train of thought, dry up, mind blank) were more likely to be mentioned in the context of novel situations, whereas feeling self-conscious and feeling small (inadequate, like a child) were more common when the person was conspicuous and were absent from descriptions of novel situations. One participant suggested there are two types of shyness:

> there's self-consciousness and an embarrassment almost and there's a shyness that's a sort of reservedness where you feel reserved and you don't want to give away too much of yourself.

Nevertheless, the overall picture from the analysis of these interviews is that while different circumstances do elicit different patterns, it is an oversimplification to conclude that there are two distinct types of shyness, in terms of either eliciting circumstances or responses.

Five participants mentioned blushing:

> I'd meet people for the first time and I would be so interested in what people were saying but I didn't feel that I could contribute and felt very sort of quiet and I'd blush easily if people spoke to me. I used to be painfully shy – sort of embarrassed and I used to blush and I'd get very tongue-tied. I didn't find it easy to speak to people, although I desperately wanted to.

> It first started with a university summer school. We sat round in a circle – we had to say who we were. When it came to me I couldn't speak. I was just shy. Shaky. I was blushing. I just couldn't speak. They were all teachers, I'm just at home and I've got two children.

> Job interviews, that's the only time I'm ever tongue-tied. When they say 'is there anything you would like to say' and I can never think of a thing to say and I can feel the colour coming up through my neck. I can feel the sweat on my forehead and on my back.

> [While working in an office] People look at me and I go absolutely red.

> Being introduced to four or six people at once and feeling overawed or people you think intellectually superior. They're relaxed, you're not, it's going to show. Blush. Stutter.

The first participant describes elements typical of shyness: it is elicited when meeting people for the first time, there is an element of conflict in that she is interested in people and 'desperately wants' to speak to them but at the same time she is inhibited and feels unable to contribute to conversation. Her characterisation of herself as a shy person includes finding it difficult to talk to people and being readily embarrassed and prone to blush. In the first four cases the blusher is momentarily the object of attention – people look at her, speak to her, it is her turn to contribute. More than this, she is put on the spot in some way, for example, when the interviewee is asked if she has any questions or, in another case, it comes round to her turn in the circle. In the fifth case, the individual is conscious of being different from the people to whom he is being introduced, of being overawed by them, so that he too is in a sense 'under the spotlight'.

Participants spoke at length about shyness. It was something with which they were all familiar and they could readily recall and describe occasions when they felt shy. There are recurrent themes across the interviews and these are similar to those identified in previous research – they exemplify the definition provided by Lewinsky at the beginning of this chapter.

Conclusion

Most research into shyness regards it as a form of fear. Buss proposed a self-conscious form of shyness that seems closer to shame and embarrassment than to fear and which may be more likely to be accompanied by a blush. However, there are uncertainties about the value of the distinction between the forms of shyness. Fear of others and shame before others must be closely related, since having the good opinion of others is fundamental to social interaction and most of us continually monitor our social performance and the reactions of others. Other than in early childhood, can fear of others not involve self-consciousness?

Shyness is close to embarrassment. Goffman (1972) discussed shyness in terms of the individual's consciousness that certain recurring situations or relationships make him or her uncomfortable. The accounts given by the interviewees in this chapter identify types of situations and interactions with particular others that make them feel uneasy and uncertain what to say or do. They acknowledge that they have little poise in these encounters. Shyness leads readily to a state of embarrassment since the shy person is exposed and there is suspension of 'self-functioning'. Shyness is closely associated with self-consciousness as the individual is aware of his shortcomings and often blames himself for creating the predicament. Furthermore, he thinks these thoughts in the presence of others. These circumstances are surely ripe for triggering a blush.

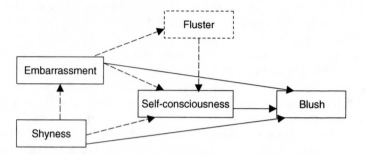

Figure 9.1   Pathways from shyness to the blush

Part III of this book has considered emotional states that are associated with the blush and has highlighted the significant part that self-consciousness plays in each of these states. Conclusions about whether blushing accompanies embarrassment but not shame or shyness seem premature, since we do not know how these states relate to one another or how blushing is triggered by any of them. It is possible that the blush expresses a heightened state of self-consciousness and accompanies any emotional state that entails this. Alternatively, it might be that the blush is specific to embarrassment (or those instances of embarrassment that entail self-consciousness) and that shame, shyness, praise and so on trigger a blush only because they produce embarrassing circumstances. That is, does embarrassment mediate the relation between shyness and the blush? (It would be helpful to know whether people blush when they are alone. There exists anecdotal evidence of this, but there has been no systematic research. This would be helpful in disentangling the contribution of embarrassment to the blush.)

Alternatively, self-consciousness might mediate the relation so that only those instances of embarrassment that entail self-consciousness trigger the blush. These possible models are outlined in Figure 9.1.

Shyness might directly trigger a blush, as indicated by the continuous line, or it might be mediated by embarrassment or self-consciousness (dotted lines). Embarrassment might have a direct link with the blush or be mediated by self-consciousness. Embarrassment does not lead necessarily to a blush but can produce fluster, uncertainty how to behave; this can produce self-consciousness if it leads the flustered person to focus attention on how the self appears. The relations in this outline model concern emotional states; it is possible that these also involve traits of shyness and embarrassability and self-consciousness. The next chapter addresses this issue.

IV
Problematising Blushing

10
Propensity to Blush

Preceding chapters have sought to identify circumstances that elicit a blush, the mechanisms that are involved and implications for the blusher and others present. Nevertheless, while the blush is a ubiquitous phenomenon, some people believe that they blush more often or more intensely than others do, and for many this creates problems so troublesome that they seek professional help. Individual differences in tendency to blush are typically assessed by means of self-report questionnaire, and three approaches to the construction of such questionnaires are now briefly described.

Measuring individual differences

The first approach involves the design of psychometric self-report scales to assess a predisposition to blush. Chapter 4 introduced the Blushing Propensity Scale (BPS) constructed by Leary and Meadows (1991), where respondents rate how likely it is that they would blush in each of the 14 hypothetical circumstances. The scale was discussed in Chapter 4 in the context of classifying blush-making situations but it has also been used to locate individuals along a single dimension of blushing propensity by summing their scores over the items. Responses are made on a five-point scale ranging from 'I never feel myself blush in this situation' to 'I always feel myself blush in this situation'. Leary and Meadows provide evidence of satisfactory internal reliability of the BPS (Cronbach's alpha = 0.86) and four-week test-retest reliability of 0.81.[1] There seem to be no gender differences in scores on the measure, which is consistent with findings from self-report items about the frequency of blushing, which find comparable rates among men and women (Shields *et al.*, 1990). This contrasts with findings on embarrassability, where women obtain higher scores on average than men (Miller, 1995).

A second type of measure assesses fear of showing somatic symptoms of anxiety. Bögels and Reith (1999) produced the Blushing, Trembling and Sweating Questionnaire (BTS-Q), which comprises several sections: the severity of the fear of blushing, trembling and sweating (6 items referring to each of these symptoms); the physical symptoms associated with blushing (6 items), trembling (4 items) and sweating (3 items); avoidance strategies used to avoid or mask blushing (10 items), trembling (3 items) and sweating (6 items); behavioural problems (6 items) and mental problems (10 items) associated with the set of symptoms; positive beliefs (10 items) and negative beliefs (54 items) about them; their frequency (a single item for each symptom). The scales have satisfactory internal reliability, with alpha coefficients ranging from 0.77 to 0.98. A clinical sample of 92 patients meeting criteria for social phobia scored significantly higher on the set of scales than a control group matched with regard to age and educational level. An indication of the validity of the measure is the finding that a clinical sample of patients whose principal concern was physical symptoms obtained significantly higher scores than patients for whom symptoms were not the main concern. This measure is of potential value for research into blushing propensity since the separate blushing sub-scales seem to have sound psychometric properties. The correlations between the blushing items and the sweating and trembling items have not been researched, so that we do not yet know the extent to which some individuals fear one symptom but not the others. Bögels and Reith (1999) report sizeable correlations between the section scores (with the exception of the positive beliefs about symptoms scale, which has small negative correlations with the other sub-scales), ranging from 0.37 to 0.81, showing that the scales have moderate discriminant validity. Finally, the fear of blushing sub-scale correlates significantly ($r = 0.56$) with the Dutch version of the BPS (Mulkens *et al.*, 1999).

A third approach asks people directly how frequently or intensely they blush. The participants in Shields *et al.*'s (1990) study were asked how often and how readily they blushed compared with their same-sex peers. Edelmann (1990b) recruited a sample of self-described chronic blushers from individuals who had written to request a fact sheet advertised in a magazine article about blushing and, among other items requesting information on their blushing and its consequences, respondents completed two six-point self-rating scales, one on the severity of their blushing and one on its effect upon their life. Crozier and Russell

(1992) asked participants to rate how frequently they blushed in comparison with others and also to report on characteristics of their blushing in a further set of six items. The items avoided reference to situations eliciting blushing, as one goal of the research was to examine the links between blushing and embarrassability in a range of situations, and any similarity of situations in blushing and embarrassability items would have biased the findings. A seven-item scale, effectively a composite of items referring to frequency of blushing, lack of control over blushing and perceived intensity of blush, was constructed by summing across the seven items. The Composite Blushing Measure (CBM) had satisfactory internal reliability (alpha = 0.82).

Personality and blushing

Self-consciousness

The discussion at the end of the previous chapter raised the question of the association between blushing and shyness, self-consciousness, embarrassability and social anxiety. Studies have investigated correlations between blushing propensity questionnaires and the Self-Consciousness Scales (SCS; Fenigstein *et al.*, 1975); these are summarised in Table 10.1. The coefficients are small where public and private self-consciousness

Table 10.1 Correlations between blushing tendency and Self-Consciousness Scale

| | | | | Correlations with | | |
Author	Blushing measure	Sample	Sample size	Public SC[a]	Private SC	Social anxiety
Crozier and Russell (1992)	CBM	Unselected	86	0.09	0.01	0.22*
Leary and Meadows (1991)	BPS	Unselected	220	0.29*	0.24*	n.a.
Bögels *et al.* (1996)	BPS	Unselected	195	0.20*	−0.04	0.58*
Edelmann (1990b)	Severity item	Chronic blushers	107	0.25*	0.18*	0.35*

Notes: [a] See text for explanation of acronyms; * Statistically significant, P < 0.05.

are concerned. Bögels *et al.* (1996) reported somewhat higher correlations between the BPS and two measures of self-focused attention (self-focus on arousal, $r = 0.38$; self-focus on interpersonal behaviour, $r = 0.30$) but it is not clear how these measures relate to the SCS scales.

The correlations between measures of a predisposition to blush and public and private self-consciousness are modest at best, and this pattern of results is inconsistent with the thesis that blushing is closely related to self-consciousness. There are several factors that might explain the failure to identify a relationship. Respondents may lack clear grounds for answering questions as they may not have readily available or interpretable cues on which to base their responses. We are not always sure whether or not we are blushing, and it may be difficult to decide whether we blush more than others do, nor can we answer with confidence whether we blush often or rarely.

Findings might be affected by limitations of the measures, although there is evidence of the predictive validity of the SCS (meta-analysis of research undertaken by Mor and Winquist [2002] concluded that the SCS is consistently related to measures of negative affect). Drummond *et al.* (2003) concluded that although research has not identified a correlation between self-report measures of blushing tendency or of blushing in an embarrassing situation and physiological measures of blushing intensity, the BPS is related in systematic ways to changes in blushing during embarrassing tasks, which suggests that it would be premature to attribute the failure to identify relations on any shortcomings in the blushing propensity measure.

As discussed in Chapter 5, there is considerable semantic overlap between embarrassment and blushing and this might influence answers to questions about blushing tendencies. Moreover, blushing has been little discussed and there exists little 'common sense' knowledge about it in contrast with, say, shyness or embarrassment, thus it may be difficult for respondents to draw upon a store of common sense in order to answer generalised questions about it. It is also the case that the reliance on correlational methods, which assess the degree to which there is a linear relationship between two variables, might obscure psychologically important non-linear relationships. A correlation between blushing propensity and self-consciousness, or between self-reports and behavioural or physiological measures, may only hold for a minority of the population, yet it could represent a robust relationship within that minority even if it does not apply beyond it.

One possible confounding factor is skin complexion. Simon and Shields (1996) reported no difference among Black, Hispanic, Asian and

White students at a Californian university in self-reported frequency of blushing, but there were complexion-related differences in the influence of colour and temperature upon the experience of blushing. Even within populations that are regarded as 'white', some people have a fair or translucent complexion that results in their blushing being highly visible and this may tend to make them more self-conscious about it. Differences among European nations in the frequency with which blushing is mentioned as a sign of embarrassment may relate to differences in the relative frequencies of light and dark complexions, since blushing was reported more often in Britain than in Mediterranean countries such as Greece and Spain (Edelmann, 1990a). Crozier and Russell (1992) found that those who believed they blushed more often than others do were significantly more likely to report that they had a fair or very fair complexion than those who thought they blushed less often; specifically, 22 of the 28 participants who described themselves as blushing more often than others and 22 out of the 30 who described themselves as blushing about the same as others reported that they had very fair or fair skin; this contrasts with non-blushers, where 16 out of 27 who claimed they blushed less often than others do reported that they had natural tan or dark skin. Interestingly, there was no association between complexion and self-reported reddening of the skin during non-blushing episodes such as physical exercise, anger, alcohol consumption or a hot environment. Shields *et al.* (1990) obtained similar results: frequent and less frequent blushers and non-blushers did not differ in reported flushing associated with physical exertion, alcohol consumption or drinking warm liquids (though blushers were more likely to report flushing after eating spicy food). Examination of the links between personality and blushing ought to take variation in skin complexion into account. The relations might only hold for those individuals whose blushing is visible or who are more conscious of their blushing and possibly more sensitive to the reactions of other people to it.

It might also be the case that personality influences awareness of blushing rather than blushing propensity. Crozier and Russell (1992) found no significant correlation between private self-consciousness and scores on their blushing measure. However, in an additional analysis the participants were assigned to groups on the basis of their reported frequency of blushing (blushers, intermediate and non-blushers) and their Private SCS scores (median split) and these formed two factors in a factorial analysis of variance where the dependent variable was ratings on the item, 'When I blush, I am immediately aware that I am doing so'.

The main effect of Private SCS was not significant but there was a significant interaction between blushing and self-consciousness: there were no differences among the groups of blushers when self-consciousness was below the median but in the high Private SCS group, blushers and the intermediate group rated themselves as more aware of blushing (respective mean ratings, 4.45 and 4.25) than the non-blushers (mean rating 3.54). Given that the ratings were made on a five-point scale, the mean scores for this combination of blushing and self-consciousness are high and demonstrate a significant effect of personality.

It is also possible that the relation holds only in particular settings rather than at the trait level. Hence I might blush whenever I am in a state of self-consciousness, or in particular kinds of self-consciousness, and never blush when I am not self-conscious. However, this systematic pattern of intra-individual variation would not necessarily be picked up by research that relies solely upon inter-individual trait measures. The fact that someone regards himself as more self-conscious than I do may be irrelevant to the relation between self-consciousness and blushing that holds for each of us.

In contrast with the equivocal results concerning self-consciousness, a consistent finding is the significant correlation between blushing tendency and various measures of social anxiety. Correlations range from 0.22 to 0.58 for the SCS social-anxiety sub-scale, which includes items referring to shyness and embarrassability. Edelmann (1991) concluded that, within a sample of chronic blushers, self-rated blushing was correlated with psychometric scales of trait and state anxiety, social phobia, depression, and 'social avoidance and distress'. Edelmann and Skov (1993) found significant correlations between the BPS and psychometric scales of social avoidance and distress and 'anxiety sensitivity' (fear of, or embarrassment about the experience of anxiety) in a sample of undergraduate students. Bögels *et al.* (1996) reported a substantial correlation coefficient of 0.63 between the BPS and scores on the Social Phobia and Anxiety Inventory (SPAI; Turner *et al.*, 1989). Bögels and Reith (1999) reported significant correlations between the BTS-Q and a Dutch version of the SPAI. Similar findings are reported in study undertaken by Drummond (1997; summarised in Chapter 3). Participants who blushed more frequently (high BPS scores) had significantly higher scores than those with low BPS scores on measures of interaction anxiousness, audience anxiousness and fear of negative evaluation.

Drummond also found that participants obtaining high and low scores on the blushing propensity measure responded differentially to the embarrassing tasks that they encountered. More frequent blushers reported a significantly greater increase in negative affect and in self-consciousness than did less frequent blushers during both tasks and they also reported a greater increase in embarrassment when singing. However, despite these group differences in self-rated reactions, the differences between the two groups in physiological measures of the intensity of the blush were slight, and the effects of the manipulation of α- and β-adrenergic blockade were also similar in the two groups.

Physiological differences

There seems to be little relation between physiological measures of the intensity of blushing and scores obtained on blushing or social anxiety scales or self-reports of embarrassment and blushing (Drummond *et al.*, 2003). This is illustrated by a study undertaken by Mulkens *et al.* (1997). They selected two groups of women participants on the basis of extreme scores on the BPS and exposed them to two episodes: watching an excerpt from a horror film and a video recording of their own performance singing a children's song, both viewings taking place in the presence of others; these episodes were interspersed with other, emotionally 'neutral' episodes. Physiological measures were made of cheek coloration (plethysmograph), facial temperature and skin conductance; participants rated their blushing intensity and fear of blushing, and the intensity of their blushing was rated by observers. There was no main effect of blushing propensity on increase in cheek coloration, facial temperature or skin conductance. Nor was there a significant interaction between blushing propensity and type of episode for any of the physiological measures. (That the failure to find differences is not due to lack of sensitivity of the measures is implied by the significant effect of type of episode, where watching the embarrassing performance elicited more blushing than watching the excerpt from the horror movie.)

On the other hand, there was a significant effect of blushing propensity on *self-report* measures of fear of blushing and blushing intensity, and a significant interaction effect between blushing propensity and type of episode. The disconnection implied by this result between the self-report measure and the physiological measures is confirmed by the low correlation between these measures. Those with a propensity to blush believe that they blush more, but do observers detect this? Observers did not pick up changes in actual blushing as reflected in the physiological measures. There was, however, a correlation between observer and participant ratings of blushing intensity but only for the low blushing propensity group. There was no equivalent correlation among the high BPS group, which might be a 'ceiling effect' due to high self-ratings of blushing intensity in that group.

To allow for the possibility that the embarrassment of watching a videotape of their singing overrode any effects of individual differences, a separate experiment undertaken by Mulkens *et al.* (1999) added a less embarrassing activity – watching a television test card in the presence of others. Participants were selected on the basis of their scores on the fear of blushing sub-scale of the BTS-Q. The findings replicated previous research, in that high scorers expressed greater fear of blushing and more intense blushing, and these differences were greater in the more embarrassing episode. Both groups obtained higher scores on the physiological measures of cheek coloration, facial temperature and skin conductance level in the more embarrassing episode. There was no interaction involving episode and group: there was no difference between the groups in physiological indices in either episode.

Nevertheless, while there exists little evidence of 'main effects' of blushing propensity on physiological measures, significant interaction effects imply that the failure to establish relations between the measures reflects the complexity of relations rather than inadequacy of measures (though this may well contribute to the pattern of findings currently available). Drummond *et al.* (2003) reported such an effect. Twenty-eight female undergraduate students high in blushing propensity and 28 low in blushing propensity undertook an embarrassing task (singing) and a control task (reading aloud) and listened to audiotapes of their performances. The order of tasks was randomised. After the first task half of the participants were informed that they had blushed and half that they had not done so; this feedback was given on a random basis and was independent of whether or not individuals had actually blushed. After each task each participant rated how embarrassed she felt and how intensely she blushed on self-rating scales; before and during the tasks the extent of blushing was assessed by a photoplethysmograph measure of blood flow at the forehead.

Blushing propensity (BPS) influenced *self-rated* embarrassment and intensity of blushing but how it did so depended on the nature of the task and the type of feedback received. Before any feedback on blushing had been given, high BPS participants reported greater embarrassment and blushing in the singing task than did those with low scores on the BPS (there were no differences on the reading task). When feedback was given its effects over-rode any effect of blushing propensity and both groups reported more embarrassment and blushing when they were told that they had blushed and less when told that they had not. When listening to their singing there was little difference between the blushing propensity groups in the blush feedback condition; however, when participants were led to believe they had not blushed, mean ratings were reduced overall but the high BPS group still had higher ratings than the low BPS group – feedback had less effect on high BPS participants' perceptions of their blushing and embarrassment.

The finding of particular interest here concerns the interaction between BPS scores and blushing feedback in their influence on measured blood flow. There were increases in blood flow relative to baseline and these were greatest in the high BPS group who had been given feedback that they had blushed; the increases were smaller in the high BPS group who had been informed that they had not blushed and in the low BPS group whatever feedback they had been given.

In summary, those with high BPS scores differ from their low scoring counterparts in ratings of their blushing and embarrassment but not on physiological measures: the differences are in self-perceptions of blushing. Yet physiological measures are not completely dislocated from blushing propensity, since providing blushing feedback to high BPS scorers is associated with a greater increase in blood flow. Whether the process involved is that feedback increases self-focused attention and thereby heightens sensitivity to proprioceptive cues is not known. There is evidence that being informed that you are blushing increases blood flow (Leary *et al.*, 1992); this study suggests that high BPS scorers are more susceptible to this effect. To look at this another way, being informed that you have blushed changes self-ratings of blushing but this is not associated with physiological changes unless you are high in blushing propensity. Why this change does not happen for everyone is a question that needs to be addressed. The introduction of feedback raises complex issues. If you believe that you are prone to blush, being told that you have done so in an embarrassing situation confirms your beliefs. If you receive feedback that you have not blushed, but you believe that you have, then you can respond in different ways to this contradictory information: you might modify your belief, you might disbelieve what you have been told, or you might experience conflict between your belief and the information (steps were taken to make the feedback convincing). How these differences translate into ratings is not known, given that there are demand characteristics operative and experimenter effects: expectations that participants should adjust their ratings in the light of task demands.

Mulkens *et al.* (1999) presented a model of fear of blushing where self-focused attention and heightened awareness of blushing are mediating factors. The model proposes that interpersonal situations evoke anxiety that produces self-focused attention. This focus makes anxious individuals more sensitive to changes in bodily states, including proprioceptive cues of blushing, which, in turn, amplifies their tendency to self-attention and intensifies their fear of blushing. This leads these individuals to over-estimate the extent of their blushing. Empirical evidence shows that individuals who obtain high scores on measures of fear of blushing and blushing propensity do over-estimate their blushing and embarrassment relative to individuals with low scores: there are reliable effects of blushing propensity upon self-reported blushing. However their estimations do not seem to relate reliably to physiological measures of the facial temperature or colour changes that presumably represent actual facial flushing. Moreover, the evidence does not support the proposed mediating role of self-focused attention, at least at the level of trait measurement, since individual differences in predisposition to blush are not correlated with measures of self-consciousness. It might be that the evidence will appear in the future. We do not have a full test of the model where the effect of self-focused attention as a mediating or moderating factor can be assessed, for example by multiple regression or structural equation modelling techniques. It is important too, as argued above, that research should assess individual differences in a range of settings and focus on intra-individual changes.

Finally, a problem in interpreting findings is that the physiological measures are difference scores rather than absolute scores, comparing the change between baseline and manipulation (Mulkens *et al.*, 1997) or representing change as a percentage of the level prior to exposure to the manipulation (Drummond *et al.*, 2003). This reliance on change scores and on aggregated data results in loss of valuable information. Common sense suggests that individuals either blush or don't blush in a given situation but we lose sight of data on individuals when scores are combined. Is it simplistic to think of blushing as an either/or phenomenon or is it on a continuum, as increases in blood flow or facial temperature would be? Are there cut-off points, for example an increase in blood flow or facial temperature that becomes noticeable when it reaches a threshold and produces awareness of the blush, and do these thresholds vary across individuals?

Shyness and embarrassability

Trait level studies find that individual differences in blushing propensity are associated with measures of social anxiety and with embarrassability. These are correlational data and we do not know the causal relations involved, whether fear of blushing induces anxiety and embarrassment or whether these bring it about. The latter explanation is compatible with Schlenker and Leary's (1982) influential conceptualisation of social anxiety in terms of self-presentation processes and, in particular, with Leary *et al.*'s (1992) interpretation of blushing as the product of undesired social attention, which is likely to be brought about when people have self-presentation concerns. Of course, even if blushing is originally brought about by these concerns, awareness of doing so will create further anxiety and additional concerns about what others will think. Thus, there can be a 'vicious circle' involving social anxiety and blushing.

The relation between blushing propensity and shyness has not been directly investigated, although there is relevant albeit indirect evidence from studies of the relations among shyness, embarrassability and different aspects of social anxiety. Miller (1995) conducted a factor analysis on correlations between the Cheek–Buss Shyness scale (introduced in Chapter 9), measures of embarrassability and a number of other trait measures including fear of negative evaluation, motivation to avoid social exclusion, approval motivation, social self-esteem, anxiousness about social interaction and various components of perceived social skill including skills of self-presentation, verbal expressiveness, expression of emotional states and sensitivity to others' emotions. Shyness was represented, along with low social self-esteem and lack of skill in self-presentation, verbal expressiveness and expression of emotional states, on a factor that Miller interpreted in terms of lack of social self-confidence. Embarrassability was represented on a separate 'social evaluation' factor along with measures of fear of negative evaluation, motivation to avoid exclusion, attentiveness to the appropriateness of one's behaviour, social sensitivity and public self-consciousness. Private self-consciousness appeared on a third 'asocial' factor along with two other measures, skill in regulating non-verbal displays and lack of skill in non-verbal communication of emotional states and attitudes. Shyness seems to be associated with low self-efficacy in the domain of social performance whereas embarrassability is more closely linked to fear of negative evaluation.

This conception of shyness as low social self-efficacy is consistent with other research findings. A multiple regression analysis undertaken in one of my early studies (Crozier, 1981a) compared fear of lacking social competence and fear of negative evaluation as predictors of shyness (measured by Stanford Shyness Survey items). Fear of lacking competence significantly predicted shyness scores but fear of negative evaluation added a negligible amount to the prediction. Similar results are reported by Jackson *et al.* (1997) who found that scores on the Cheek–Buss Shyness scale correlated with self-reports of lack of interpersonal competence and fears of social rejection but not with other measures of self-presentation concerns, namely different forms of perfectionism. Hill (1989) found that shy participants (selected on the basis of scores on Stanford Shyness Survey items) had lower self-efficacy expectancies than less shy participants for performing certain social behaviours (for example, taking the initiative in conversation, expressing disagreement and making eye contact).

Nevertheless, it is surely the case that low self-efficacy is associated with concerns about being negatively evaluated by others. Consistent with this expectation, Miller (1995) found that the interaction anxiousness scale had significant loadings on both principal factors identified in his factor analysis of personality measures, and the study of embarrassment by Sabini *et al.* (2000) found that interaction anxiousness had significant correlations with three forms of embarrassability: making a faux pas, being the centre of attention and anticipating difficult social situations. Lack of confidence in social performance is likely to be associated with anxieties about the impact that less competent behaviour will have on other people and this combination may give rise to a vicious circle, particularly if these concerns result in inhibited or awkward behaviours which produce unsatisfactory social outcomes. Even if these outcomes are not produced, shy individuals' own biased appraisals of their performance may confirm the negative view that they have of their social competence.

These analyses have brought some order to the plethora of existing measures of social anxieties. They suggest distinctions among lack of self-confidence, concerns about social evaluation and (a factor that is less straightforward to label) sensitivity to non-verbal signals and symptoms. What is lacking is knowledge of how blushing propensity relates to these factors. Given the significant correlations obtained between embarrassability and blushing it is likely that the factor representing concerns about social evaluation is related to blushing and this is consistent with our current understanding of the causes and consequences of blushing. We do not yet know whether self-confidence is related to blushing, although it would seem so since there is evidence (reported in Chapter 9) that shy people report that blushing is a symptom of their shyness. As discussed in that chapter it is not clear if there is a direct path from shyness to blushing propensity or whether the path is indirect and is mediated by evaluation concerns. It is possible that when shy individuals are in situations that induce their shyness and reticence, they become embarrassed about not knowing what to do or say and concerned about what others will think of them, and in these circumstances they may be likely to blush. This is consistent with self-reports made by shy people to the effect that self-consciousness is one of the defining features of their shyness. Alternatively, it might be important to distinguish two forms of shyness – fearful shyness and self-conscious shyness – if one is to understand the links between shyness and blushing. Perhaps blushing propensity is more closely associated with self-conscious shyness than it is with the fearful form. Tests of this hypothesis would require more effective measures of the two forms than are currently available.

Embarrassability

Leary and Meadows (1991), Crozier and Russell (1992) and Halberstadt and Green (1993) provided evidence that blushing propensity correlates significantly with embarrassability. Since embarrassability can be deconstructed into distinct scales, it would be informative to discover whether blushing propensity correlates more highly with some scales than with others as this would help us understand why some occasions of embarrassment are more likely than others to be associated with blushing.

Sabini *et al.* (2000) constructed scales to measure tendency to be embarrassed in three classes of situations: making a faux pas, sticky situations and being the centre of attention. These were described in Chapter 6 where it was also explained that correlations between scores on these scales and on a series of personality measures were investigated in order to examine the discriminative validity of the three scales and thereby provide support for the hypothesis that there are indeed three sets of circumstances that trigger embarrassment. A number of the personality measures in their study were either included in Miller's (1995) study or are similar conceptually to measures in it. While Miller identified a single social evaluation factor that had high loadings on embarrassability and interaction anxiousness along with measures relating to fear of negative evaluation, social sensitivity and exclusion avoidance, Sabini *et al.* postulated three 'embarrassability' factors, which had differential relations with the personality measures. Neuroticism and interaction anxiousness correlate with all three factors, showing a strong anxiety component in embarrassability, consistent with previous research that finds correlations between embarrassability and anxiety. Individuals who tend to be embarrassed by making a faux pas have lower and less stable self-esteem, are sensitive to social rejection and are concerned about the appropriateness of their behaviour. Those who report a tendency to be embarrassed when they are at the centre of attention obtain higher scores on audience anxiety, concern for appropriateness of behaviour and wish to avoid conflict. Those who find sticky situations more embarrassing score high on the last two of these and have less stable self-esteem.

The two studies are dissimilar; the Sabini *et al.* study has a smaller sample ($n = 152$) and relies on inspection of differences between correlations. Miller's study has a larger sample ($n = 310$) and draws upon multivariate analyses. Neither sample is large in terms of the numbers of variables that the study includes, and future research is necessary to assess the robustness of these findings. Studies of this nature are influenced by similarity of the wording of items across measures that can inflate the inter-correlations. For example, ten of the 12 items on the audience anxiousness scale refer explicitly to nervousness about speaking in front of an audience or a group and while the items in the centre of attention scale do not refer directly to nervousness they refer to similar situations in that there is an audience present and the individual is the focus of attention.

What neither study provides is direct evidence on whether the propensity to blush correlates differentially with scores on measures of embarrassability and social evaluation concerns. An attempt at this was made by Crozier and Russell (1992) who factor analysed the embarrassability scale and correlated factor scores on the resulting three factors with their measure of blushing propensity. Only scores on the first factor, the items of which refer to being observed, doing something foolish and raising an awkward topic in conversation, correlated significantly with tendency to blush. The other two factors involve items where someone else has produced the predicament and were not correlated with blushing. Nevertheless, further research is needed, given that the blush-making incidents in personal recollections and fictional sources that were identified in Chapter 5 do not offer support for the view that blushing is restricted to a single class of triggers: events that are recalled include instances of being the centre of attention, making faux pas and anticipating sticky situations. Furthermore, it would be more convincing to show these relations at the level of social situations, whether naturally occurring or contrived in the social psychology laboratory, to investigate the 'state' of blushing rather than the trait level and self-reported behavioural tendencies. As noted before, self-consciousness may be associated with blushing in specific situations but this relation may not be evident at the trait level. Intra-individual differences are not equivalent to inter-individual differences, and the covariation between self-consciousness and blushing at the state level need not be the same as the covariation at the trait level. As Asendorpf (1990b, p. 93) has cautioned in a discussion of shyness, 'Very often, interindividual correlations are interpreted as if they would tell us something about the processes that give rise to the emotional state of shyness in everybody. They do not'. Blushing can be substituted for shyness in the quotation.

Gender, blushing and shyness

Before concluding this chapter it is worth commenting on gender and blushing. The research we have reviewed throughout the book has paid little attention to gender. An overview of the literature by Simon and Shields (1996) concluded that there exists little evidence for differences between men and women in the experience of blushing, physiological measures of cheek coloration or facial temperature, or the propensity to blush. In their own questionnaire study where the sample included representatives of different ethnic groups no clear gender differences emerged in estimates of frequency of blushing, the location, latency and duration of the blush, or symptoms accompanying blushing. Shields *et al.* (1990) found differences in vascular symptoms, with females more likely to report cold hands and feet at normal room temperature and symptoms associated with Reynaud's disease (lack of blood flow to fingers, toes, ears and nose that can result in swelling and throbbing), consistent with previous research that identified a greater incidence among women of peripheral circulatory disorders. Despite these differences, the accounts of blushing given by males and females were 'virtually indistinguishable from one another' (ibid., p. 184). Subsequent to Simon and Shields' review, Bögels and Reith (1999) tested for gender differences in scores on the Dutch version of the SPAI and the BTS-Q. These questionnaires were administered to samples of participants, one sample with a diagnosis of social phobia and one without. There were no gender differences on the SPAI or on scales relating to fear of blushing, trembling or sweating.

It is possible that while there are no gender differences in the average scores of men and women the correlations between blushing propensity and other measures might be moderated by gender, implying that blushing has different implications for men and women. This has not been examined, but such findings have been obtained in studies of self-consciousness and shyness. For example, a meta-analysis of measures of self-focused attention found that the correlations between measures of self-focus and negative affect were significantly higher in studies that contained a higher proportion of female participants; this result was interpreted in terms of a greater prevalence of 'rumination' – persistent, recurrent negative thoughts and focus on depressed mood – among women (Mor and Winquist, 2002). Research into shyness has found few consistent 'main effects' of gender but has identified interaction effects suggesting that shyness has different implications and consequences for each gender. Stevenson-Hinde and Shouldice (1993) reported that parents had different attitudes towards their children's shyness, regarding it as less acceptable in boys than in girls as the children grew older. Childhood shyness can have long-term influences that affect men and women differently. In a longitudinal study Caspi *et al.* (1988) found that when shy boys reached adulthood they married, had children and entered a stable occupation at a significantly later age than their non-shy peers but there was no equivalent difference between shy and non-shy girls.

In a longitudinal investigation of early and later appearing shyness (discussed in Chapter 9), Kerr (2000) collected measures at three time periods – early childhood (up to five years), later childhood (6 to 11 years) and adolescence – and followed their sample of children into adulthood, assessing them at ages 25 and 37. The findings represent a complex pattern of significant interactions involving gender and the onset of shyness in predicting adult psychological well-being and social relationships. For example, among males, early appearing shyness was associated with less anxiety and depression and a greater sense of control at age 37 but these relationships were not found among females. On the other hand, shyness that emerges at a later age was not associated with subsequent measures of well-being and this is the case for both males and females. Early appearing shyness was not related to the perceived quality of adult relationships for either gender; shyness that develops in adolescence was associated with poorer quality of relationships and this correlation was stronger among females than among males. In short, the relationship between shyness and gender is a complex one: the relationship between shyness and adult adjustment depends on the age at which shyness emerges and the gender of the child.

Greater complexity is introduced if it is considered that changes in social and economic context will influence the pattern of findings. Kerr (2000) reports that her research in Sweden was unable to replicate the relationship between shyness and occupational status that had been found in Caspi *et al.*'s study, which was carried out in the United States.

There are differences between America and Sweden in the role of women in society and the workplace, and these differences have changed over time. There have been marked increases in the number of women entering and remaining in the full-time workforce over the period covered by these longitudinal studies and this trend could increase the impact of shyness on occupational status among women. There have been differences in expectations about relationships between the sexes and in images of sexually attractive men and women. If men were expected to take the initiative in romantic relationships then shyness would have a greater influence on men than on women. Men may be expected to be confident and assertive, while shyness and modesty could be seen as positive qualities in a woman. Shyness might not be a problem for a physically attractive woman, indeed it might be to her advantage in the eyes of at least some men, but it might be a handicap for a physically attractive man. McDaniel (2001) has explained this representation of women's shyness in terms of their traditional subordinate role in white American middle class society, their deference, submissiveness and 'purity'.

McDaniel explored changes in representations in shyness by means of an analysis of 'self-help', etiquette and dating advice books from the 1950s, the 1970s and contemporary publications. She argues that the view that shyness is an attractive quality for women is a simplification of a more complex picture, one that has changed over time. In the 1950s women were expected to demonstrate some features of shyness, namely a 'mask' of submissiveness and deference, but not to show signs of self-consciousness or fear, which would be noticed as fidgeting, looking frightened and being tongue-tied, since these would deter men. Women had an obligation to help 'boys' – who needed help because of their tendency to be shy with 'girls' – by being friendly and talkative, putting boys at their ease and protecting their delicate egos; she would have to do this without giving the impression that she was taking the initiative or assuming control in the relationship. The display of shyness was therefore strategic, but while it produced desirable outcomes for women – enabling her to catch Mr Right – it reinforced the existing imbalance of power in relationships between the sexes and maintained women in a submissive position.

The 'fifties' now seems a distant era, not least because of changes in women's role in the workplace and the family, the accessibility of reliable contraception and the dissemination of feminist analyses of gender relationships. In the 1970s self-help publications were still encouraging a display of deference and modesty while cautioning against unwanted self-consciousness and feelings of inferiority, but changes were under-way and assertiveness began to be encouraged. It now became acceptable for women to take the initiative in dating and there was less call for a strategic display of shyness; indeed, modesty could appear like unattractive prudery.

Another trend that could be detected in the publications was a concern with self-disclosure and genuineness in relationships and a belief that reticence could impede the development of authenticity and threaten the relationship. However, reticence in men was not interpreted as shyness but as reserve and this had two implications. First, reserve is not an emotional response to social interaction, and hence a sign of weakness, but a suppression of emotion, a sign of strength and control even it is not always helpful. Second, because it is reserve rather than shyness it is not the man's 'fault', requiring change on his part, but it is the responsibility of both man and woman, and calls for effort on her part to overcome it. Indeed, shyness becomes a positive quality in a man and a sign of his gentleness and sensitivity. This can be contrasted with shyness in women, which, McDaniel argues, remains problematic. No longer the strategic element of a role, it has become part of her identity.

McDaniel's analysis provides a context in which to think about findings from empirical studies about gender differences in shyness. The same behaviour – reticence – and the same motivation – fear of negative evaluation – is labelled as either shyness or reserve, depending on who displays it. These trends are detected in advice to women about dating and gender relationships, and McDaniel emphasises that her discussion is restricted to white, middle class American women, since it might not apply to other groups or societies. A cultural analysis of blushing equivalent to McDaniel's study of shyness would be valuable. Is blushing more acceptable in women and have there been changes over time in blushing that parallel changes in shyness? There is evidence from shyness surveys that the frequency with which men and women label themselves as shy and consider their shyness to be problematic seems to be increasing, and there are growing concerns about social phobia, which is discussed in the next chapter.

11
Interventions

> Subject to constant blushing [she] would not be shy before any
> one but for this infirmity and *the constant dread of an attack*.
>
> (Campbell, 1890, p. 152)

Blushing can be a source of shame and anxiety in its own right. Many
people interpret a blush as a sign of weakness or loss of control or as evidence of social incompetence, and this can lead those who believe they
are susceptible to blushing to adopt a range of coping strategies. Of
course, these anxieties are heightened not only by the awareness that
blushing is uncontrollable but also by the awareness that consciousness
of blushing can induce or intensify it. Such concerns lead many to seek
professional help and fear of blushing – erythophobia – is a common
presenting problem to medical practitioners and clinicians. There exist a
number of approaches to helping these individuals, including behaviour
therapies, pharmacological treatments and, more recently, surgical
procedures. These are briefly reviewed in this chapter.

Social phobia

The construct

Erythrophobia is a social fear, since blushing occurs in company and the
anxieties that people express about it are mostly concerned with what
others will think of them because of their visible reddening. A useful
starting point for this chapter is to introduce the construct of social phobia, since clinical approaches to social fears are now subsumed under
this heading. It was not always so, and the concept of social phobia is
relatively recent. Its origins, together with changes in diagnostic criteria,
can be traced through successive editions of the American Psychiatric

Association's *Diagnostic and Statistical Manual of Mental Disorders* (DSM). The Manual adopts a categorical system for psychological disorders: if the individual meets a specified set of criteria he or she belongs to this particular category and does not do so if the criteria are not met. The categories are distinct, defined by their own sets of criteria. Where the boundaries between categories are drawn is important, not least because of their implications for treatment. For example, it might be the consensus among clinicians that one disorder is more effectively treated by pharmacological means whereas another is better treated through psychotherapeutic interventions. The conditions and criteria have been modified in successive editions in the light of clinical practice, published empirical evidence and advocacy by interest groups within psychiatry (Healy, 2002).

The first two editions of the DSM included social fears as instances of an undifferentiated category of phobia. However, research into fear suggested a distinct category of social fear. Factor analysis of items in fear surveys regularly identified one or more social fears factors, where items refer to speaking before a group, meeting someone for the first time, being with a member of the opposite sex, making faux pas, being misunderstood and looking foolish. Influenced by such findings social phobia appeared in its own right in the third edition of the Manual (DSM-III) published in 1980. This edition indicated three classes of phobias: agoraphobia, simple phobia, and social phobia. Social phobia was characterised as a persistent fear of situations where the individual believes he or she might be subject to scrutiny by others and anticipates that his or her behaviour will lead to embarrassment or humiliation. This causes the individual a significant amount of distress because he or she recognises that the fear is excessive. This encouraged research to distinguish social phobia from other phobias and anxieties in terms of symptoms. Amies *et al.* (1983) distinguished between social phobia and agoraphobia in terms of the eliciting circumstances and the most common symptoms reported in each (further details are presented later). Reich *et al.* (1988) reported that patterns of autonomic symptoms distinguished among social phobia, panic disorder and generalised anxiety disorder. Sweating and flushing (the questionnaire did not separate the two) was reported by 71 per cent of the group meeting DSM-III criteria for social phobia and this frequency was higher than for the other two disorders.

The same edition of the Manual introduced the diagnostic category of avoidant personality disorder, characterised by social inhibition, sensitivity to criticism and social withdrawal, and there has been debate since then about the distinctions between this category and social phobia and about the relation of each with shyness. The revision of the third edition (DSM-III-R) that appeared in 1987 made a further distinction, between generalised and non-generalised social phobias. Empirical evidence had not supported the claim made in DSM-III that an individual tends to have fears about a single type of situation, for example public speaking, dating or eating in public. Some individuals report anxieties about a wide range of social situations and subsequent editions adjusted the criteria to refer to one or more social situations. The distinction can be blurred in research studies; for example fear of blushing can be characterised as a non-generalised fear (Scholing and Emmelkamp, 1999) even though a variety of different situations might elicit this fear. Further changes to the criteria have included the addition of references to the individual's fear that embarrassment or humiliation can ensue from showing signs of anxiety as well as from his or her behaviour, to the tendency to avoid situations or to respond to them with intense anxiety, and to the significant interference with the individual's everyday life caused by this anxiety or distress.

Widiger (2005) reviews definitions of the sub-types of social phobia and avoidant personality disorder that appeared in successive editions of the DSM and draws attention to continuing uncertainties about their relations and where the boundaries between them are to be located. This creates problems, since if an individual meets criteria for both disorders it raises the question of which category should have priority. This is an important issue as it has implications for choice of treatment. For example, a personality disorder is regarded as pervasive and ingrained, more resistant to change than social fears and hence less amenable than social phobia to pharmacological treatment. It might imply the need for a lengthy process of psychotherapy. Uncertainties cast doubt upon the validity of the categorical scheme, particularly if, as seems to be the case, co-occurrence of different disorders within the same individual is common (Krueger and Piasecki, 2002). It is not clear whether this is due to insensitivity of the categorical scheme, imprecision of assessment, a high frequency of the separate disorders in the population and hence a greater likelihood of co-occurrence within any individual, or due to the actual co-morbidity of different disorders reflecting the nature of the underlying conditions.

The criteria for social phobia and avoidant personality disorder share common elements. For example, both refer to concerns with embarrassment: in the case of avoidant personality disorder, one criterion refers to the avoidance of risks and novel situations because of the fear of being embarrassed (DSM-IV; American Psychiatric Association, 1994). This similarity in criteria might contribute to evidence that individuals who meet the criteria for avoidant personality disorder are highly likely to meet the criteria for generalised social phobia (Widiger, 2005).

Relation to shyness

Both categories seem to be related to extreme shyness, since this involves anxiety about social interactions – shy individuals report a range of anxiety symptoms – and a tendency to avoid or escape from them. The reticence characteristic of shyness might be due to anxiety about saying the wrong thing or creating a negative impression, or it might be a form of withdrawal in situations where the person is unwilling to leave. It is difficult to identify the causal relations between anxiety and withdrawal. Anxiety might be primary, the reason for socially withdrawn behaviour, or secondary, a consequence of shy individuals feeling unable to cope with social demands that their personality and the history of learning experiences that this trait has influenced leave them ill-equipped to face. This question of causal factors will also concern us in our discussion of treatments for fear of blushing: is blushing the source of the person's anxiety, which would be eradicated if the blushing were controlled, or is it just one symptom of social anxiety, which would be reduced but not eliminated if the symptom could be managed?

One plausible hypothesis about the relation between shyness and the social anxiety disorders is that they can be located at different points along a single dimension of intensity of anxiety. McNeil (2001) proposed that shyness spans a range from normal to pathological levels and at the extreme anxiety pole of the dimension are found, in order, non-generalised anxiety, generalised anxiety and, finally, avoidant personality disorder. According to this position, the differences between shyness and the anxiety disorders are quantitative rather than qualitative and avoidant personality disorder is a more extreme form of anxiety than social phobia. Empirical studies (for example, one reported by Chavira *et al.*, 2002) that compare scores of the same individuals on self-report questionnaire measures of shyness with diagnoses of social phobia based on a structured interview show that individuals in the sample who obtain high scores on the shyness measure are much more likely to receive a diagnosis of a social anxiety disorder than are those who obtain less extreme shyness scores. On the other hand, substantial numbers of extremely shy participants do not receive a diagnosis of a disorder and there is considerable overlap in the shyness scores of those individuals who do receive a diagnosis and those who do not.

Nonetheless, it has to be borne in mind that shyness and the anxiety disorders are different kinds of constructs. Shyness has its origins in ordinary language whereas social phobia and avoidant personality disorder are first and foremost technical constructs. These will be redefined in the light of fresh empirical evidence, as has already taken place where the DSM is concerned, but the concept of shyness does not change in this way. Thus empirical findings on the relation between shyness and social phobia are necessarily relative to the diagnostic criteria that are current at any given time. Nevertheless, the current descriptions of shyness and avoidant personality disorder seem similar; indeed, as Rettew (2000, p. 292) points out, 'there are surprisingly few examples of a personality disorder and a personality trait sharing the same degree of similarity (at least on the surface) as that found between APD and shyness'.

Prevalence

Epidemiological evidence suggests that the incidence of social phobia in the general population is high. For example, Kessler *et al.* (1994) reported the findings of the National Comorbidity Study (NCS), a survey of a large (over 8000 respondents) national sample in the United States. Trained staff conducted structured interviews; the diagnostic interview included questions based on social phobia items reflecting DSM-III-R criteria. The study reported a 12-month prevalence of 7.9 per cent and a lifetime prevalence of 13.3 per cent. These data imply that social phobia is the third most common psychiatric disorder in the United States, after major depression (17% lifetime prevalence) and alcohol dependence (14%). There is evidence that social phobia is a 'chronic and unremittent disorder' (De Wit *et al.*, 1999, p. 569). Their survey of retrospective accounts of social phobia obtained from a sample of more than 1000 respondents found that the median duration of the disorder was reported to be 25 years and in some cases was as long as 45 years. Epidemiological surveys of the general population consistently show that prevalence rates are higher among women (Furmark *et al.*, 1999), which contrasts with research that has found no consistent gender differences in shyness, but explanations for this trend have not been investigated. There is also evidence on the prevalence of social phobia in childhood and adolescence. A review by Rapee and Sweeney (2005) concluded that the prevalence in the general child population is between 1 and 2 per cent; it also reported that social anxiety is a common form of anxiety, in that the fears of one in every five children attending an anxiety clinic are social fears.

Widiger (2005) suggests that the prevalence of avoidant personality disorder in the general population is less than 2 per cent although it is a commonly diagnosed personality disorder, constituting a substantial proportion (20–25%) of patients in clinical settings. A survey undertaken in Sweden by Tillfors *et al.* (2001) involved the administration of a postal questionnaire to a random sample of the population; the questionnaire items were based on DSM-IV criteria for social phobia and avoidant personality disorder (APD). They reported that 16 per cent of their sample met the criterion they had set for social phobia of respondents reporting a high level of distress to at least one item in the questionnaire referring to a potentially phobic situation. When the frequency of individuals meeting the criteria for each disorder was examined it was found that the ratio of social phobia without APD to APD without social phobia was 7:1, replicating findings that APD is much less frequent than social phobia in the general population.

Controversies

The concept of social phobia and its treatment by medical means, particularly by pharmacological treatments, is controversial. It is argued that everyday worries about social interaction are being 'medicalized', that the definition of social phobia has been over-extended to encompass 'normal' shyness and that the incidence of these anxieties has been deliberately exaggerated, all to serve the interests of the medical profession and pharmaceutical companies – the 'medico-pharmaceutical complex'. In an article with the unambiguous title, 'Selling Shyness: How doctors and drug companies create the "social phobia" epidemic', Cottle (1999) argued that researchers exaggerate the incidence of social phobia in the general population when they conclude that it is a disorder which will affect one in eight Americans at some time in their life. She claims that the magnitude of the incidence of the disorder is a consequence of adjustments that have been made to its definition, so that it is no longer restricted to a small number of individuals with extreme anxieties but, as the title of her article suggests, it also encompasses shyness. As a consequence of this, she continues, the large numbers of the population who are shy when they meet new people, date someone, attend social gatherings and so on, come to believe that they have a medical problem and that treatment will help them cope with their 'disability'.

In the context of claims about over-estimation of the prevalence of social phobia it is noteworthy that the NCS data and Swedish data cited above are not based on detailed psychiatric diagnoses but on self-reports about social difficulties. Furmark *et al.* (1999) point out that the prevalence rates from surveys based on DSM-III-R or DSM-IV criteria are higher than those obtained with surveys based on DSM-III criteria, which could reflect an increase over time in prevalence or alternatively the changes to the criteria that were made between the editions of the Manual. The cut-off point for the social phobia 'diagnosis' is arbitrary and in the Swedish study varied from 20 per cent of the sample to 2 per cent depending on the number of items on the postal questionnaire that respondents endorsed.

Cottle's argument begs the question why social anxieties are 'every-day' or why there are substantial individual differences in self-reported anxiety such that some individuals claim to be much less confident and more fearful in social encounters than others do. Nevertheless, her argument raises important issues about influences on the identification of psychological problems and the distinction between 'normal' anxiety and 'mental disorder' and about the boundaries between them.

Much of the research in psychiatry and, in particular, pharmaceutical treatments for psychological problems has been undertaken in the United States, where health care is largely in the private sector and individuals are dependent upon insurance companies to pay for their medical treatment. It is in the interest of all stakeholders in this system to extend the definition of illness and to obtain evidence that these are treatable. In addition, it is in the interest of several stakeholders that pharmaceutical treatments can be applied to the illness. If individuals are anxious about their blushing they will have to bear the costs of seeking professional advice and treatment unless they can persuade their insurers that their problem meets professionally recognised psychiatric criteria. Health care organisations – clinics or hospitals – have to make a profit, for the benefit of their shareholders and investors and to invest in their provision in order to keep up with the pace of developments in health care. Insurers have to expand their business, to increase their market share and profits and to compete against rival companies. Pharmaceutical companies are major international corporations, constantly seeking new markets for their products. Since the development of new products is very expensive, not least because of the investment in pharmacological research and the extensive clinical trials that are a legal requirement, the expansion of markets for existing drugs is an attractive source of new revenue. The recent application of established antidepressant drugs, the selective serotonin reuptake inhibitors (SSRIs), to the treatment of social phobia is an example of this expansion and, it has been argued, an example of the extension of the concept of social phobia, since the expansion coincides with greater awareness of the prevalence and seriousness of social phobia. Healy (2002) argues that rates of diagnosis of a disorder increase in conjunction with pharmacological developments for the treatment of the disorder. He cites evidence that the rate of diagnosis of depression has increased dramatically over the past 50 years: the prevalence of depressive disorder has risen from 0.5 per cent of the population to 10 per cent and some studies suggest that 25 per cent of the population shows at least some symptoms of depression. The increase in the prevalence of social phobia is not a new phenomenon and, as was the case in depression, coincides with the availability, marketing and increased use of pharmaceutical treatments for the disorder. The more effectively a drug is marketed, the more patients become aware of it so that it can be difficult for medical practitioners to resist requests for its prescription.

This is a complex issue. On the one hand, depression and social fears can be debilitating and many who suffer these problems report the benefits of pharmaceutical intervention. On the other hand, there are anxieties about the widespread application of medication to depression and social phobia. The application of SSRIs to the treatment of social phobia has raised concerns that this reflects the needs of pharmaceutical companies to enlarge the markets for their products rather than any breakthrough in understanding the role of serotonin in social phobia.

Little is understood about the processes whereby SSRIs alleviate symptoms or about the involvement of serotonin in social phobia, and this reflects how little is known about neurotransmitters. At present there is no accepted theoretical rationale for applying an anti-depressant to the treatment of social phobia. It does not follow that the treatment efficacy of SSRIs necessarily shows that serotonin deficits play a causal role in social phobia. To take alcohol use as an analogy (setting aside for the sake of the argument the well-documented problems associated with alcohol dependence) many individuals report taking alcohol to help them cope with their shyness. A hypothetical study might have such individuals rate the effectiveness of alcohol in alleviating their symptoms and alleviation could conceivably be greater than that found in a sample that did not take alcohol. It would be misleading to infer on the basis of such (hypothetical) findings that alcohol deficits are causes of shyness and social fears and that alcohol treatment works by making good this deficit.

It is possible that SSRIs are not specifically related to social phobia but have non-specific effects on the nervous system, for example in enhancing positive mood in people whether or not they meet criteria for social phobia or depression. Suggestive evidence for this is provided by a study undertaken by Knutson *et al.* (1998), where a sample of 51 psychologically healthy volunteers who met no criteria for psychological disorders were administered either an SSRI (fluoxetine) or a placebo for four weeks in a double-blind experiment. Relative to the control group, the group who had received the SSRI had lower scores on a measure of neuroticism (trait anxiety) and increased scores on observational measures of social affiliation while working with a partner on a problem-solving task.

Concerns about the extensive marketing of medication for depression and social phobia are heightened by claims that pharmaceutical companies have withheld data from clinical trials that allegedly showed harmful side effects of SSRIs in the treatment of depression. Healy (2002, pp. 373–4) claimed that clinical trials where outcome measures involve patient-provided rating scales that are not specific to the 'disease' have not shown the efficacy of the treatment and these findings have not been published. It is argued that the side effects of this treatment have not been fully investigated or reported. In Britain, the drug regulatory agency, the Medicines and Healthcare Products Regulatory Authority, banned the prescription of SSRIs for patients under the age of 18 years in the light of growing concerns about evidence of increased risk of suicides among young people taking the medication.[1] In their submission to the Health Select Committee the Royal College of Psychiatrists expressed concerns about the completeness of evidence from clinical trials provided by pharmaceutical companies.[2] Medawar *et al.* (2002) provide a content analysis of email messages received by the BBC following a *Panorama* television programme on problems associated with the SSRI paroxetine. Messages were polarised between praise and criticism. They included accounts of accomplished suicide given by family members, attempted suicide and a range of problems reported with its use including withdrawal symptoms. Medawar *et al.* concluded that regulators assigned less weight to users' concerns about withdrawal symptoms than to clinical trials of drug effectiveness. We shall see later in this chapter that there also exist Internet websites dedicated to discussion of the problems of patients who have undergone surgery for their blushing, problems that are not emphasised in the clinical literature.

Media coverage of the increase in pharmacological interventions for social phobia has been less than helpful in describing these treatments as 'cures' or 'pills' for 'shyness'. The distinction between social phobia and shyness is not a straightforward matter and remains an issue for research. The Stanford Shyness Survey established that very large numbers, up to 50 per cent of the American population, consider themselves to be shy, and a significant proportion of these regard their shyness as problematic. The prevalence of self-attributed shyness seems to be increasing (Carducci and Zimbardo, 1997). Are all these people in need of treatment? Social anxieties are ubiquitous. Undergraduate students anticipating making a short presentation to their peers are almost all highly anxious about doing so; many experienced and effective lecturers also report anxiety symptoms before taking a class. When do these anxieties become problematic?

Blushing and social phobia

Where does blushing fit into this picture? There is no doubt that many people find their blushing troublesome and seek professional help. Internet web sites carry testimonials that present vivid depictions of the miseries caused by blushing, variously described in terms of 'suffering a condition', a 'disability' or being a 'weird person', and provide many examples of attempts to overcome the problem with one or another form of treatment. Gerlach and Ultes (2003) investigated the numbers of people presenting with problems of blushing and sweating who would meet diagnostic criteria for social phobia. Potential participants were approached via the Internet web sites of newsgroups whose members are interested in endoscopic thoracic sympathectomy; respondents completed a questionnaire based on DSM criteria for social phobia. Completed questionnaires were received from 372 individuals, 46 per cent reporting chronic blushing, 32 per cent chronic sweating and 23 per cent reporting both blushing and sweating. Sixty per cent of those with blushing concerns met the criteria for social phobia as did 54 per cent of those reporting both blushing and sweating and 27 per cent of those reporting sweating. The prevalence of social phobia in members of this sample who have problems with blushing, on its own or accompanied by sweating, is higher than that in the general population and implies high levels of anxiety among people with these concerns. Of course, important as these findings are, they are based on a self-selected sample and we cannot know how representative they are of the population of those with anxieties about blushing. Further research would be valuable.

We can approach the issue from the opposite direction and ask how many patients with social phobia report problems with blushing. The references to fear of embarrassment in DSM criteria for social phobia and avoidant personality disorder and its inclusion as a symptom of anxiety in DSM-IV suggest that blushing or subjectively excessive blushing might be a frequent presenting problem in patients with social anxiety disorders, and evidence suggests that this is the case. Amies *et al.* (1983) compared the symptoms reported by a sample of 144 patients whose principal complaints were symptoms of either social phobia or agoraphobia. There were no differences between the two groups in a number of anxiety symptoms, for example, palpitations, dry mouth, sweating, trembling, and feeling hot or cold, but there was a significant difference in blushing, which was reported by 51 per cent of those with social phobia compared to 21 per cent of those with agoraphobia. Fahlén (1997) administered a questionnaire to a sample of 63 volunteers who responded to a newspaper advertisement inviting participation in a drug trial for social phobia and who met DSM-III-R criteria for disorder about their symptoms (potential participants who also showed evidence of depressive symptoms or alcohol abuse were not included). The intensity of symptoms was rated on a scale from 0 to 4, where 4 referred to extremely intense. Blushing had the highest mean rating of all the symptoms (2.59) and 25 of the 63 participants assigned blushing the highest rating of 4. Participants classified as having generalised social phobia had higher scores on blushing (mean 2.8) than those with the non-generalised type (1.2). These studies confirm that blushing is a principal concern of individuals meeting criteria for social phobia; they do not show whether they regard it as a symptom of their problems or their primary cause.

In short, significant numbers of people who are anxious about their blushing meet diagnostic criteria for social phobia and a substantial proportion of individuals diagnosed with social phobia report blushing as a symptom. This implies that treatments for social phobia will also be applied to individuals with anxieties about blushing, and this is the case. The principal psychological interventions for social phobia, behavioural *in vivo* exposure methods and cognitive behaviour therapy have been applied to blushing. An exception is social skills training, which is based on the assumption that anxieties are caused or intensified because individuals lack the skills to contribute effectively to social interactions or because their lack of poise produces social predicaments or increases the perceived likelihood of being negatively evaluated by others, and these create anxiety; this does not seem to have been applied to blushing problems. Another common intervention for social phobia is pharmacological treatment, although there seem to be few systematic evaluations of this in the research literature on blushing. As discussed later, there has been a recent development of a surgical intervention for the treatment of worries about blushing: endoscopic thoracic sympathectomy. The next section provides brief accounts of these treatments and studies reporting clinical evaluations of them. Illustrative examples will be provided rather than an attempt at an exhaustive review; in any case the literature on blushing interventions, as opposed to treatments for social phobia, comprises scattered studies rather than an extensive body of research.

Interventions for erythrophobia

Behaviour therapies

The behaviourist paradigm has provided the basis for a number of approaches to treating social phobia and it has also been applied to blushing. One approach is based on the principle that an avoidance response can be conditioned so that anxiety about possible social situations is maintained even though the individual does not come into contact with the feared situation. It is argued that if circumstances could be arranged so that the individual encounters these situations without the feared embarrassment or humiliation ensuing, then the situations would lose their aversive qualities. One method relies simply on repeated *in vivo* exposure to the feared situation. It is essential that the individual confronts the situations rather than adopt his or her habitual response of avoiding or escaping from them. Therapists have developed supplementary techniques to prevent the individual being overwhelmed by anxiety in initial encounters, for example, teaching the patient relaxation responses that can counteract anxiety symptoms or introducing him or her to the feared class of situations in a gradual yet systematic way (a procedure called systematic desensitisation). Rather than face a feared situation in its entirety, the elements of the situation are analysed and presented to the individual in a progressive step by step procedure. An application of *in vivo* exposure to blushing is presented later, where an intervention conducted by Scholing and Emmelkamp (1993) involved exposure and cognitive behaviour therapy.

In paradoxical intention the client is encouraged to deliberately attempt to produce a blush. The assumption underlying this approach is that the onset of a blush will be viewed positively, as an achievement, rather than in a negative light. Mersch *et al.* (1992) review a number of individual case studies that have applied this technique with some success to a range of psychological problems as well as to social phobia. Their own research involved three patients meeting DSM-III-R criteria for social phobia; their primary complaints were, respectively, blushing in social situations, hand trembling in the presence of others and sweating in social situations. The patient with blushing concerns, a 39-year-old man, could trace the onset of his concern to an occasion when he was 22 years old: he was teased in front of a group of 20 people and an onlooker remarked that he was blushing. He had tried drug treatments, taking the beta-blocker, propranolol and the benzodiazepine, lorazepam, as well as resorting to alcohol. The intervention, which comprised 14 weekly one-hour sessions, involved cognitive behaviour therapy as well as paradoxical intention; the patient was advised that he had to be able to produce a blush in threatening social situations so that it would be available to be countered by practising the cognitive therapeutic techniques designed to alter anxious self-statements and reduce anxiety about blushing. If he could produce a blush, for example by imagining himself in a threatening situation, this would provide evidence that he could control his symptom and he would be less anxious about it. If he did not do so the therapist would convey disappointment, which would motivate the patient to practise inducing the symptom. When the blush has been induced, this is rewarding; also, the therapist stresses the benefits of using the self-statements to reduce the anxiety and decrease the blushing.

The goals of the intervention were to change cognitions and lessen anxiety rather than reduce the frequency of blushing. Nevertheless, the frequency of blushing in social situations, as reported in a diary kept by the patient, decreased over the course of the therapy and at follow-up 18 months later (although anxiety had increased at follow-up). Another application of this technique reported by Timms (1980), a case study with a 25-year-old woman, identified improvements in frequency of blushing and anxiety feelings at 22-month follow-up.

The technique is of interest because it focuses on the controllability of the blush; the inability to prevent or terminate a blush is commonly reported and it is a source of anxiety for many, whether or not they seek medical help. The evidence for its effectiveness is slight, particularly if it is considered that in Mersch *et al.*'s study the technique was combined with cognitive therapy, which might have contributed to any success obtained.

Cognitive behaviour therapy

Rather than regarding anxiety as a conditioned habit, the cognitive approach assumes it to be the result of aberrations in thinking. Therapy is targeted at challenging the bias and distortion represented in the assumptions and beliefs of anxious people. There are several models and techniques that are based upon empirical research into the cognitions that maintain anxiety. For example, Clark (2005) presents the concept of safety behaviours and illustrates this with the case of blushing. A 'safety behaviour' is said to be displayed when an individual takes some action that he or she believes will ward off the feared event. When this event eventually fails to happen this welcome outcome is attributed to the action that was taken, the 'safety behaviour', and consequently this will be repeated whenever a threat is thought to be imminent. For example, an individual with erythrophobia might take steps to try to reduce body temperature, apply cosmetics to mask the blush or find an alternative explanation for the redness of the face (hurrying, the hot weather and so on). These behaviours can be irrational or 'superstitious', in the sense that they may be unconnected to the outcome or can even make the feared outcome more likely to occur (by making people antic-ipate blushing and bringing it on, heightening self-awareness of their blush and thereby intensifying it, or when they act in an odd way and attract the unwanted attention of others). Helping patients identify and challenge safety behaviours plays a key role in the cognitive approach to the treatment of social phobia.

Scholing and Emmelkamp (1993) reported an intervention for prob-lems of blushing, sweating and trembling that involved combinations of *in vivo* exposure and cognitive behaviour therapy. The emphasis in the former treatment was on homework assignments (practice of behaviour that takes place outside the therapy sessions but is reported and dis-cussed in subsequent sessions), where the individual attempts to tackle situations that elicit blushing without relying on avoidance strategies. Patients nominated the situations that they feared and avoided and for each patient a hierarchy of exercises, from least to most difficult, was constructed. Sample problems are maintaining eye contact while talking about difficult topics and wearing a blouse with an open neck. Avoidance behaviours included wearing sunglasses or cosmetics as well as fleeing from the situation. The cognitive approach focused on irra-tional thinking about blushing, encouraging the client to analyse such self-statements as 'blushing means that you hide something'. A third form of treatment integrated exposure with the cognitive approach. It was explained to participants that the treatment goal was not to reduce the frequency of blushing but to diminish their fear of it. Thirty-five patients began the treatment, all with a primary diagnosis of social pho-bia (DSM-III-R) but whose principal anxieties were symptoms of blushing, sweating and trembling in social situations. Thirty patients (14 men) completed the treatment, which involved two blocks of eight one-hour sessions over a period of 12 weeks; ten patients were assigned to one of three treatment programmes: a block of exposure followed by a block of cognitive therapy; cognitive therapy followed by exposure; two blocks integrating exposure and cognitive therapy.

Pre-treatment and post-treatment measurements were recorded, with follow-up measures at three months and, for 26 participants, at 18 months (Scholing and Emmelkamp, 1996). There were four self-report composite measures: responses to feared situations, avoidance of social situations, social phobic cognitions and somatic symptoms. There were pre-post changes on all measures and gains were maintained at 18 months. There were no differences in the relative effectiveness of the three treatments. Nevertheless, results are not presented separately for the three symptoms so it is not possible to evaluate the success of treatments for those whose primary concern is with blushing or to separate reductions in anxiety about blushing from anxieties about sweating and trembling. Pre-treatment measures of participants' depression and personality disorder contributed little to the prediction of treatment outcome (Scholing and Emmelkamp, 1999).

Another cognitive approach aims to reduce the self-focused attention that is associated with social anxiety and impaired social performance and with blushing (Bögels *et al.*, 2002). Bögels *et al.* (1997) developed a form of treatment that encourages clients to focus attention on the task; this treatment is based on the assumption that task focused attention would be incompatible with focus on the self. The treatment has three phases: increasing participants' awareness of the role of attention in their erythrophobia; practice in focusing outwards in non-threatening situations (e.g., concentrating on the content of a news broadcast); practice of external focus in a typical blush-eliciting situation (these situations are presented in an order from least to most likely to produce a blush, as identified by the client). Practical exercises involve role-play during sessions and homework practice in actual social situations. In an initial evaluation of the approach data were presented for two individual case studies. There were six to eight weekly task focus practice sessions and this intervention led to changes in beliefs about blushing which were maintained at follow-up one year later. Participants also undertook cognitive therapy targeting beliefs about blushing. Changes in beliefs about blushing were not dependent on the cognitive therapy or indeed any discussion of the participant's beliefs and seemed to derive from the task focus intervention.

Mulkens *et al.* (2001) extended the study of the task concentration approach in a number of respects: they tested a larger sample of participants, compared this treatment with *in vivo* exposure, and assessed its effects on physiological measures as well as fear of blushing. Participants comprised a sample of 31 patients (7 men) with primary diagnosis of social phobia (DSM-IV) who reported fear of blushing as their prominent concern. Treatments were brief and consisted of six weekly one-hour sessions although participants were urged to undertake extensive practice outside the sessions. In terms of self-report measures relevant to fear of blushing (blushing items from the Blushing, Sweating and

Trembling Questionnaire), the approach was more effective than a waiting list control group; however it was not shown to be more effective than the *in vivo* exposure condition at follow-up six weeks or one year later. As the researchers point out, the two forms of treatment share common features including practice at encountering feared situations outside the therapy sessions. The length of treatment is also short in the context of the fears expressed by the participants, fears sufficient to seek professional help.

Notably, the treatment did not have an effect on physiological measures of blushing; there was no difference between treatment groups and control group on measures of changes in cheek coloration and temperature taken during conversation with two others (confederates of the researchers) and while giving a three-minute speech to an audience of four; nor did scores on these measures decrease from pre-test to post-test. Clearly it is difficult to know how representative these measurement occasions are of the situations that make the participants blush away from these treatment sessions and which have led them to seek treatment. Nor is there a control group of non-anxious participants to enable any effects of a potentially limited range of blushing scores to be gauged. Nevertheless, the pattern of these findings again implies the separation of actual blushing from erythrophobia.

Psychopharmacological treatment

Four principal approaches to pharmaceutical intervention for social phobia can be identified. Two approaches involve classes of drugs that have been primarily used in the treatment of depression, the MAOIs (Mono-Amine Oxidase Inhibitors) and the SSRIs. Another two classes of drugs have been widely applied to the treatment of anxiety disorders, Beta-Blockers and the Benzodiazepines.

Monoamine oxidase is a chemical found in the pre-synaptic cell. It is involved in breaking down neurotransmitters like dopamine, norepinephrine and serotonin. As the name MAOI suggests, the drug is designed to inhibit the activity of monoamine oxidase, and hence increase the levels of these transmitters at post-synaptic receptors. High levels of monoamines have been shown to be associated with positive mood and low levels with negative mood. However, there is potential for serious side effects particularly if the drug is taken with some forms of food, and patients taking the drugs have to be vigilant about their diet. Because MAOIs inhibit the breakdown of monoamines, their levels can become dangerously high. In an attempt to reduce some of these risks, a class of reversible MAOIs (RIMAs) has been developed.

Phenelzine (Nadil is a brand name for this drug) is an MAOI and Brofaromine a RIMA that have been investigated in clinical trials as treatments for social phobia.

Serotonin (5-hydroxytryptamine or 5-HT) is a neurotransmitter active in a small number of neurons in the brainstem that have a large number of target neurons. These neurons have a coordinating and modulator role and variations in the level of serotonin have multiple effects, associated with quality of mood, self-esteem, sexual activity, and levels of arousal and vigilance. Serotonin is involved in levels of behavioural arousal and vigilance. It seems to have an overall inhibitory effect and low levels result in the individual being less able to cope with stress, less effective in social behaviour and more prone to impulsive aggression. Low circulating serotonin has been linked with increased irritability, mood change, increased impulsivity and risk-taking, and a tendency among depressed patients to suicidal behaviour. SSRIs work by preventing the reuptake of serotonin into the synapse and this allows it to remain longer in the synapse, the increased concentration facilitating transmission of subsequent messages across the synapse. Several SSRIs have been investigated, including fluoxetine (Prozac is a brand name for fluoxetine), fluvoxamine (Luvox), paroxetine (Paxil and Seroxat) and sertraline (Zoloft).

Beta-adrenergic receptor antagonists (beta-blockers) inhibit activity of epinephrine and norepinephrine and reduce heart rate, sweating and subjective components of anxiety. They are extensively used to reduce stimulation of the heart, for example among patients suffering from angina. Little research has evaluated their effectiveness for social phobia although it has been more widely applied to performance anxiety, for example among sports performers and professional musicians. Hartley *et al.* (1983) found that propranolol reduced anxiety among two groups of non-clinical volunteer participants selected on the basis of obtaining either high or low scores on a measure of trait anxiety when they had to give a short speech while being filmed with a video camera. Although propranolol led to lower anxiety scores in both the high and low anxiety groups, its effect seemed to be greater on overt signs of anxiety while giving the speech as judged by observers of the participants' behaviour. Propranolol has also been studied as a treatment for social phobia although a review by Hood and Nutt (2005) concluded that the results from randomised control trials have proved disappointing. Beta-blockers have been used to block symptoms like blushing and sweating although there does not seem to be systematic research investigating their effectiveness in doing so.

Benzodiazepines affect arousal by enhancing the activity of GABA (gamma-amino-butyric-acid), which is the major neurotransmitter at inhibitory synapses of the central nervous system. High levels of GABA are associated with drowsiness and low levels with anxiety and excitement. Major reservations about using benzodiazepines concern their effects on memory and concentration, particularly if their use is sustained over the long term, and the potential for abuse of tranquillisers like diazepam (Valium). Diazepam, clonazepam (Klonopin) and chlordiazepoxide (Librium) are commonly prescribed sedatives used frequently in the treatment of anxiety. Hood and Nutt (2005) concluded that there were promising results for clonazepam in the treatment of social phobia.

There is now a considerable amount of literature on pharmacological interventions for social phobia (Hood and Nutt, 2005). In some evaluation studies these are combined with *in vivo* exposure or cognitive-behavioural treatments. Van Ameringen *et al.* (1999) claim that the SSRIs are emerging as the 'gold standard' for pharmacological treatment. Stein *et al.* (2004) undertook a systematic review of 36 studies that included a randomised control trial of pharmacological interventions (26 of these were short term, lasting 14 weeks or less) and concluded that SSRIs were more effective than RIMAs and that both were more effective than placebo conditions. Nevertheless, additional research is necessary to establish their long-term effectiveness and to understand why they are effective and why they work for some patients and not for others. Studies have been directed at generalised social phobia and outcome measures are frequently self-reports of anxiety. There seems to be little research that deals specifically with pharmacological treatments for blushing. Drott *et al.* (2002) report that 28 per cent of patients in their surgical intervention research (described later) had undergone unsuccessful pharmacological treatment: 37 per cent had used beta-blockers, 25 per cent anxiolytic (anti-anxiety) drugs, 25 per cent SSRIs and 13 per cent other anti-depressant drugs.

Surgery

There are reports in the medical literature of large-scale studies that have treated problems of blushing by a surgical procedure, endoscopic thoracic sympathectomy, that uses endoscopic techniques to divide the sympathetic chain where it overlies the second and third rib in the upper thoracic region. Pioneers in this procedure are Rex, Drott, Claes and their colleagues based at Borås Hospital in Sweden who have reported high rates of success in a series of articles in surgery and dermatology journals. The technique was originally applied to problems of excessive perspiration (hyperhidrosis) but it also resulted in patients reporting reductions in facial blushing and, according to Drott and his colleagues, when this finding was reported in the media many individuals who were seeking help for problems of excessive blushing approached them. I focus here on results for blushing rather than hyperhidrosis. Drott *et al.* (1998, p. 640) define blushing as 'facial redness likely to be mediated by the sympathetic nervous system, i.e. rapidly developing blushing in conjunction with emotional stress such as getting attention from other people'. Potential patients reported blushing as 'disabling' and were screened for other causes of facial redness, for example dermatological conditions such as rosacea. Rex *et al.* (1998) reported data from post-surgery questionnaires sent to 1152 patients, all those who had been operated upon in the period between April 1989 and April 1996; 244 of these, average age 34 years (range 15 to 67 years) had problems with facial blushing. For patients with blushing problems the average time of follow-up was 8 months after surgery, with a range from 2 months to 29 months. The questionnaires asked patients to report the degree of their blushing and sweating on visual analogue scales, with scale scores ranging from 0 (no sweating or blushing) to 10 (most exaggerated sweating or blushing). Ninety-six per cent of these patients reported a reduced rate in blushing following surgery; 85 per cent expressed total satisfaction with the operation, 13 per cent were dissatisfied to some extent, and 2 per cent regretted having had the operation.

Drott *et al.* (1998) provide more details of the impact of the surgery on patients' lives. The most common problems prior to treatment had been fear of being the centre of attention, difficulties in keeping a clear mind, and avoiding social situations such as meetings at work, parties and meeting an acquaintance on the street. Over 80 per cent of respondents reported improvement in these problems after surgery, and 72 per cent reported they were less likely to take medication for their blushing. Drott *et al.* (2002) report findings from a sample of 833 patients (63% of 1314 who had been operated upon in two hospitals in Sweden and who had been sent questionnaires). A decrease in blushing was reported by 94 per cent of the sample; the rates of improvement in the effects of blushing on everyday social life were similar to those reported in the earlier study; 35 per cent reported greater self-confidence and feeling calmer. In summary, prior to the operation patients reported high levels of fear of blushing, describing its marked effects on their social and professional life. They reported widespread use of medication and alcohol for coping with blushing. The operation produced few complications or serious side effects and there were substantial and statistically significant reductions in reported fear of blushing.

Research is not restricted to the Borås team. In a study undertaken in Finland, Telaranta (1998) described similar positive results among a sample of 42 patients who met diagnostic criteria for social phobia (51 patients had undergone surgery but only 43 had bilateral sympathectomy, one of whom did not complete the post-procedure questionnaire). All the patients reported unsuccessful experience of psychotherapy or pharmacological treatment prior to selection for the operation. Self-ratings of severity of blushing on a visual analogue scale ranging from 0 to 5 changed significantly from a pre-operative mean of 3.7 to a mean of 1.3 at four-month follow-up.

Despite the success rates claimed for surgical intervention, the procedure raises several important issues. First, the change is permanent and (so far) irreversible. Second, there are risks with any surgery performed under general anaesthetic. Third, it is possible that the gains in patient satisfaction reported a matter of months after surgery might not be maintained in the longer term, particularly if patients experience enduring side effects from the procedure (Drummond, 2000) or if it does not lead to greater self-confidence and less shyness and anxiety in social situations. If anxious individuals attribute their difficulties to the blush, a physiological reaction that is beyond their control and is in a sense 'external' to them, a matter of 'bad luck', they will be less likely to attribute their difficulties to their personality: they can externalise them. If social anxieties and lack of confidence persist even when blushing has been eradicated it might be particularly distressing to discover that social difficulties cannot be explained in this way.

The side effects can be unpleasant and potentially as embarrassing as the original blushing. Although the operation reduces sweating in the face, armpit and palms of the hands, it does lead to significant compensatory increases in sweating elsewhere in the body, including the trunk, groin and 'gustatory' sweating associated with tastes and smells (Drott *et al.*, 1998). Other possible side effects are Horner's syndrome, drooping of the eyelid, constriction of the pupil and dryness of the affected side of the face, and Raynaud's phenomenon. Drott *et al.* (2002) report few problems in their study and dissatisfaction rates were low. Across the sample as a whole, there were reported reductions in facial blushing, hand sweating and facial sweating but increases in sweating of the trunk, groin and feet. These increases were reported at two-months post-surgery follow-up; subsequently it remained at the same level for

67 per cent of the sample, increased for 18 per cent and decreased for 15 per cent. At the end of the follow-up period, 47 per cent of the sample reported at least 'moderately severe' sweating and 6 per cent reported severe sweating or regret at having undergone the treatment.

Drummond (2004) argues that the published studies do not give enough attention to the dissatisfaction expressed by a minority of patients. He draws attention to submissions to several Internet forums and support groups[3] which show that a substantial number of former patients have experienced distress and that there have been attempts to reverse the procedure to mitigate the adverse side effects. Drummond argues that the treatment should not be offered to patients whose primary problem is blushing. The Internet web site of The Center for Hyperhidrosis also does not recommend surgery for patients whose primary problem is blushing and recommends instead pharmacological treatment. It claims that the frequency of compensatory sweating is greater among patients who have undergone surgery because of facial blushing or sweating than it is among patients who are operated upon for sweating hands, and argues that this is because the sympathectomy is carried out at the T2 level (the T2 ganglion is located between the second and third ribs). Other Internet sites acknowledge the benefits of the procedure in reducing shyness and anxiety, but some former patients claim that they were not made fully aware that the side effects would be so severe and distressing. These effects are not described simply as compensatory sweating and dry hands, but are said to include a range of psychological effects, including problems with attention span, over-sensitivity to sounds and light, and fatigue. Several correspondents report that these side effects have impaired their life, reducing their capacity for physical exercise and leading on occasion to loss of employment. The My Diary section of the Patients Against Sympathetic Surgery site provides a detailed account of one patient's experiences.

One reply to these criticisms made by advocates of endoscopic thoracic sympathectomy has been that the patients they have treated seek surgery not just because they are distressed but also because many of them have experienced little success with alternative forms of interventions including psychotherapy and pharmacological treatment (Drott *et al.*, 2002; 2004). If alternative non-invasive techniques proved to be effective, the argument goes, there would be no need for surgery.

A further limitation of this approach is that the technique is directed at the physiological reaction, not the patient's interpretation of the reaction. Drott *et al.* (1998, p. 643) make this point explicitly: 'our philosophy of treatment is to abolish an important somatic expression of social phobia and pathological "shyness". Generally the patient's social and professional life was improved by the operation'. They point out that many of the patients were distressed by their blushing and had received little benefit from cognitive behaviour therapy directed at their interpretation of it. The assumption underlying the approach is that blushing is the cause of the problem, that it is inherently an unpleasant experience and that patients blush more frequently or intensely than they find acceptable. However, if the problem is fear of blushing rather than blushing per se, then this is the problem that should be addressed, and efforts should be made to improve psychological interventions intended to reduce anxiety. Indeed, as Drummond (2000) points out, individuals who are anxious about blushing may not in fact blush any more than others but may exaggerate the frequency and social significance of their reaction. This is plausible given the substantial evidence that socially anxious individuals are prone to misperception of their behaviour and its significance.

As reported in Chapter 3, there is empirical support for a disassociation between physiological indices of blushing and self-reports of experience. Mulkens *et al.* (1999) found that individuals who scored highly on self-report measures of fear of blushing reported more intense blushing in an embarrassing situation than did those with less fear but the two groups did not differ on physiological measures (these measures were responsive to the degree of social stress, thus findings are not due to insensitivity of measurement). Mulkens and her colleagues argue that fear of blushing can give rise to a 'vicious circle' where it produces heightened self-awareness that magnifies awareness of blushing, which intensifies fear of blushing and so on.

Gerlach *et al.* (2001) compared two groups of people who met diagnostic criteria for social phobia but who differed in whether they reported excessive blushing as their primary problem. The researchers took photoplethysmograph measures from three groups, one meeting DSM-IV criteria for social phobia with a primary diagnosis of blushing, a second meeting these criteria without blushing as the primary problem and a third, control group while participants watched, along with two other people, a videotape of themselves singing a children's song, held a five-minute conversation with a member of the opposite sex and delivered a five-minute speech to an audience of two others. On self-report questionnaire measures of characteristic behaviour the social phobia group reported more anxiety in social situations, greater propensity to blushing, greater embarrassability, less confidence as a speaker and more somatic complaints than members of the control group. The group with blushing as the primary problem scored more highly than the other social phobia group on the Leary and Meadows Blushing Propensity Scale and reported that they were more likely to blush when dating, attending meetings, talking to authority figures and maintaining a conversation. Therefore self-descriptions of tendencies to blush across a range of situations discriminated between the two social phobia groups and also distinguished the two groups from the control group.

However, these differences were not so definite in the experiment. Here the two groups with social phobia reported greater anxiety and embarrassment than the control group, in baseline measures and in anticipating and performing the tasks, and more blushing during all three tasks, but there was no difference between the two social phobia groups on these measures, including the measure of self-reported blushing. Moreover, there were no differences among the groups on the physiological measure of increase in blushing; only at the beginning of the videotape task did social phobics blush more than the control group. Observers did report that members of the social phobia groups blushed more and seemed more anxious during the talk; again there was no difference between the two social phobia groups. Although this study involves participants who are highly anxious in social situations, report blushing to be a problem and encounter tasks that have been shown to be embarrassing in previous research, there is little relation between self-reported anxiety and embarrassment, physiological measures of blushing and observers' perceptions of blushing. To be sure, these conclusions are based on laboratory studies rather than situations that are representative of patient's recurrent social situations, and levels of embarrassment and anxiety are elevated for both social phobia groups (mean ratings of embarrassment watching themselves on video were 7.2 and 7.7 on a ten-point scale). On the other hand, the participants with social phobia did not seem to observers of their behaviour to be blushing very much in the video task – the two groups each had a mean of 0.9 compared to 0.4 for the control group on a five-point scale ranging from 0 (not at all blushing) to 4 (extremely) – and it is possible that observers' judgments were influenced by other visible signs of anxiety. Thus even in this artificial setting the self-descriptions of blushing provided by anxious individuals exaggerate their blushing relative to observers of their behaviour and do not correspond to physiological measures.

Patients who have undergone surgery do report less blushing after the operation and this remains the case up to two years later. How has this affected their social anxiety and self-confidence? If blushing was the basis of the patients' problems then these should be greatly reduced. On the other hand, if it were but one symptom of underlying anxieties or difficulties with social situations then we might expect these to continue. It is possible that such individuals do exaggerate their blushing or its visibility even if objectively there is little basis for this belief. We have scant evidence on this issue apart from responses to the brief self-rating scales administered to participants in the Borås research, which do seem to show that difficulties are reduced for the majority of respondents. An article in the *New Yorker* magazine by Gawande (2001) reported the experience of one individual who had undergone endoscopic transthoracic sympathectomy. A successful television news presenter, her blushing while broadcasting undermined her confidence and affected her performance, despite initial attempts to mask it by wearing sweaters with a high collar and applying a green foundation cosmetic and then by undergoing pharmacological treatment and psychotherapy. The article describes her experience at Drott's clinic in Gothenburg; after surgery she had not blushed for two years and problems with compensatory sweating had diminished and no longer bothered her. She found that social situations that had made her blush no longer did so and she no longer felt self-conscious and was able to resume her job as a news presenter. Gawande posed the questions: Has her personality changed? Can a simple bodily change radically alter the person you are? What had happened to the person who was self-conscious and easily embarrassed? There were problems. She began to feel embarrassed and ashamed about having had the operation, of feeling that she was an 'impostor'. She felt self-conscious reading the news and resigned her position. However, she gradually overcame these feelings, set up a support group for people who had undergone the treatment and eventually took up work in radio broadcasting. She has no regrets about the surgery and accepts that her self-consciousness has been reduced but not eradicated. This case study suggests the value of looking in detail at the experiences of individuals who have undergone surgery and lost the capacity to blush. It is likely that there are many different stories.

It is essential for ethical reasons that people who are extremely anxious about their blushing have a clear picture of the possible costs as well as the benefits of an irreversible procedure that is not without risks. Clinical research should examine in detail cases of dissatisfaction and these case studies should be published in medical journals as well as reports of success rates. Potential patients and their advisors would then be in a better position to make an informed decision. Readers of this chapter should bear in mind that surgical intervention for problems of blushing and sweating is controversial. It is important too that research is undertaken to evaluate psychological approaches to therapy which draw upon findings that anxieties about blushing do not necessarily reflect an objective propensity to blush. More research should focus on subjectively excessive blushing as a problem in its own right rather than as a symptom of social phobia and should give due weight to individuals' anxieties about their blushing.

People's willingness to undergo surgery is understandable in the context of the enormous increase in cosmetic surgery in recent years. This is not the prerogative of the 'celebrities' who attract media coverage. The American Society for Aesthetic Plastic Surgery (2005) reported that in 2004 the number of surgical and non-surgical procedures increased by 44 per cent to nearly 11.9 million. Compared to the previous year surgical procedures increased by 17 per cent to over two million and non-surgical procedures by 51 per cent. Women had 90 per cent of cosmetic procedures. The most common surgical procedures were liposuction, breast augmentation, eyelid surgery, rhinoplasty (nose re-shaping), and breast reduction. The most common non-surgical procedure was botox injection, with nearly three million procedures carried out. Increases are occurring in Britain too. BUPA (2003) reported that 75,000 cosmetic operations were carried out per year. It also reports that a minority of operations has been unsuccessful, and £7 million had been paid in the past 13 years in compensation for 264 settled claims for surgery mistakes. Cosmetic approaches connect with treatment for blushing in the case of botox injections. The injection of botulinum toxin blocks the release of acetylcholine and has the effect of temporarily smoothing frown lines between the eyebrows, producing a more youthful appearance. Blushing support websites report the use of botox injections in temporarily paralysing the nerves that serve sweat glands, although there seem little data evaluating the effectiveness of this treatment or any side effects.

Finally, an emphasis on the adverse experience of blushing ignores evidence that blushing has positive features and these should be taken into account when evaluating interventions aimed at reducing its frequency. In the spirit of this conception of the blush one correspondent to the ETS and Reversals Discussion Forum describes people who *don't* blush as 'blush impaired'. As we have seen elsewhere in this volume, blushing can be a useful social signal and 'unblushing' can be synonymous with shamelessness, immodesty or insensitivity to the feelings of others. Admittedly this aspect would not be salient for those individuals for whom blushing is a misery and a disability, but it should not be lost sight of.

12
Conclusions

There is a dearth of systematic empirical evidence on the blush. Apart from observations he made during his voyage on the Beagle, Darwin based his claim for its universality on correspondence with colleagues across the world rather than on observations in those countries or direct contact with their inhabitants. There has been little subsequent research and what exists largely comprises students' understandings of hypothetical events, their responses to questionnaires on perceived tendency to blush and recollections of blushing episodes. An exception is the large-scale study of colour and emotion words undertaken by Casimir and Schnegg, which concluded that the blush is recognised across the world but that its implications vary relative to its visibility. A small number of studies have measured changes in blood flow in reaction to contrived embarrassing incidents. The paucity contrasts with the enormous body of research on facial expressions produced by the musculature and studies of visceral processes in 'basic' emotions such as fear.

Given the ubiquity of the blush its neglect is surprising. Admittedly, change in facial colour is much more difficult to isolate for study than is expression produced by the musculature[1] and it is only recently that physiological measurement techniques have contributed to research. The blush is associated with the self-conscious emotions, which have also been neglected relative to the basic emotions, yet even systematic studies of, say, the display of embarrassment 'write off' the blush. Scepticism about the blush as expression is reinforced by its invisibility in people with darker complexion: what is the function of an expression that cannot be seen? This disregards the point that the blusher knows that he or she is blushing (or at least believes so, since we do not always know we are doing so and some people seem to over-estimate their blushing), thus it could make an important contribution to social life even when it could not readily be seen.

There is longstanding debate in emotion research whether displays should be construed primarily in intra-individual terms, as the involuntary expression of an inner state, or in social relational terms, as conveying information about 'the state of a relationship' (Ekman, 1997, p. 33). Measurement studies focus on the blush as expression, in attempting to induce certain mental states in participants. Questionnaire studies enquire about respondents' experience of inner states but also investigate the circumstances surrounding the blush and thereby contribute to understanding its social context. The social relational approach is currently best represented by studies of the communicative function of the blush, for example those conducted by de Jong and his colleagues, inspired by Castelfranchi and Poggi's seminal analysis of the blush as non-verbal discourse. This research is not simply exploratory but manipulates descriptions of hypothetical events in order to test hypotheses about social influences on the blush, specifically about the circumstances in which the blusher appears in either a positive or negative light.

The study reported in Chapter 5 explored the notion that many instances of the blush are triggered by exposure of the self. This notion emphasises the inherently social nature of the blush, since something of the self is revealed to others. This is evident too in the episodes recalled by participants or portrayed in literary texts, with their many references to an audience, to blushers' concerns with what others think about them or discover about them, to the blush's impact on the self and others, and so on. These themes are illustrated in another literary excerpt, from George Eliot's *Daniel Deronda* (2003, p. 420):

> But she had no sooner said this than some consciousness arrested her, and involuntarily she turned her eyes towards Deronda ... He, like others, happened to be looking at her, and their eyes met – to her intense vexation, for it seemed to her that by looking at him she had betrayed the reference of her thoughts, and she felt herself blushing: she exaggerated the impression that even Sir Hugo as well as Deronda would have of her bad taste in referring to the possession of anything at the abbey: as for Deronda, she had probably made him despise her. Her annoyance at what she imagined to be the obviousness of her confusion robbed her of her usual facility in carrying it off by playful speech, and turning up her face to look at the roof, she wheeled away in that attitude. If any had noticed her blush as significant, they had certainly not interpreted it by the secret windings and recesses of her feeling. A blush is no language: only a dubious flag-signal which may mean either of two contradictories.

Awareness of being looked at makes 'Gwendolyn' conscious of the implication of her tasteless remark and how the others could interpret this – she assumes that it has created a poor impression. Yet the reference in the text to the blush follows immediately her sense that she has exposed ('betrayed') her private thoughts and precedes her belief that she will be deprecated. The description recalls Campbell's point that the blusher 'fancies others ... can read his consciousness' (Chapter 2). The blush is accompanied by mental confusion, which impacts on her ability to manage the situation as she might otherwise have done, and she is annoyed that the blush will render her confusion visible. At this point the author comments on the scene and reminds the reader that a blush is ambiguous and does not have a single meaning; in particular, those present will not necessarily receive the message that the blusher fears she has imparted. The blush might reveal her confusion and might betray her thoughts; but, Eliot suggests, even were it noticed it might not do so. Notably, Eliot refers to Gwendolyn's vexation, annoyance and fluster but makes no mention of her embarrassment, which a contemporary writer or reader might think of, or of any other emotional state. Eliot's account is in terms of social relations rather than emotional states. This scene is imagined, reflecting one nineteenth-century writer's understanding of the nature of the blush, and does not comprise data in the conventional sense. Yet the account strikes a chord with readers and the single excerpt alludes to several themes that have emerged in the analysis of blushing circumstances. It indicates issues that are worthy of systematic research.

Emotional states

Contemporary Western 'common sense' and academic psychology associate the blush with embarrassment. Psychophysiological studies create embarrassing circumstances in the attempt to induce changes in facial blood flow and skin temperature as well as in self-reported and observed embarrassment. Embarrassment is frequently mentioned in recollections of occasions in Chapter 5's questionnaire study, yet the study replicated the finding in the literature that the blush does not invariably accompany embarrassment; this raises questions whether the blush occurs in some embarrassing situations but not in others, and what it is that distinguishes these situations. Researchers who have isolated a characteristic display of embarrassment have not been convinced that the blush is integral to the display but this conclusion seems premature, as there exists scarcely any relevant evidence.

It has been puzzling that the blush is so visible when it occurs when we least wish to draw attention to ourselves. However, the puzzle assumes that embarrassment and related feelings are inherently negative. Tomkins has drawn attention to the ambivalence inherent in shame affect, which, he argues, occurs in conjunction with experiences of interest and joy, and the ashamed person is reluctant to forgo the positive aspects of the eliciting circumstances. This reluctance prevents either 'wholehearted' self-condemnation or outright hostility towards the other and remaining in the situation intensifies self-consciousness (Tomkins, 1963, p. 139):

> In the response of shame ... the self remains somewhat committed to the investment of positive affect in the person, or activity, or circumstances, or that part of the self which has created an impediment to communication. This continuing unwillingness to renounce what has been or might again be of value exposes the face of the self to pitiless scrutiny by the self or by others.

Shyness researchers have referred to this ambivalence, construing it as approach-avoidance conflict, evident in the child's 'hovering' at the fringes of the group. Tomkins provides the example of the child who hides her face at the sight of the stranger but who cannot resist peeking through her fingers. The ambivalence inherent in blush-making situations, together with the unexpectedness with which the circumstances often arise, surely contains clues to the causes of the blush.

Research has paid little attention to the blush in shame or shyness but without good reason, since historical sources and cross-cultural studies find that it is frequently associated with these states. Part III of this volume considered the blush in the context of embarrassment, shyness, shame and the relations between shame and guilt and anger. Each chapter concluded that convincing accounts of the association of the blush with these states are ignored in psychological theory, which on occasion denies that we do blush other than with embarrassment. Again, little relevant evidence is available. Nevertheless psychologists' reservations do raise issues for research. It is feasible that we only blush with shame or shyness when the circumstances that produce these states also create social predicaments that are embarrassing, that is to say, embarrassment mediates the relation between shame or shyness and the blush, as outlined in Chapter 9. No doubt this is sometimes the case, but is embarrassment essential for the blush? In Castelfranchi and Poggi's example, the Good Samaritan who gives assistance to an injured woman feels 'shame before the other' if he realises how an observer could interpret his action. Will he blush (with shame) when he realises this or does it need the presence of the other (embarrassment at being thus observed by a passer-by)? Is awareness of how he might be seen (the mental representation of the other) sufficient to produce a predicament, or does this over-extend the notions of a predicament and embarrassment?

Research into embarrassment has produced a number of classification schemes for eliciting circumstances, representing approaches that are exploratory or, in Sabini *et al.*'s study, are derived from theory (fluster and esteem accounts). Unfortunately no parallel studies have been undertaken for blushing. Chapter 5 drew upon two sources of circumstances: students' recollections and content analysis of fictional episodes. A classification scheme was devised that comprised categories of being the object of attention, characteristics of the other(s) present and the topic of conversation. There were differences between the sources. Fiction was more likely to portray episodes where two people are present, where something the other person says gives rise to a blush and where what is said concerns sexual relationships or a sexual theme more generally. Being the centre of attention was more characteristic of questionnaire responses, there was frequent mention of receiving positive attention and many references to embarrassment (which were absent in the fiction). Despite these differences the results are consistent with explanations of the blush in terms of unwanted attention and exposure. The first explanation has a theoretical basis (Schlenker and Leary's self-presentation model of social anxiety) but it faces the problem that many blush-making situations do not seem to involve public attention. A problem with the second explanation is that it is essentially descriptive and there is no theoretical basis for relating exposure to the blush. However, it seems useful to relate exposure to shame, where this is conceptualised in the broader sense of shame affect, in Tomkins's term, or in the sense used by H. B. Lewis and Scheff, which regards shame, shyness and embarrassment as variants of the same emotion, which has self-consciousness at its core. The application in Chapter 9 of the Gottschalk–Gleser shame-anxiety content analysis scheme to the recollections of blushing episodes provided a 'good fit', and nearly all the episodes could readily be classified. The episodes are replete with references to being exposed, embarrassed, ridiculed and criticised. The episodes portrayed in *North and South* are explicitly described by Gaskell (1994) as experiences of shame and include several references to blushing, not only when the precipitating circumstances are encountered but also when they are recalled or whenever other people make even oblique references to them.

One question that needs to be addressed is the relation between shame in this broader sense and what might be termed subjective exposure of the self. Is subjective exposure inevitably shaming or can there be exposure without shame? Are they separate reasons to blush or does subjective exposure mediate the influence of shame?

Although there are arguments that embarrassment is a distinct emotion (Miller, 1996) it is difficult to sustain this in the absence of clear boundaries between shame and embarrassment, cultural and historical variation in where these boundaries are set, and the tendency for native speakers in English to use the words interchangeably. If embarrassment is not a distinct emotion then its privileged status as the cause of the blush is undermined. Indeed, blushing might be regarded as an emotion in its own right as it meets many of the criteria proposed by Ekman (1992) for a distinct emotion and as applied to embarrassment by Keltner and Buswell (1997): it is distinctive in terms of antecedents (exposure), appraisal and experience (perceived lack of control; self-consciousness; cognitive disturbances) and physiological responses. It has a distinctive facial expression if this is taken to include colouring as well as changes brought about by the facial musculature. The blush is associated with embarrassment but how these are related is not known. It is assumed that embarrassment produces the blush rather than the reverse, and this is consistent with evidence about the timing of the embarrassment display. However, only one study (Shearn *et al.*, 1990) has addressed the timing of the blush, and this warrants further research. Admittedly these assertions and speculations are in need of empirical scrutiny.

Why a blush?

The blush is associated with those emotional states labelled social or self-conscious emotions; there are several explanations why these states are evoked in the class of situations that trigger them, but little is known about why they result in localised reddening. This was a puzzle to Darwin and remains so, even though recent years have seen the first systematic studies of relations among eliciting circumstances, measures of physiological changes, and blushing that is self-reported and visible to observers. The visible blush is produced by vasodilation of blood vessels that is regulated by sympathetic nervous system activity. It draws upon increased activity of the system that is involved in thermoregulation, and the controlling brain structures – the hypothalamus and amygdala – are also involved in heightened emotional arousal. It is not known why

this specific pattern of activity is triggered by stimuli that herald exposure and embarrassment. Is it a by-product of increased body temperature associated with heightened arousal or perhaps its sudden inhibition?
Perhaps the blush represents a 'false alarm' of the arousal system, an
immediate reaction of the threat-response system that is aborted. Frijda
(1986) made a similar point, speculating that the blush could be a
response of sudden inhibition of a tendency to act. Arousal might be
interrupted because the individual becomes aware that the threat is not
a physical one and requires no offensive or defensive action: attention is
focused on the self. Is it the operation of an 'early warning' so that the
blush is to shame what the startle is to fear?

One counter-argument is that the affected region is delimited and the
blush does not include the widespread reddening that accompanies
other kinds of arousal, for example, physical exercise. Another is that
the blush occurs too rapidly to be a by-product in this way and the
increase in skin temperature that follows the visible blush is produced
by the increased blood flow rather than elicited by it. Drummond's
research implies a specific sympathetically innervated mechanism for
vasodilation in the face region (as opposed to release of vasoconstrictor
tone), which implies a dedicated blush process. Nevertheless, his finding
that there was a substantial increase in measured facial blood flow
despite pharmacological blockade of β-adrenoceptors suggests that
other vasodilator mechanisms are involved. This research tends to adopt
a common sense notion of the blush without a close analysis of the phenomenon, and understanding the blush may benefit from setting aside
this notion. Further analysis of the different kinds of reddening, for
example the distinction between the classic and the creeping blush,
would be valuable. In addition, only a limited number of stimulus settings have been examined, typically those that make the participant
look foolish, whereas this represents only a sub-set of situations that are
embarrassing or make us blush and research into reports of eliciting circumstances suggests that the manipulation of circumstances related to
exposure of private information about the self might be a productive
avenue to explore.

'A dubious flag-signal'

One reason for the existence of a dedicated process might be that the
blush can serve as an effective signal. While much research has taken a
Darwinian line that the blush is essentially expressive and has no inherent communicative function, a separate strand of research has explored
the position advocated by Darwin's near contemporary, Burgess, and has

shown that the blush does alter the impression that the blusher makes on others. Castelfranchi and Poggi regard the blush as a signal of apology or appeasement and de Jong has produced supportive empirical evidence. We do not yet know whether the blush does this directly or whether we have learnt that it is a sign of the blusher's discomfort and this leads us to search for the source of his or her unease. In certain circumstances the indication of discomfort can be read as an apology and reassures observers about the actor's motives and his or her adherence to their values. It is important to keep in mind Eliot's warning that the blush provides ambiguous information and can be read in various 'contradictory' ways. It proved misleading to Jane Austen's Emma, to the boy in Frayn's *The Spies*, who blushes when accused even though he does not know what it is he is accused of, and the participant in the questionnaire study who reported that her blush following a question to the group about who was responsible for an incident led to her being blamed for it.

Mention of Burgess reminds us of the moral nature of the blush. The fears of the embarrassed and ashamed person are moral ones, concerned with the values and obligations of social life. The person who colours demonstrates his or her adherence to shared values; society would be the poorer without the blush. No doubt this interpretation is not uppermost in the thoughts of the individual suffering with erythrophobia but it is surely important that the blush should not be framed entirely in negative terms or as an 'illness'.

Blushing that ensues from praise has proved problematic for explanations of terms of emotional states, particularly explanations that focus on deficiencies of the self. This issue has been addressed in various ways in the literature: embarrassment is induced by over-praise rather than praise; the blusher is conscious of a discrepancy between the self-image and the public image; the attention creates a social predicament producing fluster and uncertainty how to behave. In short, there is an excess of explanations that are consistent with at least some of the evidence without, as yet, grounds for choosing among them. Praise and a combination of praise, exposure and embarrassment were common reasons to blush in the questionnaire study described in Chapter 5. These responses and literary examples all mention the audience for the positive attention and this is an important clue for understanding the blush in these circumstances. We should think in terms of the situation where the blush occurs and the implication of the blush for the situation rather than in terms of expression. A situation where someone is praised can be difficult to manage, and not only for the recipient.

We can distinguish two senses of a signal, a message that is intended or signs that are 'given off'. The blush makes a signal in the second sense and, like the shiver in fear or the involuntary smile of pleasure or amusement, it can convey information about ourselves that we would not wish others to have. Castelfranchi and Poggi emphasise that the blush serves useful functions for the individual, for his or her relation to the group and for the group itself, and this is a more important consideration than whether or not it is voluntary or intentional. Indeed, as Frank has also argued, its involuntary nature enhances its effectiveness since it guarantees its sincerity.

Exposure

Eliot's quotation refers to the betrayal of inner thoughts, and the notion of exposure has heuristic value in connecting the blush to the emotional states of shame and embarrassment while emphasising its social nature and the other-perspective taken by the blusher. Exposure includes 'nakedness of the self': the revelation of thoughts, feelings, motives and 'secrets'. Allusions to these are sufficient to trigger a blush and even bringing them to mind can do so. The notion is arguably more useful than the related explanations in terms of self-attention and unwanted social attention because the attention can ensue from rather than precede the blush. Leary proposed that the blush is due to unwanted social attention and several studies provide evidence consistent with this hypothesis. However, as discussed above, there are situations where the blush occurs without, or in advance of public attention, notably when an innocently mentioned topic evokes a blush because it reminds the blusher of something or it threatens to uncover information the blusher prefers to keep hidden. We are all social actors in Goffman's sense and the control of information about ourselves is essential for an effective performance.

In Chapter 4 it was suggested that blushing episodes have a common pattern: If an event X brings into the open (or threatens to do so) a topic Y, and Y is something that the individual wishes to keep hidden or believes ought to be kept hidden, X will elicit a blush. We blush when thrust 'into the spotlight' or when private aspects of the self are exposed or are threatened with revelation. This relates to the notion of the boundary between self and other. It is tempting to regard the blush as the reaction to a breach of, or a threat to this boundary and even to speculate that it is somehow appropriate that the face should be the locus of the boundary. More prosaically, it can be postulated that a blush is the expression of a specific form of arousal directly evoked by a breach of the self-other boundary. A breach is commonly threatened by being the object of attention, actual or anticipated, and hence the association between the blush and the self-conscious emotions: secrets, hiding, shrinking and fear of exposure are all markers of shame.

The deficient self

The classic blush is often triggered by a specific, typically unexpected event that poses a threat to the blusher's self-image; some individuals are more disposed than others to blush, for example because of their self-consciousness, shyness or sensitivity to the opinions of others. Questionnaire measures of individual differences in propensity to blush have been constructed but the predicted correlations between these measures and trait self-consciousness have not been found. This would seem to cast doubt on the theorised association between self-consciousness and the blush. However, findings from inter-individual studies cannot necessarily be generalised to intra-individual studies, and the question-naire and correlational approaches are crude. In particular, they min-imise the influence of mediating factors such as skin complexion with its implications for the visibility of the blush.

Blushing propensity has more substantial correlations with social anx-iety and embarrassability and there is evidence that many individuals are extremely anxious about their blushing. Chapter 11 reviewed approaches to therapeutic intervention, including psychological thera-pies, pharmacological treatments and endoscopic thoracic sympatheco-tomy. Behavioural methods, particularly cognitive therapies, have been widely applied to the treatment of social phobia but there have been only a few published applications to blushing problems. These have reported successful outcomes but the studies are small in scale and more comprehensive clinical research is needed. Pharmacological treatments have also been widely applied to social phobia but there are scarcely any published accounts of interventions for erythrophobia. Medications that have proved successful in the treatment of depression are now widely applied to social phobia but this is controversial, as discussed in Chapter 11. There is no theoretical rationale for their application to ery-thophobia. Anti-anxiety drugs have had little success with social pho-bia; despite the terminology the underlying cause might not be fear of other people but a complex set of behavioural tendencies underpinned by beliefs about the self and the social world. The same might be true of fear of blushing.

Surgical intervention is perhaps even more controversial. Nevertheless, the fact that so many are prepared to undergo surgery shows how serious a problem blushing is to those individuals. It suggests the need for psychologists to take this problem more seriously and to develop less extreme forms of intervention that will prove effective. The psychological research into the blush that is emerging and that has been reviewed in this volume has the potential to make a valuable contribution to the development of interventions, but more research is needed if this aspiration is to be realised. Those suffering with erythophobia and those who treat them with surgery ignore the positive benefits that a blush can bring. The treatment focuses on the physical origins of the problems and neglects its basis in the individual's interpretation of his or her blushing and assumptions about its social consequences. That these play a significant role in erythrophobia is supported by findings that individuals who fear blushing report more intense blushing in an embarrassing situation than do those with less fear even though they do not differ from them on physiological measures. (Admittedly more evidence is needed here too, particularly as research has concentrated on embarrassing circumstances rather than exposure.) This form of treatment assumes that blushing is a cause of anxiety and social withdrawal in its own right, which challenges the supposition that it is merely a symptom or expression of an underlying social anxiety. Longitudinal studies should investigate whether post-surgical individuals are less socially anxious in the long term.

Concluding remarks

This volume has aimed to show how psychological research can illuminate the blush; conversely, research into the blush has many potential contributions to make to psychology. As Goffman and others have shown, the analysis of uncertainties about social encounters enhances understanding of social life and how it functions routinely: understanding the blush will enrich social psychology. In addition, a major challenge to theories of emotion has been to discover whether specific emotions have distinctive central and autonomic nervous system concomitants, yet this research has ignored an emotional state that has a distinctive physiological signature and which is triggered by a delimited set of circumstances and is amenable to systematic empirical enquiry.

This book has reviewed social psychological and psychophysiological research and presented findings from a study of recalled blushing episodes. It has related the blush to studies of shame, embarrassment and shyness. It has considered the relation between blushing and social phobia and outlined treatments for erythrophobia. It is concluded nevertheless that many conceptual, theoretical and empirical issues remain unresolved and it is acknowledged that the book has posed at least as many questions as it has been able to provide answers. The blush is a puzzling and fascinating phenomenon; when we have understood it more we will have understood better the self, the emotions, the social world and the relations among them.

Notes

1 Emotion and its expression

1. The names refer to natives of Terra del Fuego, encountered during Darwin's voyage on the Beagle. The notebooks were transcribed and annotated by Paul H. Barrett; see Gruber (1974, p. 333) for the notebook entry; p. 353 for Barrett's explanatory note; p. 340 for the reference to self-attention.
2. Quoted by Cohen (1985, p. 607).
3. Patients with amygdala damage were also particularly poor at identifying the social emotions when they had to base their judgments on the eye region. Autistic people show a similar impairment and this may play a part in their difficulties in everyday social interactions.
4. See Hagemann *et al.* (2003) for discussion of the implications of this for research.

2 Self-consciousness and emotion

1. Labelling the two principal factors as types of 'self-consciousness' is confusing, given the widespread use of this term to describe a mental state rather than a trait-like construct. The items can be found in the original article and in the appendix to the book by Buss (1980); Scheier and Carver (1985) produced a revised version in order to improve the reliability of the measure.
2. Insufficient reports of experiments were available for the analysis for these studies. For example, only one study had data for the correlation between depression and public self-consciousness ($d = 0.52$).
3. Gruber (1974, p. 340).

3 What is a blush?

1. See Reynolds (2002) for evidence of the influence of menopausal flushing on self-esteem.
2. Photograph and accompanying text appeared in *The Mirror*, 4 July 2000, p. 3. A leading tennis player in the 1990s before injury ended her career prematurely – Kournikova attracted enormous media attention despite her modest results in tournaments. Coverage of Prince Harry's 'fracas' appeared, *inter alia*, in *The Guardian*, 22 October 2004, p. 3.
3. See Kalra and Thalmann (1998) for an account of computer modelling of skin colour change in different regions of the face.
4. Respiratory Sinus Arrhythmia refers to rhythmic variation in heart rate associated with respiration, where heart rate increase accompanies inspiration and decrease accompanies expiration. Its measurement provides an index of cardiac vagal tone and thus of parasympathetic nervous system activity.

5. Taylor (2004) argues that the involvement of the imagination was a factor contributing to the sudden rise in 'panic' about masturbation in the early eighteenth-century – 'man's vice of vices, sin of sins', as an anonymous text of the time called it. Taylor relates this condemnation to suspicion about the power of the imagination to distort religious feeling, confusing the love of God with earthly passions.
6. Another mammal, the bare-skinned walrus, faces the problem of maintaining body heat across the extreme changes in temperature it encounters in the cold sea and on land. The thickness of its skin, the layer of blubber, and changes in skin blood flow help regulate body temperature. Thus its skin turns pink when it is exposed to warmer temperatures, due to vasodilation of the blood vessels, bringing blood closer to the skin for cooling, and becomes paler when it enters the water, due to vasoconstriction to conserve heat (see Turco's [1987] aptly named article, *Why does a walrus blush?*).
7. Adrenergic nerves release norepinephrine at the nerve endings and activate the cardiovascular system, increasing heart rate and constricting blood vessels. Cholinergic nerves release acetylcholine (ACh) at their endings, depressing heart rate. In the adrenal medulla ACh triggers release of epinephrine and norepinephrine into the blood. Increased activity of cholinergic nerves stimulates the sweat glands causing increased sweating and the release of kinins.
8. Classification of receptors is based upon research into the effects of drugs on the system. Thus, for example, propranolol, a member of the class of drugs known as beta-blockers, reduces heart rate, cardiac output and blood pressure by blocking sympathetic influence on the ß-adrenergic receptors in the heart.
9. In laser Doppler flowmetry a laser beam is emitted and is reflected back to sensors by the movement of red blood cells moving just below the skin surface. The reflected light undergoes a frequency shift according to the Doppler equation where it is proportional to the velocity of blood cells and the frequency of the laser light. The measure is not absolute but relative, typically to a baseline measure for the individual.

4   Reasons to blush

1. Quoted by Ricks (1976, pp. 4–5).
2. Presumably this quotation is modelled on lines from Alexander Pope's poem, *Imitations of Horace* (1738):

> Let humble Allen, with an awkward shame,
> Do good by stealth, and blush to find it fame.

3. An exception is the work of Zajonc *et al.* (1989), who have proposed that the connection between the facial musculature (the expression of emotion) and the experience of emotion is mediated by changes in brain blood temperature that facilitate or inhibit neurochemical activity.

5   Occasion to blush

1. References to the blush pre-date the usage of embarrassment in the sense of perplexity and social difficulty – the Oxford English Dictionary dates this to

1774. Neither Burgess nor Darwin mentions embarrassment in the context of the blush although presumably both were aware of this usage: the Dictionary quotes a sentence by George Eliot that refers to blushing and embarrassment, dated to 1863.

6 Embarrassment

1. Analysed in December 2004.
2. Its temporal relation to gaze aversion also distinguishes it from a genuine smile. Asendorpf (1990b) has reported that when people are (judged to be) embarrassed they look away for 1.0 to 1.5 seconds *before* the termination of the apex of the smile (the apex is the phase in which the corners of the mouth are maximally pulled up). Gaze aversion that accompanies genuine smiles occurs 0.5 seconds *after* the termination of the apex of the smile.
3. This is reminiscent of Sartre's example of the man looking through the keyhole (Chapter 2) although he was ashamed because his voyeurism was exposed; the person's guilt is not at issue in embarrassment or 'shame before the other'.

7 Shame

1. Lezard, N. (2000), 'Radio review: When listening made me blush', *The Independent on Sunday*, May 28, London: Independent Newspaper CD-ROM 2000, 942.

9 Shyness

1. Clothing was rationed. Materials such as cotton, rubber and silk were scarce and military purposes had priority.
2. In a false-belief task the child judges what another child who does not have access to his or her knowledge understands of a situation. For example, Ioan sees an object being moved in Parveen's absence and he has to decide whether Parveen will look for it in the old or the new place when she returns. If Ioan realises that Parveen will look in the original place he will have passed the test and be said to have acquired a theory of mind.

10 Propensity to blush

1. This is confirmed by other studies. Edelmann and Skov (1993) report alpha of 0.91 and Bögels *et al.* (1996) alpha of 0.92. Bögels *et al.* (1997) report a test-retest reliability of 0.93 for a Dutch revision of the scale.

11 Interventions

1. *The Guardian*, 11 June 2003, p. 9.
2. *The Guardian*, 7 December 2004, p. 11.

3. Internet sites include:

ESFB Channel	http://www.esfbchannel.com
The Center for Hyperhidrosis	http://www.sweaty-palms.com/blushing.html
Patients Against Sympathetic Surgery	http://www.ets-sideeffects.netfirms.com
Swedish Support Group	http://home.swipnet.se/sympatiska/sideeff.htm
ETS and Reversals Discussion Forum	http://p069.ezboard.com/betsandreversals

12 Conclusions

1. This resembles the state of research into aesthetic experience, where psychological research into music has been more productive than research into the visual arts due, in part, to the difficulties of notating and manipulating qualities of paintings such as colour; musical stimuli have proved more amenable.

References

Ackroyd, P. (1994), *Dan Leno and the Limehouse Golem*, London: Sinclair-Stevenson.

Adolphs, R., Baron-Cohen, S. and Tranel, D. (2002), 'Impaired recognition of social emotions following amygdala damage', *Journal of Cognitive Neuroscience* 14, 1264–74.

American Psychiatric Association (1994), *Diagnostic and Statistical Manual of Mental Disorders (Fourth edition)*, Washington, DC: American Psychiatric Association.

American Society for Aesthetic Plastic Surgery (2005), '11.9 million cosmetic procedures in 2004', http://www.surgery.org/press/news-release.php?iid=395. Accessed 17 October 2005.

Amies, P. L., Gelder, M. G. and Shaw, P. M. (1983), 'Social phobia: A comparative case study', *British Journal of Psychiatry* 142, 174–9.

Asendorpf, J. B. (1989), 'Shyness as a final common pathway for two different kinds of inhibition', *Journal of Personality and Social Psychology* 57, 481–92.

—— (1990a), 'Development of inhibition during childhood: Evidence for situational specificity and a two-factor model', *Developmental Psychology* 26, 721–30.

—— (1990b), 'The expression of shyness and embarrassment', in W. R. Crozier (ed.), *Shyness and Embarrassment: Perspectives from Social Psychology*, Cambridge: Cambridge University Press, pp. 87–118.

Austen, J. (1966), *Emma*, Harmondsworth, Middlesex: Penguin (First published in 1816).

Averill, J. R. (1982), *Anger and Aggression: An Essay on Emotion*. New York: Springer-Verlag.

Banerjee, R. and Yuill, N. (1999), 'Children's understanding of self-presentational display rules: Associations with mental-state understanding', *British Journal of Developmental Psychology* 17, 111–24.

Barstow, S. (1982), *A Kind of Loving*, London: Book Club Associates (First published in 1960).

Beidel, D. C., Turner, S. M. and Dancu, C. V. (1985), 'Physiological, cognitive and behavioral aspects of social anxiety', *Behaviour Research and Therapy* 23, 109–17.

Bell, C. (1806), *Essays on the Anatomy of Expression in Painting*, London: Longman.

Bell, G. H., Emslie-Smith, D. and Paterson, C. R. (1976), *Textbook of Physiology and Biochemistry (Ninth Edition)*, Edinburgh: Churchill Livingstone.

Benedict, R. (1946), *The Chrysanthemum and the Sword: Patterns of Japanese Culture*, Boston, MA: Houghton Mifflin.

Bergler, E. (1944), 'A new approach to the therapy of erythrophobia', *Psychoanalytic Quarterly* 13, 43–59.

Billig, M. (2001), 'Humour and embarrassment: Limits of "nice-guy" theories of social life', *Theory, Culture & Society* 18, 23–43.

Blackmore, R. D. (1999), *Lorna Doone*, Oxford: Oxford University Press Paperbacks (First published in 1869).

Bögels, S. M., Alberts, M. and de Jong, P. J. (1996), 'Self-consciousness, self-focused attention, blushing propensity and fear of blushing', *Personality and Individual Differences* 21, 573–81.

Bögels, S. M. and Lamers, C. T. J. (2002), 'The causal role of self-awareness in blushing-anxious, socially-anxious and social phobics individuals', *Behaviour Research and Therapy* 40, 1367–84.

Bögels, S. M., Mulkens, S. and de Jong, P. J. (1997), 'Task concentration training and fear of blushing', *Clinical Psychology and Psychotherapy* 4, 251–8.

Bögels, S. M. and Reith, W. (1999), 'Validity of two questionnaires to assess social fears: The Dutch Social Phobia and Anxiety Inventory and the Blushing, Trembling and Sweating Questionnaire', *Journal of Psychopathology and Behavioural Assessment* 21, 51–66.

Bögels, S. M., Rijsemus, W. and de Jong, P. J. (2002), 'Self-focused attention and social anxiety: the effects of experimentally heightened self-awareness on fear, blushing, cognitions, and social skills', *Cognitive Therapy and Research* 26, 461–72.

Browne, J. (1985), 'Darwin and the expression of the emotions', in D. Kohn (ed.), *The Darwinian Heritage*, Princeton: Princeton University Press, pp. 307–26.

Burgess, T. H. (1839), *The Physiology or Mechanism of Blushing; Illustrative of the Influence of Mental Emotion on the Capillary Circulation; with a General View of the Sympathies, and the Organic Relations of those Structures with which they seem to be Connected*, London: John Churchill.

BUPA (2003), Cosmetic surgery–who can you trust?, http://www.bupa.co.uk/health_information/html/health_news/Accessed 25 April 2005.

Buss, A. H. (1980), *Self-consciousness and Social Anxiety*, San Francisco: Freeman.

—— (1986), 'A theory of shyness', in W. H., Jones, J. M. Cheek and S. R. Briggs (eds), *Shyness: Perspectives on Research and Treatment*, New York: Plenum, pp. 39–46.

Buss, A. H., Iscoe, I. and Buss, E. H. (1979), 'The development of embarrassment', *Journal of Psychology* 103, 227–30.

Campbell, H. (1890), *Flushing and Morbid Blushing*, London: H. K. Lewis.

Carducci, B. J. and Zimbardo, P. G. (1997), 'Are you shy?', in M. H. Davis (ed.), *Annual editions: Social Psychology 1997/98*, Guilford, CT: Dushkin/Brown & Benchmark, pp. 35–41.

Carver, C. S. and Scheier, M. F. (1987), 'The blind men and the elephant: Selective examination of the public-private literature gives rise to a faulty perception', *Journal of Personality* 55, 525–40.

Casimir, M. J. and Schnegg, M. (2002), 'Shame across cultures: The evolution, ontogeny and function of a "moral emotion" ', in H. Keller, Y. H. Poortinga and A. Schölmerich (eds), *Between Culture and Biology: Perspectives on Ontogenetic Development*, Cambridge: Cambridge University Press, pp. 270–300.

Caspi, A., Elder, G. H., Jr. and Bem, D. J. (1988), 'Moving away from the world: Life-course patterns of shy children', *Developmental Psychology* 24, 824–31.

Castelfranchi, C. and Poggi, I. (1990), 'Blushing as a discourse: Was Darwin wrong?', in W. R. Crozier (ed.), *Shyness and Embarrassment: Perspectives from Social Psychology*, New York: Cambridge University Press, pp. 230–51.

Chavira, D. A., Stein, M. B. and Malcarne, V. L. (2002), 'Scrutinizing the relationship between shyness and social phobia', *Journal of Anxiety Disorders* 16, 585–98.

Cheek, J. M. and Buss, A. H. (1981), 'Shyness and sociability', *Journal of Personality and Social Psychology* 41, 330–9.

Clark, D. M. (2005), 'A cognitive perspective on social phobia', in W. R. Crozier and L. E. Alden (eds), *The Essential Handbook of Social Anxiety for Clinicians*, Chichester, Sussex: Wiley, pp. 193–218.

Clark, D. M. and Wells, A. (1995), 'A cognitive model of social phobia', in R. Heimberg, M. Liebowitz, D. A. Hope and F. R. Schneier (eds), *Social Phobia: Diagnosis, Assessment, and Treatment*, New York: Guilford Press, pp. 69–93.

Cohen, D. and Gunz, A. (2002), 'As seen by the other ... : Perspectives on the self in the memories and emotional perceptions of Easterners and Westerners', *Psychological Science* 13, 55–9.

Cohen, I. B. (1985), 'Three notes on the reception of Darwin's ideas on natural selection (Henry Baker Tristram, Alfred Newton, Samuel Wilberforce)', in D. Kohn (ed.), *The Darwinian Heritage*, Princeton: Princeton University Press, pp. 589–608.

Cooley, C. H. (1983), *Human Nature and the Social Order*, London: Transaction Books (First published in 1902).

Cottle, M. (1999), 'Selling shyness', *The New Republic* 221, 5 (August 2) 24–9.

Crozier, W. R. (1981a), 'Shyness and self-esteem', *British Journal of Social Psychology* 20, 220–2.

—— (1981b), 'Do photographs of facial displays provide a sound basis for classifying the basic emotions?', *Current Psychological Research* 1, 199–202.

—— (2004), 'Self-consciousness, exposure and the blush', *Journal for the Theory of Social Behaviour* 18, 121–8.

Crozier, W. R. and Garbert-Jones, A. (1996), 'Finding a voice: Shyness in mature students' experience of university', *Adults Learning* 7, 195–8.

Crozier, W. R. and Russell, D. (1992), 'Blushing, embarrassability, and self-consciousness', *British Journal of Social Psychology* 31, 343–9.

Csikszentmihalyi, M. (1990), *Flow: The Psychology of Optimal Experience*. New York: Harper & Row.

Cupach, W. R. and Metts, S. (1990), 'Remedial processes in embarrassing predicaments', in J. A. Anderson (ed.), *Communication Yearbook 13*, Newbury Park, CA: Sage, pp. 323–52.

Cutlip, W. D. and Leary, M. R. (1993), 'Anatomic and physiological bases of social blushing: Speculations from neurology and psychology', *Behavioural Neurology* 6, 181–5.

Damasio, A. (2004), *Looking for Spinoza*. London: Vintage.

Darwin, C. (1872), *The Expression of the Emotions in Man and Animals*, London: John Murray.

—— (1877), 'A biographical sketch of an infant', *Mind* 2, 285–94.

de Jong, P. J. (1999), 'Communicative and remedial effects of social blushing', *Journal of Nonverbal Behavior* 23, 197–217.

de Jong, P. J., Peters, M. and de Cremer, D. (2003), 'Blushing may signify guilt: Revealing effects of blushing in ambiguous social situations', *Motivation and Emotion* 27, 225–49.

de Jong, P. J., Peters, M., de Cremer, D. and Vranken, C. (2002), 'Blushing after a moral transgression in a prisoner's dilemma game: Appeasing or revealing?', *European Journal of Social Psychology* 32, 627–44.

Demoulin, S., Leyens, J.-P., Paladino, M.-P., Rodriguez-Torres, R., Rodriguez-Torres, A. and Dovidio, J. F. (2004), 'Dimensions of "uniquely" and "non-uniquely" human emotions', *Cognition and Emotion* 18, 71–96.

De Wit, D. J., Ogborne, A., Offord, D. R. and MacDonald, K. (1999), 'Antecedents of the risk of recovery from DSM-III-R social phobia', *Psychological Medicine* 29, 569–82.

Dickerson, S. S. and Kemeny, M. E. (2004), 'Acute stressors and cortisol responses: A theoretical integration and synthesis of laboratory research', *Psychological Bulletin* 130, 1–37.

Dickerson, S. S., Kemeny, M. E., Aziz, N., Kim, K. H. and Fahey, J. L. (2004), 'Immunological effects of induced shame and guilt', *Psychosomatic Medicine* 66, 124–31.

Drott, C., Claes, G., Olsson-Rex, L., Dalman, P., Fahlén, T. and Göthberg, G. (1998), 'Successful treatment of facial blushing by endoscopic transthoracic sympathecotomy', *British Journal of Dermatology* 138, 639–43.

Drott, C., Claes, G. and Rex, L. (2002), 'Facial blushing treated by sympathetic denervation – longstanding benefits in 831 patients', *Journal of Cosmetic Dermatology* 1, 115–19.

—— (2004), 'Endoscopic transthoracic sympathecotomy ... and no regrets. Reply to Dr Drummond', *Journal of Cosmetic Dermatology* 2, 48.

Drummond, P. D. (1996), 'Adrenergic receptors in the forehead microcirculation', *Clinical Autonomic Research* 6, 23–7.

—— (1997), 'The effect of adrenergic blockade on blushing and facial flushing', *Psychophysiology* 34, 163–8.

—— (1999), 'Facial flushing during provocation in women', *Psychobiology* 36, 325–32.

—— (2000), 'A caution about surgical treatment for facial blushing', *British Journal of Dermatology* 142, 177–99.

—— (2004), 'Endoscopic transthoracic sympathecotomy for blushing', *Journal of Cosmetic Dermatology* 2, 45.

Drummond, P. D., Camacho, L., Formentin, N., Heffernan, T. D., Williams, F. and Zekas, T. E. (2003), 'The impact of verbal feedback about blushing on social discomfort and facial blood flow during embarrassing tasks', *Behaviour Research and Therapy* 41, 413–25.

Drummond, P. D. and Lim, H. K. (2000), 'The significance of blushing for fair-and dark-skinned people', *Personality and Individual Differences* 29, 1123–32.

Drummond, P. D. and Mirco, N. (2004), 'Staring at one side of the face increases blood flow on that side of the face', *Psychophysiology* 41, 281–7.

Duval, S. and Wicklund, R. A. (1972), *A Theory of Objective Self-awareness*. New York: Academic Press.

Edelmann, R. J. (1987), *The Psychology of Embarrassment*, Chichester, Sussex: Wiley.

Edelmann, R. J. (1990a), 'Embarrassment and blushing: A component-process model, some initial descriptive and cross-cultural data', in W. R. Crozier (ed.), *Shyness and Embarrassment: Perspectives from Social Psychology*, New York: Cambridge University Press, pp. 204–29.

—— (1990b), 'Chronic blushing, self-consciousness, and social anxiety', *Journal of Psychopathology and Behavioral Assessment* 12, 119–27.

Edelmann, R. J. (1991), 'Correlates of chronic blushing', *British Journal of Clinical Psychology* 30, 177–8.

Edelmann, R. J. and Skov, V. (1993), 'Blushing propensity, social anxiety, anxiety sensitivity and awareness of bodily sensations', *Personality and Individual Differences* 14, 495–8.

Ekman, P. (1972), 'Universals and cultural differences in facial expressions of emotions', in J. Cole (ed.), *Nebraska Symposium on Motivation, 1971* 19, Lincoln, NE: University of Nebraska Press, pp. 207–83.

—— (1992), 'An argument for basic emotions', *Cognition and Emotion* 6, 169–200.

—— (1997), 'Should we call it expression or communication?' *Innovations in Social Science Research* 10, 333–4.

—— (2003), *Emotions Revealed*, London: Weidenfeld & Nicolson.

Ekman, P. and Friesen, W. (1978), *The Facial Action Coding System*, Palo Alto, CA: Consulting Psychologists Press.

Eliot, G. (1976), *The Mill on the Floss*, London: Dent, First published in 1860.

—— (2003), *Daniel Deronda*, London: Penguin, First published in 1876.

Fahlén, T. (1997), 'Core symptom pattern of social phobia', *Depression and Anxiety* 4, 223–32.

Feldman, S. (1941), 'On blushing', *Psychiatric Quarterly* 15, 249–61.

Fenigstein, A., Scheier, M. F. and Buss, A. H. (1975), 'Public and private self-consciousness: Assessment and theory', *Journal of Consulting and Clinical Psychology* 43, 522–7.

Folklow, B. and Neil, E. (1971), *Circulation*, New York: Oxford University Press.

Fontaine, J. R. J., Poortinga, Y. H., Setiadi, B. and Markam, S. S. (2002), 'Cognitive structure of emotion terms in Indonesia and The Netherlands', *Cognition and Emotion* 16, 61–86.

Frank, R. H. (1988), *Passions within Reason: The Strategic Role of the Emotions*, New York: Norton.

—— (2000), *Microeconomics and Behavior (Fourth edition)*, New York: McGraw Hill.

Frayn, M. (2001), *The Spies*, London: Faber and Faber.

Fridlund, A. J. (1994), *Human Facial Expression*, New York: Academic Press.

Frijda, N. (1986), *The Emotions*, Cambridge: Cambridge University Press.

Fuller, R. (1956), *Image of a Society*, Harmondsworth: Penguin, 1956.

Furmark, T., Tillfors, M., Everz, P.-O., Marteinsdottir, I., Gefvert, O. and Fredrikson, M. (1999), 'Social phobia in the general population: Prevalence and sociodemographic profile', *Social Psychiatry and Psychiatric Epidemiology* 34, 416–24.

Gaskell, E. (1994), *North and South*, London: Penguin, First published in 1854.

Gawande, A. (2001), 'Crimson tide', *The New Yorker*, 12 February.

Gerlach, A. L. and Ultes, M. (2003), 'Überschneidung von Socializer Phobie und ubermässigem Schwitzen und Erröten – eine internetbasierte Studie', in R. Ott and C. Eichenberg (eds), *Klinische Psychologie im Internet*, Göttingen: Hogrefe Verlag, pp. 327–41.

Gerlach, A. L., Wilhelm, F. H., Gruber, K. and Roth, W. T. (2001), 'Blushing and physiological arousability in social phobia', *Journal of Abnormal Psychology* 110, 247–58.

Gerlach, A. L., Wilhelm, F. H. and Roth, W. T. (2003), 'Embarrassment and social phobia: The role of parasympathetic activation', *Journal of Anxiety Disorders* 17, 197–210.

Gilbert, P. (2002), 'Body shame: A biopsychosocial conceptualisation and overview with treatment implications', in P. Gilbert and J. Miles (eds), *Body Shame: Conceptualisation, Research and Treatment*, Hove: Brunner-Routledge, pp. 3–54.

Goffman, E. (1972), *Interaction Ritual*, Harmondsworth, Middlesex: Penguin.

Gottschalk, L. A. and Gleser, G. C. (1969), *The Measurement of Psychological States Through the Content Analysis of Verbal Behavior*, Berkeley: University of California Press.

Gruber, H. (1974), *Darwin on Man: A Psychological Study of Scientific Creativity. Together with Darwin's Early and Unpublished Notebooks transcribed and annotated by Paul H. Barrett*, London: Wildwood House.

Hackmann, A., Surawy, C. and Clark, D. M. (1998), 'Seeing yourself through others' eyes: A study of spontaneously occurring images in social phobia', *Behavioural and Cognitive Psychotherapy* 26, 3–12.

Hagemann, D., Waldstein, S. R. and Thayer, J. F. (2003), 'Central and autonomic nervous system integration in emotion', *Brain and Cognition* 52, 79–87.

Halberstadt, A. G. and Green, L. R. (1993), 'Social attention and placation theories of blushing', *Motivation and Emotion* 17, 53–64.

Harré, R. (1983), *Personal Being: A Theory for Individual Psychology*, Oxford: Blackwell.

Harré, R. (1990), 'Embarrassment: A conceptual analysis', in W. R. Crozier (ed.), *Shyness and Embarrassment: Perspectives from Social Psychology*, New York: Cambridge University Press, pp. 181–204.

Harris, P. R. (1990), 'Shyness and embarrassment in psychological theory and ordinary language', in W. R. Crozier (ed.), *Shyness and Embarrassment: Perspectives from Social Psychology*, New York: Cambridge University Press, pp. 59–86.

Harter, S. and Whitesell, N. R. (1988), 'Developmental changes in children's understanding of single, multiple and blended emotion concepts', in C. Saarni and P. L. Harris (eds), *Children's Understanding of Emotion*, New York: Cambridge University Press, pp. 82–107.

Hartley, L. R., Ungapen, S., Davie, I. and Spencer, D. J. (1983), 'The effect of beta adrenergic blocking drugs on speakers' performance and memory', *British Journal of Psychiatry* 142, 512–7.

Healy, D. (2002), *The Creation of Psychopharmacology*, Cambridge, MA: Harvard University Press.

Hill, G. J. (1989), 'An unwillingness to act: Behavioral appropriateness, situational constraint, and self-efficacy in shyness', *Journal of Personality* 57, 871–90.

Hirsch, C. R., Clark, D. M., Mathews, A. and Williams, R. (2003), 'Self-images play a causal role in social phobia', *Behaviour Research and Therapy* 41, 909–21.

Hood, S. D. and Nutt, D. J. (2005), 'Psychopharmacological treatments: An overview', in W. R. Crozier and L. E. Alden (eds), *The Essential Handbook of Social Anxiety for Clinicians*, Chichester, Sussex: Wiley, pp. 287–320.

Ishiyama, F. I. (1984), 'Shyness: Anxious social sensitivity and self-isolating tendency', *Adolescence* 19, 903–11.

Izard, C. E. (1971), *The Face of Emotion*, New York: Appleton-Century-Crofts.

—— (1972), *Patterns of Emotions*, New York: Academic Press.

—— (1977), *Human Emotions*, New York: Plenum Press.

Izard, C. E. and Hyson, M. C. (1986), 'Shyness as a discrete emotion', in W. H. Jones, J. M. Cheek and S. R. Briggs (eds), *Shyness: Perspectives on Research and Treatment*, New York: Plenum, pp. 147–60.

Jackson, T., Towson, S. and Narduzzi, K. (1997), 'Predictors of shyness: A test of variables with self-presentation models', *Social Behavior and Personality* 25, 149–54.

James, W. (1884), 'What is an emotion?', *Mind* 9, 188–205.

Kagan, J. (1994), *Galen's Prophecy*, London: Free Association Books.

Kalra, P. and Thalmann, N. M. (1998), *Modeling of vascular expressions in animation*, Geneva: MIRAlab, University of Geneva, http://www.miralab.unige.ch/papers/21.pdf.

Karch, F. E. (1971), 'Blushing', *Psychoanalytic Review* 58, 37–50.

Keltner, D. (1995), 'Signs of appeasement: Evidence for the distinct displays of embarrassment, amusement, and shame', *Journal of Personality and Social Psychology* 68, 441–54.

Keltner, D. and Anderson (2000), 'Saving face for Darwin: The functions and uses of embarrassment', *Current Directions in Psychological Science* 9, 187–92.

Keltner, D. and Buswell, B. N. (1997), 'Embarrassment: Its distinct form and appeasement functions', *Psychological Bulletin* 122, 250–70.

Keltner, D. and Harker, L. A. (1998), 'The forms and functions of the nonverbal signal of shame', in P. Gilbert and B. Andrews (eds), *Shame*, New York: Oxford University Press, pp. 78–98.

Kerr, M. (2000), 'Childhood and adolescent shyness in long-term perspective: Does it matter?', in W. R. Crozier (ed.), *Shyness: Development, Consolidation and Change*, London: Routledge, pp. 64–87.

Kessler, R. C., McGonagle, K. A., Zhao, S., Nelson, C. B., Hughes, M., Eshleman, S., Wittchen, H.-U. and Kendler, K. S. (1994), 'Lifetime and 12-month prevalence of DSM-III-R psychiatric disorders in the United States', *Archives of General Psychiatry* 51, 8–19.

Knutson, B., Wolkowitz, O. M., Cole, S. W., Chan, T., Moore, E. A. *et al.* (1998), 'Selective alteration of personality and social behavior by serotonergic intervention', *American Journal of Psychiatry* 155, 373–9.

Krueger, R. F. and Piasecki, T. M. (2002), 'Toward a dimensional and psychometrically-informed approach to conceptualising psychopathology', *Behaviour Research and Therapy* 40, 485–99.

Laederach-Hofmann, K., Mussgay, L., Büchel, B., Widler, P. and Rüddel, H. (2002), 'Patients with erythrophobia (fear of blushing) show abnormal autonomic regulation in mental stress situations', *Psychosomatic Medicine* 64, 358–65.

Leary, M. R. (2004), 'Digging deeper: The fundamental nature of "self-conscious" emotions', *Psychological Inquiry* 15, 129–31.

Leary, M. R., Britt, T. W., Cutlip, W. D. and Templeton, J. L. (1992), 'Social blushing', *Psychological Bulletin* 107, 446–60.

Leary, M. R. and Buckley, K. E. (2000), 'Shyness and the pursuit of social acceptance', in W. R. Crozier (ed.), *Shyness: Development, Consolidation and Change*, London: Routledge, pp. 139–53.

Leary, M. R. and Downs, D. L. (1995), 'Interpersonal functions of the self-esteem motive: The self-system as a sociometer', in M. Kernis (ed.), *Efficacy, Agency and Self-Esteem*, New York: Plenum, pp. 123–44.

Leary, M. R., Landel, J. L. and Patton, K. M. (1996), 'The motivated expression of embarrassment following a self-presentational predicament', *Journal of Personality* 64, 619–36.

Leary, M. R. and Meadows, S. (1991), 'Predictors, elicitors, and concomitants of social blushing', *Journal of Personality and Social Psychology* 60, 254–62.

Leary, M. R., Rejeski, W. J., Britt, T. and Smith, G. E. (1994), *Physiological differences between embarrassment and social anxiety*, Unpublished manuscript, Wake Forest University, Winston-Salem, NC.

LeDoux, J. E. and Phelps, E. A. (2000), 'Emotional networks in the brain', in M. Lewis and J. M. Haviland-Jones (eds), *Handbook of Emotions (Second edition)*, London: Guilford Press, pp. 157–72.

Lewinsky, H. (1941), 'The nature of shyness', *British Journal of Psychology* 32, 105–13.

Lewis, H. B. (1971), *Shame and Guilt in Neurosis*, New York: International Universities Press.

Lewis, M. (1992), *Shame: The Exposed Self*, New York: Free Press.

—— (2000), 'Self-conscious emotions: Embarrassment, pride, shame, and guilt', in M. Lewis and J. M. Haviland-Jones (eds), *Handbook of Emotions (Second edition)*, London: Guilford Press, pp. 623–36.

—— (2001), 'Origins of the self-conscious child' in W. R. Crozier and L. E. Alden (eds), *International Handbook of Social Anxiety*, Chichester, Sussex: Wiley, pp. 101–18.

Lewis, M. and Ramsay, D. (2002), 'Cortisol response to embarrassment and shame', *Child Development* 73, 1034–45.

Li, J., Wang, L. and Fischer, K. W. (2004), 'The organisation of Chinese shame concepts', *Cognition and Emotion* 18, 767–97.

Lupton, D. (1998), *The Emotional Self*, London: Sage.

Marshall, P. J. and Stevenson-Hinde, J. (2005), 'Behavioral inhibition: Physiological correlates', in W. R. Crozier and L. E. Alden (eds), *The Essential Handbook of Social Anxiety for Clinicians*, Chichester, Sussex: Wiley, pp. 57–80.

Maynard Smith, J. and Harper, D. (2003), *Animal Signals*, Oxford: Oxford University Press.

McDaniel, P. (2001), 'Shrinking violets and Caspar Milquetoasts: Shyness and heterosexuality from the roles of the fifties to the rules of the nineties', *Journal of Social History* 34, 547–68.

McNeil, D. W. (2001), 'Terminology and evolution of constructs related to social phobia', in S. G. Hofmann and P. M. DiBartolo (eds), *From Social Anxiety to Social Phobia*, Boston, MA: Allyn and Bacon, pp. 8–19.

Mead, G. H. (1934), *Mind, Self, and Society*. Chicago: University of Chicago Press.

Medawar, C., Herxheimer, A., Bell, A. and Jofre, S. (2002), 'Paroxetine, Panorama and user reporting of ADRs: consumer intelligence matters in clinical practice and post-marketing drug surveillance', *International Journal of Risk & Safety in Medicine* 15, 161–9.

Mellander, S., Andersson, P.-O., Afzelius, L.-E. and Hellstrand, P. (1982), 'Neural beta-adrenergic dilation of the facial vein in man: Possible mechanisms in emotional blushing', *Acta Physiologica Scandinavica* 114, 393–9.

Mellings, T. M. B. and Alden, L. E. (2000), 'Cognitive processes in social anxiety: The effects of self-focus, rumination and anticipatory processing', *Behaviour Research and Therapy* 38, 243–57.

Mersch, P. P. A., Hildebrand, M., Lavy, E. H., Wessel, I. and van Hout, W. J. P. J. (1992), 'Somatic symptoms in social phobia: A treatment method based on rational emotive therapy and paradoxical interventions', *Journal of Behavior Therapy and Experimental Psychiatry* 23, 199–211.

Miller, R. S. (1987), 'Empathic embarrassment: Situational and personal determinants of reactions to the embarrassment of others', *Journal of Personality and Social Psychology* 53, 1061–9.

—— (1992), 'The nature and severity of self-reported embarrassing circumstances', *Personality and Social Psychology Bulletin* 18, 190–8.

—— (1995), 'On the nature of embarrassability: Shyness, social evaluation, and social skill', *Journal of Personality* 63, 315–39.

—— (1996), *Embarrassment: Poise and Peril in Everyday Life*. New York: Guilford Press.

—— (2001), 'Shyness and embarrassment compared: Siblings in the service of social evaluation', in W. R. Crozier and L. E. Alden (eds), *International Handbook of Social Anxiety*, Chichester, Sussex: Wiley, pp. 281–300.

Miller, R. S. and Tangney, J. P. (1994), 'Differentiating embarrassment and shame', *Journal of Social and Clinical Psychology* 13, 273–87.

Mor, N. and Winquist, J. (2002), 'Self-focused attention and negative affect: A meta-analysis', *Psychological Bulletin* 128, 638–62.

Mulkens, S., Bögels, S. M., de Jong, P. J. and Louwers, J. (2001), 'Fear of blushing: Effects of task concentration versus exposure in vivo on fear and physiology', *Anxiety Disorders* 15, 413–32.

Mulkens, S., de Jong, P. J. and Bögels, S. M. (1997), 'High blushing propensity: Fearful preoccupation or facial coloration?', *Personality and Individual Differences* 22, 817–24.

Mulkens, S., de Jong, P. J., Dobbelaar, A. and Bögels, S. M. (1999), 'Fear of blushing: Fearful preoccupation irrespective of facial coloration', *Behaviour Research and Therapy* 37, 1119–28.

Nigro, G. and Neisser, U. (1983), 'Point of view in personal memories', *Cognitive Psychology* 15, 467–82.

O'Brien, E. (1963), *The Country Girls*, Harmondsworth, Middlesex: Penguin.

O'Connor, F. (1973), *The Holy Door and Other Stories*, London: Pan.

O'Farrell, M. A. (1997), *Telling Complexions: The Nineteenth-Century Novel and the Blush*, Durham, NC: Duke University Press.

Ortony, A., Clore, G. L. and Collins, A. (1988), *The Cognitive Structure of Emotions*, Cambridge: Cambridge University Press.

Parrott, W. G. and Smith, S. F. (1991), 'Embarrassment: Actual vs. typical cases, classical vs. prototypical representations', *Cognition and Emotion* 5, 467–88.

Patterson, G. (2005), *That Which Was*, London: Penguin.

Pavlidis, I., Eberhardt, N. L. and Levine, J. A. (2002), 'Seeing through the face of deception', *Nature* 415, 35.

Petronio, S. (2000), 'The boundaries of privacy: Praxis of everyday life', in S. Petronio (ed.), *Balancing the Secrets of Private Disclosures*, Mahwah, NJ: Lawrence Erlbaum Associates, pp. 37–49.

Pinker, S. (1994), *The Language Instinct*, New York: HarperCollins.

—— (1997), *How the Mind Works*, London: Penguin.

Poulson, C. (2000), *Shame: The Master Emotion?*, University of Tasmania School of Management, Working Paper Series.

Rapee, R. and Sweeney, L. (2005), 'Social phobia in children and adolescents: Nature and assessment', in W. R. Crozier and L. E. Alden (eds), *The Essential Handbook of Social Anxiety for Clinicians*, Chichester, Sussex: Wiley, pp. 133–51.

Reddy, V. (2000), 'Coyness in early infancy', *Developmental Science* 3, 186–92.

—— (2001), 'Positively shy! Developmental continuities in the expression of shyness, coyness, and embarrassment', in W. R. Crozier and L. E. Alden (eds), *International Handbook of Social Anxiety: Concepts, Research and Interventions Relating to the Self and Shyness*, Chichester, Sussex: Wiley, pp. 77–99.

Reich, J., Noyes, R. and Yates, W. (1988), 'Anxiety symptoms distinguishing social phobia from panic and generalized anxiety disorders', *Journal of Mental and Nervous Disease* 176, 510–13.

Rettew, D. C. (2000), 'Avoidant personality disorder, generalized social phobia, and shyness: Putting the personality back into personality disorders', *Harvard Review of Psychiatry* 8, 283–97.

Rex, L. O., Drott, C., Claes, G., Göthberg, G. and Dalman, P. (1998), 'The Borås experience of endoscopic thoracic sympatheticotomy for palmar, axillar, facial hyperhidrosis and facial blushing', *European Journal of Surgery* Supplement 580, 23–6.

Reynolds, F. (2002), 'Exploring the long-term experience of vasomotor instability: A 5 year follow-up study of distress, perceived control and catastrophizing', *Counselling Psychology Quarterly* 15, 73–83.

Ricks, C. (1976), *Keats and Embarrassment*, Oxford: Oxford University Press.

Roth, P. (2001), *The Dying Animal*, London: Jonathan Cape.

Russell, J. A. and Yik, S. M. (1996), 'Emotion among the Chinese', in M. H. Bond (ed.), *The Handbook of Chinese Psychology*, Hong Kong: Oxford University Press, pp. 166–88.

Sabini, J., Garvey, B. and Hall, A. L. (2001), 'Shame and embarrassment revisited', *Personality and Social Psychology Bulletin* 27, 104–17.

Sabini, J., Siepmann, M., Stein, J. and Meyerowitz, M. (2000), 'Who is embarrassed by what?', *Cognition and Emotion* 14, 213–40.

Sabini, J. and Silver, M. (1997), 'In defense of shame: Shame in the context of guilt and embarrassment', *Journal of the Theory of Social Behaviour* 27, 1–15.

Sartre, J.-P. (1966), *Being and Nothingness*, Translated by Hazel E. Barnes, New York: Washington Square Press, Originally published as *L-Être et le néant*, Paris 1943.

Scheff, T. J. and Retzinger, S. M. (2001), *Emotions and Violence: Shame and Rage in Destructive Conflicts*, Lincoln, NE: iUniverse.

Scheier, M. F. and Carver, C. S. (1985), 'The self-consciousness scale: A revised version for use with general populations', *Journal of Applied Social Psychology* 15, 687–99.

Scherer, K. R. (1993), 'Studying the emotion-antecedent appraisal process: An expert system approach', *Cognition and Emotion* 7, 325–55.

Schlenker, B. R. and Leary, M. R. (1982), 'Social anxiety and self-presentation: A conceptualization and model', *Psychological Bulletin* 92, 641–69.

Schmidt, L. A. and Fox, N. A. (1994), 'Patterns of cortical electrophysiology and autonomic activity in adults' shyness and sociability', *Biological Psychology* 38, 183–98.

Scholing, A. and Emmelkamp, P. M. (1993), 'Cognitive and behavioural treatments of fear of blushing, sweating or trembling', *Behaviour Research and Therapy* 31, 155–70.

—— (1996), 'Treatment of fear of blushing, sweating or trembling: Results at long-term follow-up', *Behavior Modification* 20, 338–56.

Scholing, A. and Emmelkamp, P. M. (1999), 'Prediction of treatment outcome in social phobia: A cross-validation', *Behaviour Research and Therapy* 37, 659–70.

Schulkin, J., Thompson, B. L. and Rosen, J. B. (2003), 'Demythologizing the emotions: Adaptation, cognition and visceral representations of emotion in the nervous system', *Brain and Cognition* 52, 15–23.

Semin, G. R. and Manstead, A. S. R. (1981), 'The beholder beheld: A study of social emotionality', *European Journal of Social Psychology* 11, 253–65.

—— (1982), 'The social implications of embarrassment displays and restitution behavior', *European Journal of Social Psychology* 12, 367–77.

Shearn, D., Bergman, E., Hill, K., Abel, A. and Hinds, L. (1990), 'Facial coloration and temperature responses in blushing', *Psychophysiology* 27, 687–93.

Shields, S. A., Mallory, M. E. and Simon, A. (1990), 'The experience and symptoms of blushing as a function of age and reported frequency of blushing', *Journal of Nonverbal Behavior* 14, 171–87.

Silver, M., Sabini, J. and Parrott, W. G. (1987), 'Embarrassment: A dramaturgic account', *Journal for the Theory of Social Behaviour* 17, 47–61.

Simon, A. and Shields, S. A. (1996), 'Does complexion color affect the experience of blushing?', *Journal of Social Behavior and Personality* 11, 177–88.

Smith, A. (1759/2002), *The Theory of Moral Sentiments*, London: A. Millar (2002 edition), Cambridge: Cambridge University Press.

Stein, D. J. and Bowyer, C. (1997), 'Blushing and social phobia', *Medical Hypotheses* 49, 101–8.

Stein, D. J., Ipser, J. C. and van Balkom, A. J. (2004), 'Pharmacotherapy for social phobia (Cochrane Review)', *The Cochrane Library, (Issue 4)*, Chichester, Sussex: John Wiley.

Stevenson-Hinde, J. and Shouldice, A. (1993), 'Wariness to strangers: A behavior systems perspective revisited', in K. H. Rubin and J. B. Asendorpf (eds), *Social Withdrawal, Inhibition, and Shyness in Childhood*, Hillsdale, NJ: Erlbaum, pp. 101–16.

Strathern, A. (1977), 'Why is shame on the skin?', in J. Blacking (ed.), *The Anthropology of the Body*, London: Academic Press, pp. 99–110.

Tangney, J. P. (2003), 'Self-relevant emotions', in M. R. Leary and J. P. Tangney (eds), *Handbook of Self and Identity*, New York: Guilford, pp. 384–400.

Tangney, J. P. and Fischer, K. W. (eds) (1995), *Self-conscious Emotions: The Psychology of Shame, Guilt, Embarrassment, and Pride*, New York: Guilford.

Tangney, J. P., Miller, R. S., Flicker, R. and Barlow, D. H. (1996a), 'Are shame, guilt, and embarrassment distinct emotions?', *Journal of Personality and Social Psychology* 70, 1256–69.

Tangney, J. P., Wagner, P. E., Barlow, D. H., Marschall, D. E. and Gramzow, R. (1996b), 'Relation of shame and guilt to constructive versus destructive responses to anger across the lifespan', *Journal of Personality and Social Psychology* 70, 797–809.

Taylor, B. (2004), 'Too much. A review of Solitary Sex: A Cultural History of Masturbation by Thomas Laqueur', *London Review of Books* 26, 9, 22–24.

Taylor, G. (1985), *Pride, Shame and Guilt: Emotions of Self-assessment*, Oxford: Clarendon.

Telaranta, T. (1998), 'Treatment of social phobia by endoscopic thoracic sympatheticotomy', *European Journal of Surgery* 164, Supplement 580, 27–32.

Tillfors, M., Furmark, T., Ekselius, L. and Fredrikson, M. (2001), 'Social phobia and avoidant personality disorder as related to parental history of social anxiety: A general population study', *Behaviour Research and Therapy* 39, 289–98.

Timms, M. W. H. (1980), 'Treatment of chronic blushing by paradoxical intention', *Behavioural Psychotherapy* 8, 59–61.

Tomkins, S. S. (1963), *Affect, Imagery, Consciousness. Vol. 2: The Negative Affects*, New York: Springer.

Tracy, J. L. and Robins, R. W. (2004), 'Putting the self into self-conscious emotions: A theoretical model', *Psychological Inquiry* 15, 103–25.

Turco, K. (1987), 'Why does a walrus blush?', *Alaska Science Forum* 830, http://www.gi.Alaska.edu/Science Forum/ASF8/830.html. Accessed 14 December 2004.

Turner, B. and Rennell, T. (1995), *When Daddy Came Home*, London: Hutchinson.

Turner, S. M., Beidel, D. C., Dancu, C. V. and Stanley, M. A. (1989), 'An empirically derived inventory to measure social fears and anxiety: The Social Phobia and Anxiety Inventory', *Psychological Assessment* 1, 35–40.

Updike, J. (1970), *Bech: A Book*, London: Andre Deutsch.

—— (2000), *Licks of Love*, London: Penguin.

Van Ameringen, M., Mancini, C., Oakman, J. M. and Farvolden, P. (1999), 'Selective serotonin reuptake inhibitors in the treatment of social phobia: The emerging gold standard', *CNS Drugs* 11, 307–15.

Wicker, F. W., Payne, G. C. and Morgan, R. D. (1983), 'Participant descriptions of guilt and shame', *Motivation and Emotion* 7, 25–39.

Widiger, T. (2005), 'Social anxiety, social phobia, and avoidant personality', in W. R. Crozier and L. E. Alden (eds), *The Essential Handbook of Social Anxiety for Clinicians*, Chichester, Sussex: Wiley, pp. 219–40.

Wierzbicka, A. (1992), 'Talking about emotions: Semantics, culture, and cognition', *Cognition and Emotion* 6, 285–319.

Yuill, N. and Banerjee, R. (2001), 'Children's conceptions of shyness', in W. R. Crozier and L. E. Alden (eds), *International Handbook of Social Anxiety*, Chichester, Sussex: Wiley, pp. 119–36.

Zahavi, A. (1975), 'Mate selection–A selection for a handicap', *Journal of Theoretical Biology* 53, 205–14.

Zahn-Waxler, C. and Robinson, J. (1995), 'Empathy and guilt: Early origins of feelings of responsibility', in J. P. Tangney and K. W. Fischer (eds), *Self-conscious Emotions: The Psychology of Shame, Guilt, Embarrassment, and Pride*, New York: Guilford, pp. 143–73.

Zajonc, R. B., Murphy, S. T. and Inglehart, M. (1989), 'Feeling and facial efference: Implications of the vascular theory of emotion', *Psychological Review* 96, 395–416.

Zimbardo, P. G. (1977), *Shyness: What it is. What to do about it*, Reading, MA: Addison-Wesley.

Index

Printed in the United States
105437LV00001B/103/A

9 781403 946751